Introducing
Microsoft Windows 95

Brent Ethington

(and the Microsoft Windows 95 Team)

PUBLISHED BY
Microsoft Press
A Division of Microsoft Corporation
One Microsoft Way
Redmond, Washington 98052-6399

Library of Congress Cataloging-in-Publication Data
Introducing Microsoft Windows 95 / Microsoft Corporation.
p.   cm.
Includes index.
ISBN 1-55615-860-2
1. Operating systems (computers) 2. Microsoft Windows 95
I. Microsoft Corporation.
QA76.76.O63I64   1994
005.4 ' 469--dc20   94-41890
                                                                                    CIP

Printed and bound in the United States of America.

1 2 3 4 5 6 7 8 9 QMQM 0 9 8 7 6 5

Distributed to the book trade in Canada by Macmillan of Canada, a division of Canada Publishing Corporation.

A CIP catalogue record for this book is available from the British Library.

Microsoft Press books are available through booksellers and distributors worldwide. For further information about
international editions, contact your local Microsoft Corporation office. Or contact Microsoft Press International
directly at fax (206) 936-7329.

Contents

Microsoft WinNews—Get the Latest Information on Microsoft Windows

Windows 95 is continuing to evolve as we get closer to the release of the product. To help keep you informed of the latest information on Windows, Microsoft has created the WinNews information forum, an easily accessible electronic distribution point for new white papers, press releases, and other pertinent documentation. If you have a modem or access to the Internet, you can always get up-to-the-minute information on Windows 95 directly from Microsoft on WinNews. Use the following electronic addresses to access further information:

CompuServe	GO WINNEWS
Internet	ftp.microsoft.com/peropsys/win_news
Worldwide Web	http://www.microsoft.com
GEnie	WINNEWS Download area in Windows RTC
Prodigy	Jumpword WINNEWS
AOL	Keyword WINNEWS

To subscribe to Microsoft's WINNEWS Electronic Newsletter, send e-mail to enews@microsoft.nwnet.com with the words SUBSCRIBE WINNEWS in your message.

This document is provided for informational purposes only. The information contained in this document represents the current view of Microsoft Corporation on the issues discussed as of the date of publication. Because Microsoft must respond to change in market conditions, it should not be interpreted to be a commitment on the part of Microsoft and Microsoft cannot guarantee the accuracy of any information presented after the date of publication.

INFORMATION PROVIDED IN THIS DOCUMENT IS PROVIDED "AS IS" WITHOUT WARRANTY OF ANY KIND, EITHER EXPRESS OR IMPLIED, INCLUDING BUT NOT LIMITED TO THE IMPLIED WARRANTIES OF MERCHANTABILITY, FITNESS FOR A PARTICULAR PURPOSE, AND FREEDOM FROM INFRINGEMENT. The user assumes the entire risk as to the accuracy and the use of this document. This document may be copied and distributed subject to the following conditions: 1) All text must be copied without modification and all pages must be included; 2) All copies must contain Microsoft's copyright notice and any other notices provided therein; and 3) This document may not be distributed for profit.

Acknowledgments

Special thanks to the contributors to this book, including (but not limited to):

Russ Arun
Richard Barton
Joe Belfiore
Andreas Berglund
Eric Bidstrup
Jeff Camp
Ina Chang
Brad Chase
Joyce Cox
Deborah Epstein-Celis
Dhiren Fonseca
Pat Fox

Richard Freedman
Andy Hill
Jean Kaiser
Bill Koszewski
Keith Laepple
Greg Lowney
Peggy McCauley
Yusuf Mehdi
George Moore
Doralee Moynihan
John Parkey
Dave Pollon

Rob Price
Victor Raisys
Jim Reitz
Brad Silverberg
Bob Taniguchi
Jeff Thiel
Mike Tuchen
Bill Veghte
Rogers Weed
Christian Wildfeuer

Dedicated to the Windows 95 Project Team—
for the development of one really cool operating system!

Foreword

Microsoft Windows 95 is the next major release of Windows from the Personal Systems Division at Microsoft. It's an integrated and complete Windows operating system that starts with the basic functionality found today in MS-DOS, Windows, and Windows for Workgroups. It improves ease of use, enhances workgroup functionality, makes it easier to find and share information, enables new application capabilities, and offers advanced operating system performance. The phrase "integrated and complete" is key—it means that Windows 95 is the first high-volume desktop release of Windows that does not sit on top of (or require any version of) MS-DOS. Windows 95 will be a compelling upgrade for existing Windows users and a compelling new computing environment for people who have not yet moved to Windows.

The development of Windows 95 began in early 1992 with a core group of developers. Over the course of several months, this group defined the mission for what was to become Windows 95. They closely examined the feature set of the existing versions of Windows and considered how computers would be used and what technologies would be common when Windows 95 was to be delivered, and beyond. They looked at the capabilities of existing PC hardware and the promise of new capabilities in a platform for the future. Their vision of the future included the following elements: PCs must be easier to use in order to expand the world of computing; PC hardware must be easier to install and configure to reduce the need for support and shorten the time required to set up and add peripherals; capabilities such as multimedia must be enhanced and made easier to use because more PCs will be used in the home; PCs must be easier to manage in networked environments; communication facilities such as access to electronic information from online services and the Internet must be more accessible; support for mobile computing must deliver easy access to remote information and leverage the dynamic nature of docking/undocking operations; and an operating system infrastructure must be developed that can be easily extended to accommodate future application requirements and yet be backwards-compatible with existing standards and existing software and hardware.

The mission of Windows 95, derived from these observations, defined a mainstream Windows operating system that would make PCs easier to use, would be faster and more powerful, would integrate network connectivity and manageability, and would preserve the users' investment in software and hardware. Windows 95 delivers on this mission.

To make PCs easier to use, we provided a new shell, integrated Plug and Play into the operating system, included wizards to guide users through system operations, and delivered a consistent user interface across all operating system components and namespaces. The increased speed and power come from a modern 32-bit operating system with preemptive multitasking, threads, and a platform for a new generation of 32-bit applications. Windows 95 is a complete operating system that is not limited by MS-DOS and has all the benefits of a completely self-contained graphical operating system. In the area of connectivity—either in a LAN, a WAN, or a mobile dial-up environment—we made connecting to remote resources as easy as connecting to local resources, and we built in access to electronic information for electronic mail and online services. And finally, we made Windows 95 compatible with the software and hardware that users own today.

Windows 95 offers something for everybody. The administrator in a corporation with more than 10,000 PCs will gain from improved manageability; the person in a branch office with 10 PCs will benefit from built-in networking and dial-up remote access. The home PC user will gain from improved and built-in multimedia functionality, and the small business owner will profit from built-in peer networking. Windows 95 offers features and capabilities to make you more productive and keep you in touch with the evolving world of online information and e-mail. Windows 95 will change the industry and the way people use PCs in a way that no other operating system release ever has. We are excited about the possibilities that Windows 95 offers, and we hope you are too.

This book, *Introducing Microsoft Windows 95*, provides insight into Windows 95 from a unique perspective—straight from the project team that developed it. Enjoy!

Brad Silverberg
Senior Vice President, Personal Systems Division
Microsoft Corporation
Redmond, Washington
November 1994

Introduction

As the successor to Microsoft's MS-DOS, Windows 3.1, and Windows for Workgroups 3.11, Windows 95 is the next major release of the standard operating system for desktop and portable PCs. This release offers something for everyone, including a more intuitive way to work, new capabilities such as "surfing the information highway," and better support for managing an installation site with hundreds of PCs.

Where We've Been

Over the past decade, the PC industry has delivered innovative, cost-effective products that have made the personal computer a widely used tool both in the office and in the home. The development of these products was made possible by a number of key advances during the 1980s and early 1990s:

- The adoption of MS-DOS as an operating system standard for PCs, which provided a platform for application development

- Rapid decreases in price and increases in performance made possible by innovative PC components, especially the Intel i386 and i486 microprocessors

- The wide adoption of the Microsoft Windows operating system, which provided an appealing graphical user interface and multitasking capabilities and made possible a new generation of graphical applications, thereby making PCs much easier to use

Where We Are Today

Although the PC has made dramatic gains over the past decade, a number of limitations prevent current users from taking full advantage of their PCs and discourage others from beginning to use them:

- **PCs are still not easy enough to use.** Learning how to use the PC is difficult because the PC does not lend itself to learning through experimentation. The wrong set of keystrokes can, for example, inexplicably cause programs to disappear. As a result, learning basic processes such as launching or switching between applications is frustrating. Configuring the PC is also difficult; for example, tasks such as connecting to a printer or adding a CD-ROM drive are too complicated.

- **Users want software that takes full advantage of the power of their hardware.** The performance delivered by hardware—the CPU, video system, CD-ROM drive, video subsystem, and so on—is constantly accelerating. And new hardware, such as wireless, PCMCIA, and MPEG, continuously arrives on the market. Users want their software to fully exploit all this power.

- **Connecting to a network is hard.** The two primary PC operating systems, MS-DOS and Windows, were not designed with easy connection to a network in mind. Consequently, the basic task of connecting a PC to a server and to other PCs is still a challenge, in spite of the prevalence of networks in organizations of all sizes.

- **PCs are expensive to support.** The cost of hardware is small relative to the cost of installing, configuring, and maintaining a PC and of training and supporting users. These costs must be reduced to make PCs a more cost-effective tool for business.

Where We're Headed

Windows 3.1 moved the PC platform forward by making PCs easier to use. Yet the problems of today's users indicate that the ease, power, and overall usefulness of the PC must be further increased. Windows 95 raises the PC platform to new levels in the following ways:

- **Windows 95 makes PCs even easier to use.** Windows 3.1 put a friendly interface on top of MS-DOS to make common PC tasks easier. With Windows 95, the goal is to make those tasks more intuitive, or where possible, automatic. For example, adding and configuring new hardware devices has been simplified. Windows 95 automatically loads the appropriate drivers, sets IRQs, and notifies applications of the new capabilities of the hardware device without any action by the user. A redesigned user interface, highlighted by the Windows Taskbar, makes computing more automatic for novices. (Usability tests show a ten-fold improvement over Windows 3.1 in the time it takes to complete certain common tasks, such as starting an application.) The interface also makes the power of the PC more discoverable for intermediate and advanced users.

- **Windows 95 is a faster and more powerful operating system.** Ease on the surface requires power and speed at the core, and the modern, 32-bit architecture of Windows 95 meets these requirements. Freed from the limitations of MS-DOS, Windows 95 preemptively multitasks for better PC responsiveness; for example, users will no longer have to wait while the system copies files. It also delivers increased robustness and protection for applications and provides the foundation for a new generation of easier, more powerful, multithreaded 32-bit applications. And most important, Windows 95 delivers this power and robustness on today's average PC platform while scaling itself to take advantage of additional memory and CPU cycles.

- **Windows 95 integrates network connectivity and manageability.** Windows 3.1 gave users the power to make better use of their PCs, but it did not make the same strides for MIS organizations. Windows 95 addresses this deficiency by providing a system architecture that makes basic network connectivity easy. By integrating high-performance, 32-bit client support into the operating system—including the 32-bit Microsoft Client for Novell NetWare Networks—Windows 95 goes beyond simple connectivity to enable the central management and control of the PC. User profiles, policies, and the ability to leverage server-based security make it much easier for MIS organizations to administer and support large numbers of PCs.

Windows 95 is more than the next generation of Windows; it is a catalyst that will move the PC industry to a higher level. The release of Windows 95 is expected to spawn not only a new generation of PCs and peripherals that support Plug and Play, but also a new generation of powerful 32-bit Windows–based applications.

How We Get There

The development of Windows 95 has been guided by the primary principle that all technological improvements must translate into practical benefits for users, and that these benefits must be easily and inexpensively available to everyone. This principle has produced the following results:

- **Compatibility with existing MS-DOS–based and Windows–based applications.** Because Windows 95 is designed to add significant value to any PC without requiring additional software or hardware, compatibility with existing applications is essential. Windows 95 not only supports the enormous range of existing MS-DOS–based and Windows–based applications, it goes a step further by fixing key compatibility deficiencies of Windows 3.1; for example, it provides much better support for demanding MS-DOS–based applications (such as certain types of games, which can now be run from Windows).

- **Compatibility with existing hardware.** The wide range of hardware available for Windows 3.1—from scanners to plotters to fax modems to video capture boards—is enormously valuable to users. While providing support for new, easier-to-use peripherals through Plug and Play, Windows 95 preserves the huge investment of users and manufacturers by maintaining compatibility with existing peripherals and their associated device drivers.

- **Performance equal to or better than that of Windows 3.1.** In keeping with the goal of adding value to existing PCs without requiring additional hardware and software, Windows 95 matches or exceeds the performance of Windows 3.1 on today's average PC (386DX with 4 MB of RAM). As more memory is added to the PC, performance scales faster than Windows 3.1. As a result, access to all the new features in Windows 95 should not incur any performance penalty.

- **Safe, hassle-free upgrade and migration.** Windows 95 makes the upgrade process as easy as possible by providing a Setup program that installs cleanly over Windows 3.*x*. Windows 95 includes the Windows 3.1 Program Manager and File Manager so that users can migrate to the new user interface at their own pace.

The mission of Windows 95 is to go beyond making PCs easier to use and make them truly usable. A truly usable PC is more intuitive and automatic, integrates the latest technologies, offers superior responsiveness and stability, and is compatible with today's existing software and hardware. Windows 95 also aims to make the upgrade and transition easy, without pain and without loss of performance or capability. This book details the specific benefits of the many Windows 95 innovations, underscoring improvements over Windows 3.1. You'll see as you read through the chapters that the size and scope of Windows 95 is awesome, and that its features are worthy of its mission.

C H A P T E R   1

The Microsoft Windows Operating System Family

The Microsoft Windows operating system family provides users and developers with a rich set of services that take full advantage of the broad range of available hardware platforms, from small form-factor portable systems to multiprocessor servers. Windows 95 is for users of Intel–based desktop and laptop PCs. Windows NT Workstation and Windows NT Server are advanced operating systems for workstations and network servers, respectively, and support both Intel and reduced instruction set computing (RISC) microprocessors, as well as symmetric multiprocessing (SMP).

The scaleable architecture of the Windows operating system family supports the same user interface, applications, and development tools across an ever-expanding range of hardware. At the same time, the Windows operating systems meet the spectrum of customer requirements, from productivity applications to powerful, secure, mission-critical applications.

Windows 95 and Windows NT Workstation

Because it is not currently possible to have one operating system that fully exploits the broad range of available hardware, the Microsoft Windows operating system family, shown in Figure 1, has two distinct design points: one centered on mainstream systems, and the other centered on leading-edge systems.

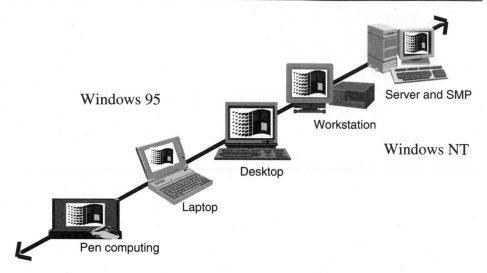

Figure 1. A consistent platform for development, deployment, and training

For mainstream systems (currently represented by products such as subnotebook and entry-level desktop machines), Windows 95 delivers responsive performance for a broad range of applications while conserving the amount of system resources used. Windows 95 is designed for use on Intel–based PCs and supports the Intel 80386DX, 80486, and Pentium processors used in mainstream desktop and portable PCs.

For leading-edge systems, Windows NT fully exploits the capabilities of the hardware and provides the most advanced services for the most demanding applications. Windows NT is designed for use on Intel–based and workstation PCs—for example, a MIPS R4400 or Digital Alpha AXP–based system, a dual-processor workstation, or a multiprocessor RISC server.

Because of the requirements placed on new enterprise solutions, all major operating system developers—including Microsoft, IBM, Sun (and most UNIX vendors), and Novell—have recognized the necessity of moving to a micro-kernel architecture for their leading-edge operating systems. Microsoft made this commitment over five years ago and began shipping Windows NT to developers in July 1992 with general availability in July 1993. This architecture allows vendors to enhance systems to respond to the rapidly changing requirements of evolving business solutions while maintaining the flexibility needed to exploit new hardware and peripherals.

Both Windows 95 and Windows NT Workstation provide a common base of functionality that is required by all customers, including ease of use, power, connectivity and manageability. Microsoft is committed to and will deliver parity in basic functionality (such as the user interface) to each platform as quickly as possible.

The differences between the two platforms are a result of their different design goals. Windows 95 is focused on making computing easier for anyone using a wide range of personal and business applications on desktop and portable computers. To protect their current investment, these users require the highest level of compatibility with today's applications and device drivers. Windows NT Workstation is focused on providing the most powerful desktop operating system for solving complex business needs. For developers; technical/engineering/financial users; and business operations application users, Windows NT Workstation delivers the highest level of performance to support the most demanding business applications. It also provides the highest levels of reliability, protection, and security for critical applications while exploiting the latest hardware innovations, such as RISC processors and multiprocessor configurations. This focus on solving business needs is also reflected in the emphasis on maintenance and regular system updates.

Over time, as mainstream systems become more powerful, technologies implemented first in the leading-edge Windows operating system will migrate to the mainstream operating system. Sometimes technical innovations will appear first in the mainstream operating system because of timing of releases or because some features improve ease of use for general users. However, the guiding principle for product planning is that the leading-edge operating system will provide a superset of the functionality of the mainstream operating system.

For application developers, Microsoft provides only one Windows programming platform, defined by Win32—the 32-bit Windows application programming interface—and OLE. By following a few simple guidelines, developers can write a single application that runs across the Microsoft Windows operating system family. Optionally, developers can target a specific operating system whose functionality is important to a particular application, but targeting is not a requirement.

Which Operating System?

The decision about which of the Microsoft Windows operating systems to deploy should be based on the tasks to be accomplished. The two operating systems provide a complementary set of capabilities that can accommodate a broad range of usage scenarios.

Windows 95 Usage Scenarios

The following examples illustrate scenarios where Windows 95 is the best choice.

- Most office environments require people to perform a variety of general tasks, such as word processing, database queries, or spreadsheet analyses, using productivity applications, such as the Microsoft Office suite. These people may also be using applications that are specific to their particular business. Their companies have an installed base of personal computers, peripheral devices and applications, and Windows 95 allows them to maximize their investment in that computing infrastructure.

- Many companies have employees who spend a high percentage of their working hours away from the office—for example, at customer sites, in hotels, or out in the field—and rely on personal computers to help them perform their jobs. Windows 95 meets the requirements of these mobile computer users for the same application and device compatibility as their office-based colleagues, but also places lower demands on their hardware, including amount of memory, battery power, and use of disk space.

- Most users of computers in the home find them both challenging and unfriendly. However, they want to be able to take advantage of new capabilities, such as multimedia, and to easily access online information services. Windows 95 is easy for all family members to use, yet has the power to do what they want to do. Built into the operating system are rich multimedia capabilities; the highest levels of compatibility for running MS-DOS–based applications, such as games; and connectivity to information services, such as the Internet or other online services. In addition, technology such as Plug and Play allow some users to effortlessly add new components, such as printers, modems, and other peripherals, to their systems.

Windows NT Workstation Usage Scenarios

The following examples illustrate scenarios where Windows NT Workstation is the best choice.

- Engineers, scientific researchers, statisticians, and other technical users often need to use processing-intensive applications for data analysis and large design activities. Windows NT Workstation, with its support for SMP and its portability to high-performance platforms, such as those based on Pentium, Alpha, or MIPS CPUs, can provide the performance of a leading-edge workstation or minicomputer at a fraction of the cost. Moreover, with Windows NT Workstation, users can also run personal productivity applications on their systems.

- For industries that need to protect sensitive data or application files, such as banking and defense, Windows NT Workstation provides a secure desktop. The NTFS file system, combined with appropriate security procedures, helps prevent unauthorized access to systems and data, and the security model in Windows NT Workstation is designed to be compliant with C2-level certification. With these features, a single Windows NT system can be shared by multiple users and still maintain security for all files on the system.

- Many companies require high levels of availability and performance and cannot afford downtime, regardless of which application is running. Often these types of systems are being "right-sized" from mini and mainframe systems. For example, many manufacturing companies use 16-bit applications to manage their production lines. With Windows NT Workstation, these Win16–based applications can be run in separate address spaces (often referred to as separate virtual machines). Then even if one application fails, the other applications continue to run. Windows NT Workstation also provides complete protection for 32-bit applications and automatic recovery (reboot, if necessary) if the system goes down.

Evaluating Windows 95

As you compare Windows 95 with other operating system products on the market, including Windows 3.1, you should examine the following areas to help identify the operating system that best meets your needs and the needs of your system's users:

- Ease of use
- Performance
- Compatibility of device and application support
- Support for networking and connectivity
- Support for manageability and administration
- Support for communications and messaging
- Support for mobile services and remote access

In the following sections, we briefly discuss these evaluation criteria. The remaining chapters in this book show how Windows 95 provides the best desktop operating system for mainstream platforms in each of these areas.

Ease of Use

It is important to look at the ease-of-use aspects of an operating system from the perspectives of both a novice and an experienced user. Novice users include both people who have never used a PC and people who have used one infrequently, often because they find PCs intimidating. Novices might have trouble moving around the user interface and might need more information or coaching—for example, from an online Help system. Experienced users generally interact with more areas of the operating system than novice users, and they demand flexibility, speed, and power.

As you evaluate the ease of use of an operating system, it's helpful to answer these questions:

- Is the operating system easy to learn and use and efficient for the widest range of users?

- Can users discover new features and new, more efficient ways of performing tasks as they become more experienced?

- Does the operating system make it easy for novice users to complete common tasks, such as starting new applications, switching between two or more active applications, or manipulating files?

- Is the operating system flexible enough that experienced users can customize it to reflect the way they interact with the computer?

Performance

The term *system performance* refers to how the operating system performs overall while performing a set of broad tasks—for example, running a group of applications and programs that are normally run simultaneously. The term *performance* also refers to the ability of individual system components or subsystems to perform a more narrow set of tasks—for example, file input/output (I/O) operations.

Several available suites of benchmarks test the ability of operating systems to complete a set of tasks that are designed to mimic real-world use of a particular PC/operating system combination. These benchmark suites produce numbers that represent the responsiveness of the operating system for a given set of commercially available applications. You can run the same set of applications in your environment and use the benchmark information to determine the relative performance of various operating systems.

However, benchmark suites don't tell the whole story. In addition to running application benchmark suites, you should isolate and separately test various components and subsystems of the operating system to obtain low-level results that indicate how well the operating system can support the services used by applications. Areas commonly isolated and benchmarked on standalone PCs include the performance of the local file system for disk and file I/O, the performance of the graphics subsystem and video display drivers for graphics and text I/O, and the performance of the printing subsystem for printing I/O. In addition, you should test desktop operating systems in networked environments for their ability to support network I/O throughput for the supported network clients, as well as server functionality responsiveness (if supported by the operating system).

All operating systems perform at their best on a PC that has the maximum amount of RAM. However, most users' PCs have less than the maximum amount. You should run performance tests against different hardware configurations, including memory ranges from 4 MB to 16 MB and PCs containing Intel 80386DX, 80486, and Intel Pentium–based CPUs. Because different hardware resources deliver different performance testing results, it's important to test not only on more than one PC configuration, but also on hardware that is currently mainstream in the industry.

As you evaluate the performance of an operating system, it's helpful to answer these questions:

- Does the operating system perform well on a wide variety of hardware and software?

- How well does the operating system complete benchmark tests on a suite of applications on a given hardware platform?

- How well does the operating system complete benchmark tests on individual components and device drivers provided as part of the system?

- Does the operating system perform well as far as network connectivity for supported network clients or provided network server functionality is concerned?

Compatibility of Device and Application Support

When it's time to replace an old operating system, a key question to consider is "Can my company still use its existing hardware and software with the new operating system?" Your company has probably invested a large amount of money in applications, printers, modems, and other PC-related peripheral devices. It's important to find out whether the replacement operating system can run with the existing hardware and software.

It's also important to know how broad a range of devices is supported by the operating system you choose. No doubt, as your company grows, your hardware needs will grow too. Your choice of an operating system should not unreasonably restrict the peripheral devices your company can buy later. The operating system you choose should include ample device drivers, not only to support the devices you currently own, but also those you will buy in the future.

When examining device support of an operating system, consider the number of devices supported, the industry standards that the operating system supports, and compatibility with existing device drivers shipped with earlier operating systems or with the devices themselves.

As you evaluate the device and application support of an operating system, it's helpful to answer these questions:

- Does the operating system provide broad support for your company's existing hardware and the associated MS-DOS–based and Windows–based device drivers?

- Are devices easily recognized, installed, and configured by the operating system?

- Does the operating system allow you to run your existing MS-DOS–based or Windows–based applications as well as MS-DOS 6.*x* or Windows 3.1?

- Does the operating system allow the easy exchange of information among applications, or does it support advanced interapplication communication mechanisms?

- Does the operating system provide services for new types of applications, such as multimedia, remote access, and communications-related applications?

Support for Networking and Connectivity

In a corporate environment, an operating system must be able to provide network support for a broad base of clients. You should compare each operating system's ability to support connectivity in a heterogeneous environment, as well as how successfully network functionality and other areas of the system, such as the user interface, are integrated in each operating system. Bear in mind that, in general, companies are not looking for the incorporation of proprietary network functionality in an operating system. They want the operating system to support industry-wide standards so that they don't have to rely on a single vendor to support a multivendor environment.

As you evaluate the networking support of an operating system, it's helpful to answer these questions:

- Is the operating system an open, layered networking architecture that lets you mix and match best-of-breed components at every layer?

- Does the operating system have built-in, native support for popular networks?

- Does the operating system natively support a wide range of network transports, such as TCP/IP and IPX/SPX; industry-wide communication protocols, such as RPC, NetBIOS, DCE, and named pipes; and existing network device standards, such as NDIS and ODI?

- Does the operating system provide a simple, consistent user interface for accessing the network and using network resources?

- Does the operating system support an open architecture that allows third-party and network operating system vendors to easily integrate or add network connectivity enhancements or application support?

Support for Manageability and Administration

PCs are now one of the largest expenses of an MIS organization. Medium and large businesses invest tens of thousands of dollars each year, not only on the hardware and software for new and existing computer systems, but also for setup and administration of these systems. Currently, the available tools for managing and administering PCs in a networked environment have little consistency and almost no integration.

Standards organizations are now working to simplify system administration by developing standard methods for managing PCs. These standards will mean better and more integrated management tools for the network administrator. For an administrator to reap any benefits, however, the operating system must support management mechanisms that adhere to existing standards or its infrastructure must be designed for adaptability to a new standard.

As you evaluate the support for manageability and administration of an operating system, it's helpful to answer the following questions:

- Does the operating system provide the tools and platform infrastructure for supporting management mechanisms that adhere to existing industry standards, such as SNMP, and is it flexible enough to support future standards, such as DMI?

- Does the operating system provide tools and mechanisms for MIS organizations and administrators to customize and control the functionality and capabilities on the desktop?

- Does the operating system provide support for managing desktop PCs remotely over a network?

Support for Communications and Messaging

With the explosive growth of services such as CompuServe, America Online, and the Internet, the increase in demand for an operating system that provides access to online and mail services has been dramatic. The support and services provided by an operating system can open the door to the Information Age, allowing users to discover new communications and messaging possibilities.

As you evaluate the communications and messaging support of an operating system, it's helpful to answer these questions:

- Does the operating system support high-speed communications and background multitasking capabilities?

- Does the operating system provide support for communication hardware; for new communication functionality, such as sharing communication ports; for unified device configuration; and for emerging communications technology?

- Does the operating system provide support for industry-standard messaging services?

- Does the operating system provide broad communication and messaging capabilities, such as faxing, dial-up access to resources, and access to online information services, and consolidated information access?

Support for Mobile Services and Remote Access

To realize seamless mobility, users must be able to easily communicate and remain productive, whether they are in the office, at a customer site, or at home. Users must be able to communicate with coworkers and clients regardless of their location. In addition, transitions from home computer to portable computer to office computer must not cause interruptions in workflow. Including support for mobility services as part of the operating system ensures tight integration and connectivity between portable computers and desktop PCs, allowing minimal work interruptions as users switch from one location and/or computer to another.

As you evaluate the support for mobile services of an operating system, it's helpful to answer these questions:

- Does the operating system support remote access to the key services or information you need on your corporate network?

- Does the operating system have robust support for the dynamic nature of mobile hardware, such as PCMCIA, power management, and docking stations?

C H A P T E R   2

An Overview of Windows 95

Windows 95 is an extremely feature-rich operating system. Virtually every aspect of Windows 95 reflects improvements over Windows 3.1 and Windows for Workgroups. This book discusses the areas of technology that make up Windows 95, focusing on the following features, functionality, and components:

- The Windows 95 user interface
- Base system architecture
- Robustness
- Support for running MS-DOS–based applications
- Plug and Play
- Device support
- Networking
- Systems management
- Printing
- Communications
- Mobile computing services
- Microsoft Exchange: e-mail, fax, and more
- The Microsoft Network online information service
- Multimedia services
- Installation and setup of Windows 95
- International language support
- Accessibility
- Applications and utilities

Where appropriate, each discussion includes the following:

- **A summary of improvements in Windows 95 over Windows 3.1.** This section provides a quick overview of ways in which Windows 95 addresses Windows 3.1 problems or improves upon Windows 3.1 functionality. These discussions also apply to Windows for Workgroups, even though Windows for Workgroups may not be explicitly identified.

- **A Try It! section.** You are encouraged to see for yourself that Windows 95 is a flexible, powerful, and robust operating system by following brief sets of instructions for performing specific tasks.

Key New Features

As you read this book, it's important to keep in mind the needs of the marketplace and how Windows 95 meets those needs. This section briefly outlines some of the key new features in Windows 95 and the problems they solve. Because the scope of the new features is broad and their appeal is wide, they are organized here in terms of improvements over Windows 3.1 in the following areas:

- Ease of use
- Speed and power
- Compatibility

The features are further organized by benefiting group:

- End-users
- MIS organizations

Ease of Use

For End-Users

For end-users and MIS organizations alike, improvements in ease of use in Windows 95 fix the problems identified in Windows 3.1. For example, less-experienced users found overlapping windows and tasks such as minimizing and maximizing windows too complex, while more experienced users craved greater efficiency. But the improvements go beyond simply solving these problems, by also encompassing hardware, connectivity, and applications. Windows 95 offers these solutions:

- **A new user interface (UI).** A shower of improvements greatly enhances ease of learning, usability, and efficiency for all users, no matter what their level of expertise. Novice users can get started more quickly, and experienced users can fully unlock the power of their PCs.

- **Plug and Play.** The goal of Plug and Play is simple: When a user installs a new hardware device, it works.

- **Long filenames.** Signaling the end of cryptic 8.3 filenames, long filenames are just one example of the many usability improvements in Windows 95.

For MIS Organizations

MIS organizations find their jobs increasing in difficulty as the number of PCs in a given corporation grows more rapidly than their support staff. In addition, the introduction of Windows 3.1 led to a series of security, reliability, and management issues because of its lack of integrated connectivity and lack of management infrastructure. The following features of Windows 95 attack these problems:

- **Built-in networking.** Whether a company is running NetWare or Microsoft networks; IPX/SPX, TCP/IP or NetBEUI; NDIS or ODI, Windows 95 has native, integrated support for its network. And additional LANs are easily supported.

- **The Registry.** By holding all pertinent information about the system—installed hardware, installed software, and user preferences and rights—and by exposing its contents remotely through a wide variety of industry standard interfaces—SNMP, DMI, Win32 plus RPC—the Registry provides the foundation for a highly manageable PC.

- **User Profiles and System Policies.** Windows 95 can provide different operating system and UI functionality depending on who has logged onto a PC. For example, a network administrator can prevent a particular user from deleting program items no matter which PC that user logs onto, or the administrator can enforce a policy that requires everyone in a particular group to have passwords of at least six characters.

- **Pass-through user-level security.** A PC running Windows 95 can be configured to require that remote users and their passwords be passed through to and validated by a NetWare server or Windows NT Advanced Server before those users are allowed to carry out certain tasks, such as changing the PC's Registry or accessing its files, either over the network or remotely. This user-level security allows the existing network-based namespace to be leveraged.

- **Network backup agents.** Windows 95 includes agents that support industry-leading server backup products, making it easier to back up information stored on PCs throughout the network.

Speed and Power

For End-Users

A major area of concern for end-users is improving the efficiency and power with which they use Windows. Users want to get their work done faster. They want to be able to run more than one application or computer process at a time instead of waiting for their PCs to finish one task before starting another. They want to be more effective without sacrificing system stability or performance. And perhaps most important of all, they want to escape the feeling that they take advantage of only a small fraction of their PCs' capabilities.

Windows 95 is designed to anticipate and exploit key emerging trends and technologies. For example, the need for seamless mobile computing is becoming more important as more hardware power is packed into smaller and lighter designs and more users work at home or on the road. The explosion of the home market has increased the demand for more powerful multimedia applications, which necessitates better multimedia support from the operating system.

The following features of Windows 95 bring more power and speed to users:

- **True preemptive multitasking.** Windows 95 can preemptively multitask 32-bit applications smoothly and efficiently.

- **Scaleable performance.** As the amount of RAM increases, the performance of Windows 95 increases more rapidly than that of Windows 3.1 because of the high-performance, 32-bit architecture of Windows 95.

- **Support for 32-bit applications**. Support for the Win32 API in Windows 95 means that users can look forward to a new generation of easier, more powerful multithreaded 32-bit applications.

- **Increased robustness**. New features mean greater robustness and protection for existing MS-DOS and Windows–based applications, and the highest level of protection for new 32-bit Windows–based applications.

- **Mobile computing anywhere**. Windows 95 provides both a remote networking client that allows dial-up access to any network (including the Internet) running IPX/SPX, TCP/IP or NetBEUI over PPP, and a dial-in server that lets any PC running Windows 95 act as a secure, single-line dial-in gateway to a network.

- **Faster printing**. The new 32-bit printing subsystem in Windows 95 means users spend less time waiting for print jobs to spool and finish.

- **High-performance multimedia components**. Both the video playback engine (Video for Windows) and CD-ROM file system (CDFS) are new 32-bit components that deliver smoother video and sound reproduction.

- **More memory for MS-DOS–based applications**. The use of protected-mode device drivers and file systems in Windows 95 means users will routinely have 600 KB or more of free conventional memory available in each MS-DOS session, even if they are connected to a network, using a CD-ROM drive, a mouse, and so on.

For MIS Organizations

Because MS-DOS and Windows were not designed for networked environments, their use in those environments can result in a string of problems well known to MIS professionals. These problems include not having enough real-mode memory to run mission-critical MS-DOS–based applications, and instability under Windows 3.1—for example, turning off a Novell NetWare server completely hangs all connected machines running Windows.

The following features of Windows 95 are just some of the solutions that will make the job of MIS organizations easier:

- **32-bit NetWare connectivity**. Windows 95 includes a 32-bit network client for NetWare that is fast and reliable and has a zero footprint in conventional memory. Windows 95 also includes a similar client for Microsoft Networks.

- **Multiple network support**. A PC running Windows 95 can have multiple network clients (to connect concurrently to a Novell NetWare server, a Windows NT Server, and so on) and multiple transports (including IPX/SPX, TCP/IP, and NetBEUI) loaded and running simultaneously, providing connectivity in a heterogeneous environment.

- **Universal information client**. Microsoft Exchange, the universal information client provided with Windows 95, is integrated seamlessly into the user interface and provides a wide range of plug-in services, such as e-mail, online services, group applications, and so on. Thus the user has a single interface with the outside world of information, and the MIS administrator has a single client that supports multiple e-mail and other systems. Windows 95 includes support for services such as Microsoft Mail for e-mail, Microsoft At Work fax software for faxing, and Internet mail.

Compatibility

For End-Users

If an operating system upgrade requires new software, more memory, or new hardware, then the upgrade's cost is far higher than just its purchase price. Currently, users often have to wait a substantial amount of time—usually until their next PC purchase—before they can benefit from new technology. One of the biggest goals of Windows 95 was to make it possible for everyone to stay up to date with the latest version of Windows.

The following features were included in Windows 95 with this goal in mind:

- **Compatibility with existing MS-DOS–based and Windows–based applications.** Windows 95 works with and even improves today's software.

- **The same or better performance.** Windows 95 runs PCs with at least a 386DX processor and 4 MB of RAM at least as fast as Windows 3.1 does—faster in many cases. Windows 95 requires no additional RAM to maintain performance.

- **Backwards compatibility with existing hardware devices.** Windows 95 supports existing hardware and device drivers while enabling next generation, easier-to-use hardware through Plug and Play.

For MIS Organizations

In terms of cost, MIS organizations also have problems upgrading to a new operating system. However, maintaining compatibility with existing hardware and software is even more important, not only because of the larger scale of the upgrade, but also because different operating systems might be used by different groups within the organization. Having to support more than one operating system multiplies the problems MIS organizations face. MIS professionals also worry about the need to migrate users to a new operating system quickly, easily, and in an orderly way and about retraining users.

Windows 95 addresses these needs through the following features:

- **Network compatibility.** In addition to its 32-bit Microsoft Client for Novell NetWare networks, Windows 95 is compatible with existing real-mode network clients and existing logon procedures, such as the scripts used by NetWare.

- **A self-paced guided tour and Windows 3.1 help.** Windows 95 offers a guided tour to help novice users and users new to Windows 95 find their way around. In addition, an online help system that eases the transition of Windows 3.1 users to Windows 95 is only a mouse-click away.

- **Inclusion of the Windows 3.1 Program Manager and File Manager.** An explicit Windows 95 goal is to allow MIS organizations and users to switch to the new user interface at their own pace. In keeping with this goal, Windows 3.1 users can opt to continue working with Program Manager and File Manager until they feel comfortable with the new interface.

C H A P T E R   3

The Windows 95 User Interface

When you first boot Microsoft Windows 95, you know immediately that the old world of Windows running on top of MS-DOS is no more. Gone are the character-mode boot messages that held meaning only for a very small minority of computer users. Instead, you are graphically carried to the desktop of the new Windows 95 user interface (UI).

More than any other part of the operating system, the UI defines the user's overall experience. The easier, more powerful, and more compelling the UI, the better the user feels about computing and the more productive the user is likely to be. A great UI helps the computer industry grow because it makes computing easier and more natural for *all* people, from the novice user to the power user.

This chapter discusses the design process that produced the UI in Windows 95 and then introduces the components of the UI, organized into the following categories:

- **Easy.** Outlines UI features that make Windows 95 easy to learn and use, especially for those new to Windows.

- **Powerful.** Outlines UI features that make Windows 95 more powerful, efficient, and customizable for the experienced Windows user.

- **Compatible.** Outlines UI features that make Windows 95 easy to learn and to use for those familiar with Windows 3.1.

Designing the Windows 95 User Interface

The overarching goal of the UI in Windows 95 is to make PCs even easier to use for *all* people. Fulfilling this goal is a challenge because different people work in very different ways. Novices want learning how to perform a task to be easy, even at the expense of efficiency. However, experienced users want to do more with their PCs, and they want efficiency and flexibility. In addition, users upgrading from Windows 3.1 want to make the transition without throwing out everything they have already learned.

Windows 95 meets these disparate needs by being scaleable—that is, by being able to fit the proficiency and preferences of the individual user. For novices, the most common and essential features of Windows 95, such as launching an application, task switching, and finding a file, are easily "discoverable" via the Taskbar, with its Start button and push-button task switching. For experienced users, Windows 95 promotes efficiency, customizability, and control via such power-user capabilities as the Windows Explorer, rich secondary mouse-button clicking, properties sheets, and shortcuts.

Design Methodology

The UI in Windows 95 was not constructed from a blueprint drawn from a master specification. It started with clear objectives, guiding design principles, and a skilled team. The design process started with the basic question, "How can the UI in Windows 3.1 be improved?" That question launched a continuous cycle of discarding old ideas, conceiving new ideas, and learning—a constantly iterating design-usability test-redesign loop like the one shown in Figure 2.

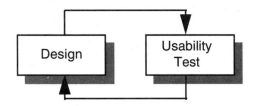

Figure 2. The design loop of Windows 95

Improving the Windows 3.1 User Interface

There was no shortage of information about how the Windows 3.1 UI might be improved. The table on the following page summarizes key findings.

The following mechanisms were used to compile this feedback data:

- **Usability tests.** The Microsoft Usability Lab, described on the following page, is primarily used for testing usability of new designs. However, to better understand how people use Windows 3.1 and to establish a baseline, several phases of testing were dedicated to Windows 3.1.

- **Focus groups.** Several focus groups were conducted with different levels of users to identify the problems people have with Windows 3.1.

- **Educator feedback program.** A team of UI designers and testers visited 12 independent software education companies. More than any other group of users, software educators understand the everyday usage challenges faced by novice and intermediate users. The educators were asked questions such as, "What are the five hardest tasks for students to learn in Windows?" and "What five changes would you make to Windows to make it easier to learn?" The educators also tested prototypes of the UI in Windows 95.

- **Suggestion database.** Thousands of UI suggestions from Windows 3.1 users and corporate customers were compiled and analyzed, along with beta-tester UI feedback.

How Can the Windows 3.1 UI Be Improved?	
Make It ...	**Problem Areas**
Easier to learn for novices	• Window management (overlapping and minimized windows) is confusing. • Hierarchical views (like those in File Manager) are confusing. • Double-clicking to launch applications is not discoverable. • Task switching is not discoverable. As a result, many users never run multiple applications.
More efficient and customizable for experienced users	• There is too much "middle management," with confusing and overlapping functionality between Program Manager, File Manager, Print Manager, Windows Setup, and Control Panel. • 8.3 filenames are restrictive. • The UI is not customizable. • Network and connectivity integration is poor.

Putting New Designs to the Test

Conducting extensive live tests in a variety of settings with a variety of subjects has been key to engineering a state-of-the-art UI. A large portion of the total development budget of Windows 95 has been expended on this critical activity, and Windows 95 is probably the most usability-tested product ever. The following methods have been used to test the UI in Windows 95:

- **Formative testing in the Usability Lab.** Conducted primarily in the groundbreaking Microsoft Usability Lab, formative testing collects data as test subjects perform specific tasks, such as launching a program, finding a file, and installing a printer. The Usability Lab has nine testing suites, each with a one-way mirror, cameras, and other equipment for observing and recording users as they work. Central to the Lab's operations is online data-collection software that helps specialists collect cognitive and quantitative process data as subjects work through the sets of tasks.

Usability tests are observed firsthand by the design team and are essential in future designs. At the time this book was being written, more than 1000 hours of usability testing in 48 phases with more than 400 participants had been conducted. The experience of test subjects has ranged from novice users to intermediate/advanced users, so the test results focus on new computer users as well as users familiar with Windows.

- **Summative testing**. Conducted at customer sites and in the Usability Lab, summative testing involves testing the UI as a whole with real users over longer periods of time.

- **UI-expert and industry-expert review**. In the fall of 1993, a panel of UI experts and industry experts was assembled to review and critique the UI in Windows 95. In addition, four independent consultants each spent large blocks of time with Windows 95 and gave extensive feedback.

Easy to Learn

This section describes the features of the UI that are designed to make learning Windows 95 easy for novices.

The Desktop: Neat, Clean, and Logical

After users start their computers, they are presented with the Windows 95 desktop shown in Figure 3. It's neat and clean and displays only a few graphical objects.

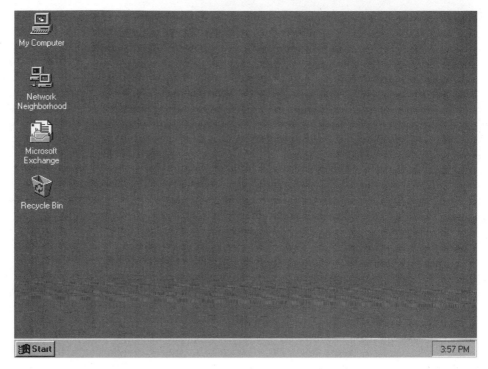

Figure 3. The desktop

The simplicity of the desktop appeals to all users' sense of organization, but it also serves to focus the novice user on the following essential elements:

- **The Taskbar.** Users can quickly start a program or open a document by clicking the Start button. And they can easily switch between tasks.

- **My Computer.** Browsing a PC is now logical and easy.

- **The Network Neighborhood.** In the world of mapped drives and complex interfaces, users can't browse their network. With the Network Neighborhood, they can easily browse the network, regardless of which network provider (such as Windows NT Server, a NetWare server, or Windows 95 itself) is being used.

- **The Recycle Bin.** The Recycle Bin allows users to recover deleted files and easily return them to their original location on the local system.

The Taskbar: Home Base

More than any other feature, the Taskbar, which is shown in Figure 4, exemplifies the order-of-magnitude improvement in ease of use and ease of learning of the UI in Windows 95. It is the UI's anchor. Its mission is to make 95 percent of what a typical user wants to do with the operating system easy to accomplish at all times. The Taskbar started out specifically as a program launcher and task switcher for novices. However, because of its simplicity and power, the Taskbar is also popular with experienced users, who can take advantage of its many other capabilities.

Figure 4. The Taskbar

The two key features of the Taskbar are the Start button and push-button task switching, which are examined in the next two sections.

The Start Button: Up and Running in Seconds

Usability tests on Windows 3.1 have shown that launching Write takes a new Windows user an average of nine minutes. With Windows 95, launching WordPad takes a new user an average of three minutes. If only the users that launch WordPad via the Start button (rather than by another means) are counted, the average launch time drops below one minute!

The main reason for this dramatic 3x–9x speed improvement is the Start button, which is shown in Figure 5. Without knowing about double clicking or complex hierarchies, a novice user of Windows 95 can quickly launch a program and get to work.

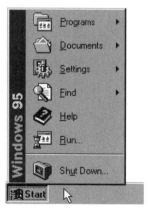

Figure 5. The Start button and its menu

However, the Start button is much more than a super-efficient program launcher. Its capabilities include the following:

- **Programs.** The Start button's Programs menu allows users to quickly launch programs. This menu is the equivalent of Program Manager in Windows 3.1, and in fact, when a PC running Windows 3.1 is upgraded to Windows 95, the contents of the program groups in Program Manager are transferred to the Programs menu.

- **Documents.** The Start button's Documents menu contains a list of the last 15 documents opened. This menu provides very quick access to the information most recently worked with and helps prevent time-consuming and frustrating browsing. It also helps users think of their work in terms of documents (a concept known as *document-centricity*), rather than applications.

- **Settings.** The Start button's Settings menu allows users to quickly change or view the PC's settings and options, including the Control Panel (for computer settings), the Start menu, and the Printers folder. It also allows users to customize the Taskbar to suit personal working preferences—for example, to specify which programs should be included on the Start button's Programs menu.

- **Find.** The Find item in Windows 95 goes far beyond the Search feature of File Manager in Windows 3.1. Searches do need not conform to the *.* searching syntax, and criteria such as last modification date, size of file, and actual text within a document can be used to find information.

- **Help.** Help has been overhauled in Windows 95 and is easily accessible via the Start button.

- **Run.** The Start button's Run item provides enhanced command-line type functionality.

- **Shutdown.** The Shutdown item provides easily accessible and safe shutdown, restart, and logoff.

Task Buttons: Task Switching Made Simple

Novices need to have powerful features presented to them in a simple and compelling way, otherwise they won't use these features. Research conducted with active Windows users indicates that fewer than 50 percent frequently use more than one application at a time and only 20 percent frequently use ALT+TAB task switching. These powerful features of Windows 3.1 are simply not discoverable.

The objective of the Taskbar is to make switching among multiple applications as simple as changing channels on a television set. Every open window has a button on the Taskbar, allowing the user to see which documents and applications are currently open. Switching applications is a simple matter of selecting the desired "channel" on the Taskbar. No more minimized program icons; no more disappearing windows. The user can see all the active tasks simply by looking at the Taskbar, the *TV Guide* of Windows 95. When a task is minimized into the Taskbar or maximized from the Taskbar, animation helps new users understand "where" the task goes.

Task buttons resize themselves automatically depending on the number of active tasks. If the buttons get too small to be useful, the user can customize the Taskbar. In fact, a host of other Taskbar configuration options allow the user to customize it in other ways, including the following:

- **Reposition.** The Taskbar can be dragged to any perimeter position on the screen.

- **Resize.** The width of the Taskbar can be widened by dragging its inside edge.

- **Auto Hide.** The Taskbar can be hidden and made to appear on the screen only when the mouse hits the screen edge, by selecting Settings and then Taskbar from the Start menu.

In addition to making task switching dramatically easier and more accessible via the Taskbar, the UI in Windows 95 includes an updated version of the familiar ALT+TAB "cool switch." It now displays an iconic road map of all active tasks to prevent users from getting lost in an infinite ALT+TAB loop, as was common under Windows 3.1.

Try It!

Customize the Start Button

1. Click *Start*, and then *Settings*, and then *Taskbar*.

2. On the *Change Start Menu* property sheet, select the programs you want to appear either at the *Start* button's first level or on the *Programs* menu.

3. Close the property sheet and check your new configuration by clicking the *Start* button.

Hint: You can also add a program to the *Start* button by dragging a shortcut defined for the program to the button.

Test a Novice

1. Find a stopwatch and a friend or family member who is a computer novice.

2. Sit the novice down at a PC that is running Windows 95 with no programs loaded and a clean desktop.

3. Ask the novice to start an application that you know is listed on the *Programs* menu. Note the time taken to successfully start the application.

4. Try the same task on a PC running Windows 3.1.

5. Compare the times to complete the task. The time using Windows 95 should be the same or faster than the time using Windows 3.1.

Display the Start Menu

- Press CTRL+ESC, and the *Start* menu pops up.

My Computer: An Easier Model for File Management and Browsing

File management and browsing in Windows 3.1 are not intuitive. Fewer than 55 percent of Windows users regularly use File Manager, and File Manager is especially confusing and intimidating for novice users.

Designing a discoverable and comfortable model for browsing and file management for the novice user has been a priority for the UI design team because of the observed difficulties with Windows 3.1. Several significantly different designs have been tested and thrown out. In the course of this testing, the design team made the following discoveries about basic file management and browsing:

- Exposed hierarchies are intimidating and unintuitive.

- Dual-pane views—hierarchy on the left and contents on the right—are also intimidating and unintuitive. Novices have difficulty understanding the connection between the logical tree hierarchy pane and the contents pane.

- An object-oriented UI works well for basic tasks but not for complex ones. The general belief is that the more object oriented a UI is, the easier it is to use. However, this is not the case. Although the direct manipulation of screen objects to achieve logical results is important for basic tasks (such as dragging a file from a folder to the desktop), direct manipulation to carry out more advanced tasks (such as dragging a file to a printer icon) is not intuitive. On the other hand, selecting an object with the mouse and then browsing menus or buttons for actions to perform on that object is intuitive.

- Large icon views are much more comfortable than list views.

- Whether novice users can find what they are looking for and whether they feel comfortable and "grounded" along the way are the defining characteristics of a good browsing experience. Efficiency and speed are less important.

The My Computer default browsing model is the result of this testing. A folder or drive can be opened by double-clicking it, or by selecting it and choosing Open from the File menu. The default browsing model brings up a new window in large icon view, as shown in Figure 6 on the following page.

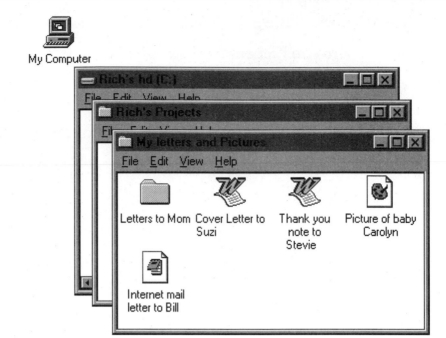

Figure 6. Browsing My Computer

To many advanced users this behavior seems cumbersome. "Why not open in list view?" they ask. "Why create a new window that just clutters up my screen?" "Why not open in a dual-pane view? It's much more efficient for me." "Why not turn the Toolbar on by default?" All of these possible default models and more were tested thoroughly and discarded because they caused confusion and stress for novices. Novices respond best when they are presented only with essential information and when they can easily "get back" to where they just were, so the default model was designed to meet these needs.

(Experienced users can select from multiple configuration options by choosing Options from the View menu. Also for experienced users, Windows 95 has a very powerful dual-pane browsing application called the Windows Explorer. In addition, File Manager from Windows 3.1 is still available and can be run for backward compatibility.)

The new capabilities of the default browsing model should not be overlooked in this discussion of simplicity. Folders can be created within folders. Files and folders respond logically to being dragged and dropped. Files and folders can be cut, copied, and pasted just like text and objects within applications can. Views can be customized, and each window "remembers" how it was last configured and opens automatically in that view. The best way to discover the capabilities of the default browsing model is to explore it, or better yet, watch a novice user explore it.

Try It!

Browse Folders with a Single Window

1. Double-click *My Computer*.

2. From the *View* menu, choose *Options*. On the *Folder* property sheet, select the *Browse folders with a single window that follows you as you open each folder* option.

3. Turn on the Toolbar by choosing *Toolbar* from the *View* menu.

4. Now double-click the icon for your hard drive. No new window opens.

Long Filenames: Greater Flexibility When Naming Files

By far the most-requested file system feature since Microsoft first released MS-DOS is support for long filenames, but until Windows 95 long filenames have not been possible. Windows 95 allows filenames of up to 255 characters. An example is shown in Figure 7. Eliminating the need to conform to the 8.3 naming convention results in obvious and large gains in usability. However, to ensure backward compatibility with existing MS-DOS and Win16–based applications, extensions have not been eliminated entirely; they are simply hidden from view by default.

Long File
Name with No
Extension

Figure 7. A sample long filename

Files can be renamed in place in Windows 95 by selecting the file, clicking the filename, and typing the new name. The hidden file extension is not affected when a file is renamed. Files can also be renamed from within the new common dialog boxes, including the Open and Save dialog boxes.

Try It!

Display the File Extensions

1. From any folder, choose *Options* from the *View* menu.

2. Select the *View* tab.

3. Deselect the checkbox for the *Don't display MS-DOS file extensions for files that are properly registered* option.

The Network Neighborhood:
Accessing Networking Features

This section discusses how the network client in Windows 95 makes browsing networks not only possible but easy, regardless of the network provider (Windows NT Server, Novell NetWare, Windows 95, and so on). For more details about the networking capabilities of Windows 95, see Chapter 9, "Networking."

Network browsing is accomplished by means of the Network Neighborhood, which sits on the desktop and logically represents the resources not available via My Computer. Its icon is shown in Figure 8.

Network
Neighborhood

Figure 8. The Network Neighborhood icon

Browsing the network via the Network Neighborhood is as easy as browsing a local hard disk.

- **Top-level configuration.** The Network Neighborhood can be configured by the network administrator to display only those PCs, servers, and printers that are in the user's immediate workgroup. Top-level configuration insulates the user from the vastness of large corporate networks. The user can still browse the larger network by opening Entire Network from within the Network Neighborhood. (Until Windows 95, browsing the larger network was not possible.) When a user browses a server, network connections are made without drive "mapping" (the assigning of new drive letters to a specific network resource).

- **Systemwide support for UNC pathnames.** This technology makes obsolete the process of mapping drives and allows natural network browsing via the Network Neighborhood. UNC pathname support allows a whole host of usability improvements of which network browsing is just one.

- **The Network Control Panel tool.** This tool consolidates all networking configuration in one location, and thereby eliminates the difficulty of configuring networking under Windows 3.1 and Windows for Workgroups 3.x.

- **Easy drive mapping.** A Map Network Drive button on the Windows Explorer and browsing window toolbars make drive mapping available in Windows 95. (Power users can also right-click My Computer.) Mapped drives appear as connections in My Computer.

- **Networking and mobility.** The UI in Windows 95 was designed from the ground up with networking and remote access in mind. For example, when a file is copied over a slow-link (a modem connection), the Copy dialog box includes an *Estimated time to completion* status message.

- **Networking integration with new common dialog boxes.** The new common dialog boxes, which are standardized in applications that make use of them, provide a consistent way to open and save files on network resources as well as on local drives. In addition, the Network Neighborhood can be browsed directly from the common dialog boxes, and the majority of basic file management tasks can be performed from them.

Try It!

Create a Shortcut to a Network Folder on the Desktop

1. Browse the *Network Neighborhood* until you find an often-used network folder.

2. Point to the folder, hold down the right mouse button, and drag the folder to the desktop.

3. Choose *Create Shortcut Here*.

4. Close the network window.

5. Double-click the shortcut. The network folder opens in a new window. The shortcut will be available every time you boot Windows 95.

Use the UNC Path to "Run" a Favorite Network Folder

1. From the *Start* menu, choose *Run*.

2. Type the full UNC path to your favorite network folder, such as *\\MKTG\PROGRAMS\SARAHB*, and press ENTER. The folder opens in a new window, with no drive mapping.

Create a New Folder from Within Common Dialog Boxes

1. Click the *Start* button, and then choose *Programs*, *Accessories*, and *WordPad*. (WordPad is the word processing equivalent in Windows 95 of Write in Windows 3.1. It uses the common dialog boxes.)

2. From the *File* menu, choose *Open*, and click the *Look in* drop-down box, which provides access to the entire PC hierarchy, including the Network Neighborhood.

3. From the *File* menu, choose *Save*, and click the *Create New Folder* icon. Unlike in Windows 3.1, where you have to start File Manager or exit to the MS-DOS command prompt to a create a new folder, you can create a folder when you save a document.

The Recycle Bin: Easy Deleting and Undeleting of Files

The Recycle Bin is an easily recognizable metaphor for being able to "throw away" files and then recover them by simply removing them from the bin. Files deleted in Windows 95, or deleted from the common dialog boxes in applications that support them, are moved to the Recycle Bin. Users can remove an item from the Recycle Bin and drag or cut/copy/paste it to another location, or they can restore it to its original location by choosing Undo Delete from the Edit menu.

The Recycle Bin graphically indicates whether it is empty or contains items. Information about "deleted" items is available in the Recycle Bin's details view, as shown in Figure 9.

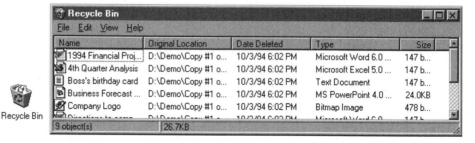

Figure 9. The Recycle Bin with deleted items and the Recycle Bin details view showing additional information

Focus on Documents: Working the Way Users Work

OLE introduced the concept of "document-centricity" by incorporating in-place editing of objects. In a document-centric environment, the application window changes and the document stays the same, so that software works the way people work, rather than vice-versa.

The UI in Windows 95 picks up on the concept of document-centricity in the following subtle but powerful ways:

- **Windows as views of objects**. When the user opens an object from anywhere in the UI, a new window opens. Logically, the title of the new window is the same as that of the object's icon. For example, when the icon of a Microsoft Word document called My Document is double-clicked from the anywhere in the UI, a new window opens entitled My Document—Microsoft Word.

- **Document creation from within folders and in the Windows Explorer**. From within any folder in Windows 95 or from the desktop, users can create new files in place by choosing New from the File menu and then selecting a file type. An icon like the one shown in Figure 10 is then created to represent the new file. This flexibility makes it very convenient to manage files based on projects, rather than at the whim of an application.

Figure 10. The icon for a new Word document

Try It!

Create a New WordPad Document from Within a Folder

1. Select a project folder in which you want to create a new WordPad document.

2. From the *File* menu, choose *New* and then select *WordPad Document*.

3. Type a name and press the ENTER key.

4. Double click the new document to open it in WordPad.

Hint: This functionality can also be accessed by right-clicking from within any folder or on the desktop.

Backtracking: Undoing File Operations

When working with files on your system, how many times have you said to yourself, "I didn't mean to do that!" after accidentally deleting, renaming, moving, or copying a file that you didn't intend to? Windows 95 has a simple answer for putting things back the way they were. Windows 95 provides a multilevel undo feature that allows users to undo one or more of their preceding actions. Users can undo file deletions, renames, moves, or copies by simply choosing Undo from the Edit menu of any UI window, as shown in Figure 11 on the following page.

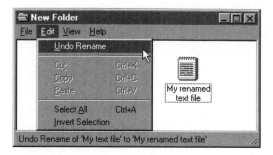

Figure 11. The Undo command on the Edit menu, which can be used to undo file operations

Try It!

Undo a File Operation

1. Open a folder and select a file.

2. Rename the selected file.

3. From the *Edit* menu, choose *Undo Rename* to undo the rename operation.

Undo Multiple File Operations

1. Open a folder and select a file.

2. Rename the selected file.

3. Drag the file from the folder to the desktop.

4. Delete the file.

5. Go back to the folder you first opened.

6. From the *Edit* menu, choose *Undo Delete* to undo the delete operation.

7. Choose *Undo Move* from the *Edit* menu to undo the move operation.

8. Choose *Undo Rename* from the *Edit* menu to undo the rename operation.

Wizards: Guides to Powerful Capabilities

Originally developed in Microsoft's Applications Group and used in applications such as Microsoft Word and Microsoft Excel, Wizards are a proven tool that make it easy for all classes of user to take advantage of powerful but complex functionality. The Wizards guide a user through a series of questions, which are posed to the user in a friendly and straightforward way, and walk the user through a process like the one shown in Figure 12.

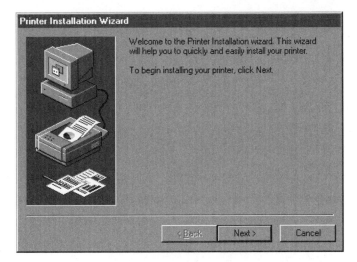

Figure 12. The Printer Installation Wizard, which walks the user through the printer installation process

Windows 95 uses Wizards throughout the operating system to assist all types of users. For example, Wizards are used to perform the following operations:

- Displaying Setup options to the user during the installation process
- Adding a new device to the system, such as a printer or modem
- Setting up remote access in the Network Neighborhood
- Creating a shortcut for an application
- Installing a new application
- Creating a Briefcase for synchronizing files between two PCs
- Creating a workgroup post office for use with the Microsoft Exchange e-mail client

A New Help Engine: Accessible and Useful Online Information

Online Help has been completely retooled in Windows 95. It underwent extensive usability testing and the result is a significantly easier-to-use and easier-to-learn Help system. Additionally, it is now dramatically easier for independent software vendors (ISVs) and corporate customers to customize and develop Windows help files. Following are brief descriptions of the major features of the new Help system in Windows 95:

- **Simplified interface.** Help in Windows 3.1 was difficult to learn and to use. It had three main functions: Contents, Search, and Glossary. The Contents view was not well organized and presented, and there was some ambiguity about which functions to use when. Windows 95 behaves much more intuitively and more like a real reference book. It only has two Tabs: Contents and Index.

- **The Contents tab.** Organized like a book's table of contents, the Contents tab displays top level "chapters" (iconically represented as books) from which users can "drill down" to subtopics (iconically represented as pages). Many chapters also have Tips and Tricks subsections that have proved popular in lab testing.

- **Short Help topics.** Topics all fit in one small window, so users don't have to scroll through large, complicated help information.

- **Shortcut buttons.** New shortcut buttons make using Help even easier in Windows 95. Some Help topics contain shortcut buttons, like the one shown in step 1 in Figure 13, that take users to the referenced area in Windows 95. For example, a user who is searching for help on how to change the date on a PC can "jump" right to the Clock Control Panel tool from within Help.

Figure 13. A Help shortcut button (in step 1)

- **What's This? button.** All Control Panel tools in Windows 95 have a ? button at the right end of their title bars. When the user clicks this button, the pointer changes to a question mark. Clicking any object in the dialog box with this pointer brings up a short description of the object. Users can also access the question-mark pointer by right-clicking within a Control Panel tool.

Try It!

Use Help's Shortcut Button to Change the Desktop Color

1. From the *Start* menu, choose *Help*.

2. Select the *Index* tab.

3. Type *display*. Double-click the *background pictures or patterns, changing* topic.

4. Click the *Properties for Display* shortcut button to move directly to this property sheet.

Transition Aids: Easy Migration to the Windows 95 User Interface

Windows 95 provides several aids for helping both users new to Windows and users of Windows 3.1 become productive quickly in the Windows 95 UI. Usability tests indicate that, with little or no additional training, users can complete common tasks under Windows 95 as quickly as they did under Windows 3.1, or even quicker. Windows 95 offers the following self-paced aids:

- **Quick tutorial of Windows 95.** This tutorial walks users through the basics of Windows 95 and covers topics such as starting programs, task switching between open windows, finding information on the local computer, and using the online Help system. The tutorial is designed for both novice users and experienced Windows users and shows how to complete common tasks.

- **Transition aids for Windows 3.1 users.** The Help system provides additional Help topics designed to make the transition to the UI in Windows 95 easier for Windows 3.1 users. These Help topics answer common questions to help users familiar with the components of Windows 3.1 quickly and easily find the respective tools or commands in Windows 95.

- **Readily available information in the online Help system.** The Help system in Windows 95 is designed to provide the information needed to complete the desired task. Topics include How To, Tips and Tricks, and Troubleshooting categories. Help is always available and can be easily accessed by choosing Help from the Start menu.

Powerful Features

Experienced users glean many of the same benefits from the taskbar and the Start button—quickly launching a new program, quickly switching to another task, and so on—as novices. However, experienced users need more, including the following:

- They need a powerful way to browse and manage file hierarchies, whether they are local or not.

- They need to be able to customize the UI to suit their needs and tastes.

- They need to be able to take shortcuts to get tasks done more quickly and efficiently.

- They need to be able to *do* more.

The new UI in Windows 95 definitely enables the experienced user to do more, as the following sections show.

The Windows Explorer: For File Management and Information Browsing

The Windows Explorer, shown in Figure 14, has been described as "File Manager on steroids." It is powerful, flexible, efficient, and extensible. It also solves many of File Manager's fundamental problems, such as having different windows for different drives. For many power users of Windows 95, the Windows Explorer will be the primary interface for navigating through information.

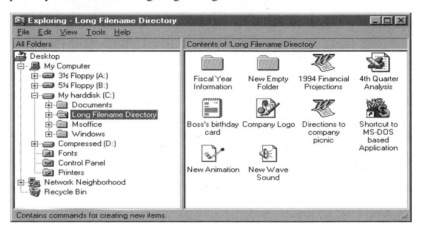

Figure 14. The Windows Explorer

The best way to understand the Windows Explorer is to experience it firsthand. However, here is an overview of its major features:

- **Single view of a world of information**. The Windows Explorer is the eyes of any PC running Windows 95. With it, users can view the entire namespace (all resources, local or connected) from the equivalent of 10,000 feet, or they can zoom down to the equivalent of 10 inches. My Computer and the Network Neighborhood can be browsed and managed, quickly and easily.

- **Flexible and customizable.** Via the Windows Explorer toolbar and the View menu, users can view folder contents in several ways, including large icon, small icon, list, and details views. Folder contents can easily be sorted by name, size, type, and modification date by selecting the column title. Users can also map network drives from the Windows Explorer toolbar.

- **Rich information about objects in details view.** Details view provides a wealth of context-sensitive information about folder contents. For example:

  - Files retain their identifying icons.

- Drive sizes and free space (even mapped network drives) are reported in My Computer.

- Descriptions of Control Panel tools are provided.

- Jobs in the print queue are listed in the Printers folder.

- Comments on other computers in the Network Neighborhood can be viewed.

All the powerful right-click and properties features described in the next two sections are supported in the Windows Explorer.

Try It!

Copy a File to a Different Drive Without Opening a New Window

1. Right-click *My Computer* and choose *Explore*. Maximize the window.

2. Select a file that you want to copy to a network or floppy drive.

3. Move to the left pane in the Windows Explorer and use the + icons to the left of the folder and drive icons to find the network folder to which you want to copy the file. Do not click the destination folder.

4. Go back to the right pane where the file is currently stored and drag or cut/copy/paste the file to the destination folder.

Operations like this one could not be performed in Windows 3.1 without opening two or more File Manager windows.

Right-Click to Create a New Folder

1. In the *Windows Explorer*, right-click an unused space inside a folder in which you want to create a new folder.

2. Choose *New Folder*.

Shortcuts: For Accessing Objects

Shortcuts are an extremely powerful tool for increasing efficiency. They are especially useful in a networked environment. Users can create a shortcut to any object, such as a file, program, network folder, Control Panel tool, or disk drive, and place it anywhere in the UI or in an application. Opening the shortcut opens the object that the shortcut is "pointing" to. For example, if a user creates a shortcut to My Network Folder on a network server and drops the shortcut on the local desktop, opening the shortcut actually opens My Network Folder. Shortcuts are represented by icons that have a small "jump" arrow in the lower-left corner, as shown in Figure 15 on the following page.

Figure 15. Shortcut icons for a folder and a program

Shortcuts are created by selecting an object and choosing Create Shortcut from the File menu or by right-clicking the object and choosing Create Shortcut. After creation, shortcuts can be renamed. If the shortcut is for an object that was created after installation of Windows 95 and the object is renamed, Windows 95 changes the shortcut definition to reflect the new name. For example, if a user creates a shortcut on the local desktop to \\Server\Share\Public Folder and the folder is subsequently renamed, the shortcut will still work. A shortcut can be deleted without affecting the object to which it points.

Uses for shortcuts are virtually limitless, but the following are some common powerful uses for shortcuts:

- **Shortcuts in the Programs folder.** Shortcuts are an extension of the icons that in Program Manager groups in Windows 3.1. The icons simply pointed to an executable file somewhere in the file system. In Windows 95, the icons that appear on the Start button's Programs menu, which can be customized by choosing Settings and then Start Menu from the Start menu, also appear as shortcuts in the Programs folder. When a shortcut is added to or deleted from the Programs folder, it is also added to or deleted from the Programs menu. As a result, users can keep shortcuts to all favorite programs in one central place, regardless of where the programs are actually stored.

- **Shortcuts on the desktop.** Power users can create shortcuts to commonly accessed files, programs, drives, folders, and utilities right on their desktops. This capability is especially powerful with network resources because no complicated browsing or drive mapping is required to access network folders.

- **Embedded shortcuts in applications.** A shortcut to a large file stored on the network can be dragged to an e-mail message. When the message recipient double-clicks the shortcut, the network file opens. This process is much more efficient than embedding the actual file in an e-mail message because the message is smaller, and embedding shortcuts cuts down on file version proliferation.

Try It!

Discover Where the Start Button's Programs Menu Is Stored

- From the *Start* menu, choose *Settings* and then *Start Menu*. The Start Menu folder, which is a sub-folder of the Windows folder, opens. The Programs folder contains the items that appear on the Start button's Programs menu.

The shortcuts and folders are those that appear on the Programs menu. Adding or deleting shortcuts and folders changes the items that appear on the menu.

Properties: For Customizing All Objects

Property sheets are a pervasive feature in Windows 95. All objects in the UI carry context-sensitive properties that can be accessed and customized by choosing Properties from the File menu or by right-clicking the object and choosing Properties. Good, consistent, easily accessible property sheets have been a favorite of power-user testers. Try the following examples to see how property sheets work.

Try It!

Rename a Hard Drive

1. In the *Windows Explorer* or *My Computer*, right-click to select your hard disk and choose *Properties* to open a property sheet like the one shown in Figure 16.

2. In the *Label* box, type a new name and choose *OK*.

3. From the *View* menu, choose *Refresh*.

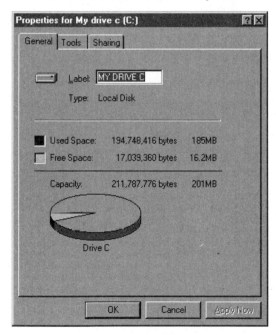

Figure 16. The properties for a disk drive

Share a Folder

1. In the *Windows Explorer*, right-click a folder you want to make available to others on your network and choose *Properties*.

2. Select the *Sharing* tab.

3. Select *Shared As*, and then complete the other fields in this dialog box.

Customize a Shortcut Icon

1. Click the *Start* button and choose *Settings* and *Start Menu*.

2. Open the *Programs* folder.

3. Right-click any shortcut and choose *Properties*.

4. Select the *Shortcut* tab.

5. Click the *Change Icon* button.

6. Select a new icon for the shortcut and choose *OK*.

7. From the *View* menu, choose *Refresh*.

Right-Clicking: For Performing Actions on Objects

Right-clicking, like properties, is a pervasive, context-sensitive feature of Windows 95. (In this book, "right-clicking" refers to clicking the secondary mouse button. Most right-handed people set their mouse options to use the left button as primary and the right button as secondary.) Usability tests have shown that right-clicking as a shortcut way of performing common actions on an object is a very popular power-user feature. However, in general, right-clicking is not a feature that novices discover or remember, so the vast majority of functions that can be performed by right-clicking can also be performed by choosing the corresponding menu commands.

The power of right-clicking can be explored by carrying out the following examples.

Try It!

Right-Click the Desktop to Customize It

1. Right-click a blank space on the desktop.

2. Choose *Properties*.

Minimize or Tile All Open Windows

1. Right-click a blank space on the *Taskbar*.

2. Choose *Minimize All* or *Tile Horizontally*.

3.   To undo this operation, right-click a blank space on the *Taskbar* and choose either *Undo Minimize All* or *Undo Tile*.

Create a Shortcut

1.   Right-click an object for which you want to create a shortcut.

2.   Choose *Create Shortcut*.

Drag a File and Create a Shortcut

1.   Right-click and drag a file from the *Windows Explorer* onto the desktop. A menu like the one shown in Figure 17 appears.

2.   Choose *Create Shortcut(s) Here*.

Figure 17. The menu that appears when a file is dragged using the right mouse button

Right-Click a Screensaver to Test It

1.   Choose *Find Files or Folders* from the *Start* menu.

2.   Type *bezier* and choose *Find Now*.

3.   Right-click *Bezier*.

4.   Choose *Test*.

Close a Task from the Taskbar

1.   Right-click the *Task* button for a window or program you want to close.

2.   Choose *Close*.

Access the Property Sheet for an Open Window

1.   Right-click the mini-icon in the upper-left corner of any window.

2.   Choose *Properties*.

The Control Panel: The Consolidated Control Center

The objective of the Control Panel is to consolidate all command, control, and configuration functions in one location. With Windows 3.1, these functions were difficult to find, use, and remember—for example, video resolution was changed in Windows Setup, but a printer was installed by selecting the Control Panel's Printers icon. As shown in Figure 18, in Windows 95 distinct graphics make all important functions instantly recognizable and previews are offered where appropriate.

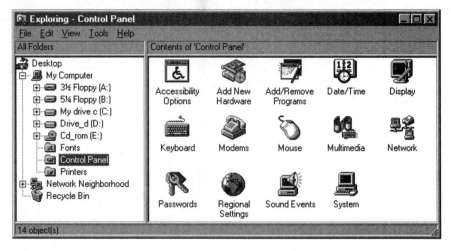

Figure 18. The large icon view of the Control Panel in the Windows Explorer

The individual functions available through the Control Panel tool are discussed in the relevant sections of this book—for example, the Network tool is discussed in Chapter 9, "Networking." However, one Control Panel tool, Display, controls the configuration of the UI in Windows 95 and allows users to customize the UI itself. As shown in Figure 19, its property sheet has the following four tabs:

- **Background.** Allows pattern and wallpaper configuration and preview.

- **Screen Saver.** Allows screen saver configuration and preview.

- **Appearance.** Allows configuration and preview of all of the user interface metrics (fonts, sizes, colors, and so on).

- **Settings.** Allows configuration of monitor resolution and color palette size.

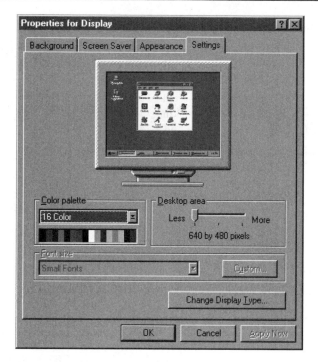

Figure 19. The display properties

Try It!

Switch the Display Resolution

Dynamic resolution switching allows the resolution of the display to be changed without having to restart Windows 95 or reboot the PC. This feature depends on several factors, including the type of video card and the selected color palette.

1. Choose *Settings* and then *Control Panel* from the *Start* menu.

2. Open the *Display* icon.

3. Select the *Settings* tab.

4. Set *Color Palette* to *256 colors* and click *Apply Now* to restart your PC.

5. After your PC restarts, repeat steps 1 and 2 to reopen the Display icon.

6. Choose another video resolution that is supported by your card by sliding the *Desktop Area* slider bar. For example, change the desktop area size from 640 x 480 to 1024 x 768.

7. Click *Apply Now*.

8. Now try playing an AVI clip.

Finding Files or Folders: Easy and Efficient

A powerful new Find utility is built into Windows 95. As shown in Figure 20 and Figure 21, it goes far beyond the minimal functionality of File Manager's Search utility in Windows 3.1.

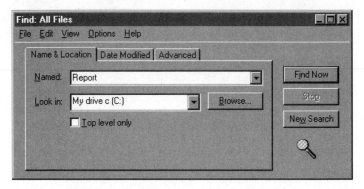

Figure 20. Finding files or folders in Windows 95

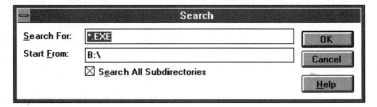

Figure 21. Searching in Windows 3.1

The Find utility includes the following features:

- **Partial name searches.** Type *rep* in the Find Files Named window, and all files and folders with *rep* somewhere in their names are found.

- **Searches on last modification date.** Because files can be searched on their last modification dates, users can perform searches such as *Find all Word documents modified in the last 3 days.*

- **Full-text searches.** Documents containing specified text can be searched for.

- **Saving of search results.** Complex or useful searches can be saved.

- **File management from the search results pane.** Operations such as renaming files or viewing file properties can be carried out within the results pane in the same way as in the Windows Explorer.

Try It!

Save the Results on a Complex Search

1. Click the *Start* button, and choose *Find* and then *Files or Folders*.

2. Type a partial string that you know will be present in many files, such as *rep* or *doc*.

3. Select the *Date Modified* tab.

4. Select *Modified during the previous seven days*.

5. Select the *Advanced* tab.

6. If necessary, select a file type.

7. Click *Find Now*.

8. When the find operation is complete, choose *Save Search* from the *File* menu. (Notice that because the Find feature is 32-bit preemptively multitasked, you have control and can go perform other tasks while Find is running.) A *Find Results* icon is automatically created on the desktop.

9. Double-click the *Find Results* icon.

The Printers Folder: Consolidated Printer Control

The Printers folder, shown in Figure 22, offers one-stop shopping for printer management and configuration. It replaces the troublesome Print Manager and Printers dialog box in the Windows 3.1 Control Panel, which is shown in Figure 23 on the following page.

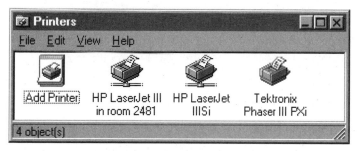

Figure 22. The Printers folder in Windows 95

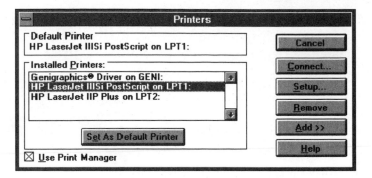

Figure 23. The Printers dialog box in Windows 3.1

The Printers folder is discussed in more detail in Chapter 11, "Printing."

Font Settings: More Powerful Font Management and Preview

The Fonts folder represents a single namespace in which all fonts used in the system can be installed or manipulated. (If any fonts are identified in the WIN.INI file, Windows 95 moves them to the Fonts folder on startup, so all fonts in the system reside in a single location.) Different views of the Fonts folder present additional information about the fonts installed in the system, as shown in Figure 24.

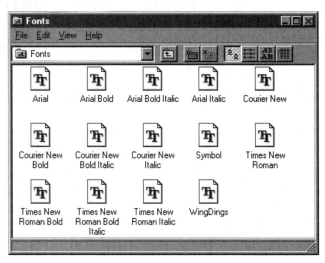

Figure 24. The large icon view of the Fonts folder

Operations can be performed on fonts in the same way they are performed on other file system objects. For example, a font can be removed from the Fonts folder by dragging it to another location, a font can be deleted from the system by deleting it from the

Fonts folder, and a font can be added to the system by dragging it from another location into the Fonts folder.

Try It!

Preview the Fonts

1. Open *My Computer* and double-click the *Fonts* folder, or open the *Fonts* icon in the *Control Panel*.

2. Right-click the font you want to preview.

3. Choose *Open*. Samples of the selected font are displayed and may be printed.

Quick Viewers: Examining Files Without Opening Them

The Quick Viewers allow users to preview a file from the UI without having to open the application that created the file. In fact, users don't even have to have the application that created the file on their system. As a result, documents can be sent over a network or through e-mail. Figure 25 shows a quick view of a Microsoft Excel worksheet.

 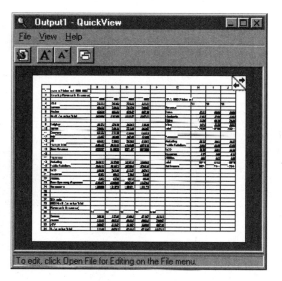

Figure 25. A quick view of a Microsoft Excel worksheet

For more information about the Quick Viewers in Windows 95, see Chapter 20, "Applications and Utilities."

Try It!

Quick-View a File

1. Right-click an icon for a file created by a registered application—for example, a bitmap, a text file, or a WordPad document.

2. Choose *Quick View*.

Compatibility

Compatibility is a requirement for Windows 95. It is a no-excuses, "no-brainer" upgrade from Windows 3.1. Overall, compatibility is most important for third-party software and hardware. However, it also applies to the UI. The UI in Windows 95 must be compatible with the way current Windows and MS-DOS users work, and it must scale itself to the level and preferences of individual users.

For Users of Windows 3.1

Of primary importance is that new UI features be easy for current Windows 3.1 users to learn at their own pace. In addition, UI visual elements and operations in Windows 95 must be consistent, to the extent possible, with the elements users are already familiar with in Windows 3.1. In addition to providing aids for users migrating from Windows 3.1, Windows 95 also includes tools familiar to Windows 3.1 users. For example, the system menu in the upper-left corner of most windows, and keyboard shortcuts such as ALT+F4, ALT+TAB, CTRL+X, CTRL+C, and CTRL+V, are present in Windows 95, easing the requirement for relearning or retraining.

With minimal changes in appearance, Program Manager and File Manager run under Windows 95 and are easily accessible via the Start button. As of this writing, the designs for access and default configuration of these Managers is not yet set. For example, when a user who has upgraded boots Windows 95 for the first time, the Program Manager window might be open. Or the Start button might have a Windows 3.1 Compatibility menu item that will launch Program Manager and File Manager. Regardless of the final design, many help and learning devices will be specifically designed for the upgrade, such as a Click Here to Begin arrow that zooms to the Taskbar when the user first boots Windows 95.

For Users of MS-DOS

Users of the command line in MS-DOS won't have to give it up when they move to the graphical UI of Windows 95. In fact, "command-line junkies" will find that the usability and power of the MS-DOS command prompt have been dramatically improved. New command-line functionality includes the following:

*   Launching Windows–based applications

- Opening documents from a command-line

- Scaling the size of the MS-DOS command prompt

- Using cut/copy/paste operations to integrate information from MS-DOS and Windows–based applications

- UNC pathname support

See Chapter 6, "Support for Running MS-DOS–based Applications," for more information.

CHAPTER 4

Base System Architecture

Ease on the surface requires power and speed at the core, and the modern, 32-bit architecture of Windows 95 meets these requirements. Freed from the limitations of MS-DOS, Windows 95 preemptively multitasks for better PC responsiveness—for example, users no longer have to wait while the system copies files—and delivers increased robustness and protection for applications. Windows 95 also provides the foundation for a new generation of easier, more powerful multithreaded 32-bit applications. And most important, Windows 95 delivers this power and robustness on today's average PC platform while scaling itself to take advantage of additional memory and CPU cycles.

The mission of Windows 95 is to deliver a complete, integrated operating system that offers modern, 32-bit operating system technology and includes built-in connectivity support. In addition to the high-level mission of Windows 95, market requirements dictate delivery of a high performance, robust, and completely backward-compatible operating system that provides a platform for a new generation of applications.

This chapter discusses the base system architecture used by Windows 95. The base architecture covers low-level system services for managing memory, accessing disk devices, and providing robust support for running applications.

Summary of Improvements over Windows 3.1

Improvements made to the base architecture of Windows 95 result in many benefits to users. Following is a summary of some of the key improvements:

- **A fully integrated 32-bit protected-mode operating system.** The need for a separate copy of MS-DOS has been eliminated.

- **Preemptive multitasking and multithreading support.** System responsiveness and smooth background processing have been improved.

- **32-bit installable file systems.** Systems such as VFAT, CDFS, and network redirectors provide better performance, use of long filenames, and an open architecture that supports future growth.

- **32-bit device drivers.** Available throughout the system, these drivers deliver improved performance and intelligent memory use.

- **A complete 32-bit kernel.** Included are memory management, scheduler, and process management.

- **Improved system-wide robustness and cleanup.** This more stable and reliable operating environment also cleans up after an application ends or crashes.

- **More dynamic environment configuration.** The need for users to tweak their systems is reduced.

- **Improved system capacity.** Included are better system resource limits to address the problems Windows 3.1 users encountered when running multiple applications.

A Fully Integrated Operating System

The first thing that users of Windows 3.1 and MS-DOS will notice when they turn on their computers is the lack of an MS-DOS command prompt from which they would formerly have invoked Windows. Windows 95 is a tightly integrated operating system that features a preemptive multitasking kernel which boots directly into the graphical UI and also provides full compatibility with the MS-DOS operating system.

Many of the components of Windows 95 overcome limitations inherent in MS-DOS and Windows 3.1. However, these improvements do not come at the cost of compatibility with existing software, hardware, or computing environments.

A Preemptive Multitasking Operating System

The job of the operating system is to provide services to the applications running on the system and, in a multitasking environment, to provide support that allows more than one application to run concurrently. In Windows 3.1, multiple applications ran concurrently in a *cooperative* multitasking manner. The Windows 3.1 operating system required an application to check the message queue every once in a while to allow the operating system to give control to other running applications. Applications that did not check the message queue on a frequent basis effectively hogged all the CPU time and prevented switching to another running task.

Windows 95 uses a *preemptive* multitasking mechanism for running Win32–based applications, and the operating system takes control away from or gives control to another running task depending on the needs of the system. Unlike Win16–based applications, Win32–based applications do not need to *yield* to other running tasks in order to multitask in a friendly manner. (Win16–based applications are still cooperatively multitasked for compatibility reasons.) Windows 95 provides a

mechanism called *multithreading* that allows Win32–based applications to take advantage of the preemptive multitasking nature of the operating system and that facilitates concurrent application design. In operating-system terms, a running Win32–based application is called a *process*. Each process consists of at least a single *thread*. A thread is a unit of code that can get a time slice from the operating system to run concurrently with other units of code. It must be associated with a process, and it identifies the code path flow as the process is run by the operating system.
A Win32-based application can *spawn* (or initiate) multiple threads for a given process. Multiple threads enhance the application for the user by improving throughput and responsiveness and aiding background processing.

Because of the preemptive multitasking nature of Windows 95, threads of execution allow background code to be processed in a smooth manner. For example, a word processing application (process) can implement multiple threads to enhance operation and simplify interaction with the user. The application might have one thread of code responding to the keys pressed on the keyboard by the user to enter characters in a document, while another thread is performing background operations such as spell-checking or pagination, and yet another thread is spooling a document to the printer in the background.

Some available Windows 3.1 applications provide functionality similar to that just described. However, because Windows 3.1 does not provide a mechanism for supporting multithreaded applications, the application developer has to implement a threading scheme. The use of threads in Windows 95 facilitates the adding of asynchronous processing of information to applications by their developers.

Applications that use multithreading techniques can also take advantage of improved processing performance available from a symmetric multiprocessing (SMP) system running Windows NT, which allows different portions of the application code to run on different processors simultaneously. (Windows NT uses a thread as the unit of code to schedule symmetrically among multiple processors.)

For information about how Windows 95 runs MS-DOS–based applications in a preemptive manner (as Windows 3.1 does today), Win16–based applications in a cooperative manner (as Windows 3.1 does today), and Win32–based applications in a preemptive manner (as Windows NT does today) see later sections in this chapter.

No CONFIG.SYS or AUTOEXEC.BAT?

Windows 95 doesn't need the separate CONFIG.SYS or AUTOEXEC.BAT file required by MS-DOS and Windows 3.1. Instead, Windows 95 is intelligent about the drivers and settings it requires and automatically loads the appropriate driver files or makes the appropriate configuration settings during its boot process. If a CONFIG.SYS or AUTOEXEC.BAT file is present, the settings in these files are used to set the global environment. For example, the default search path or the default appearance of the command prompt can be defined by using the appropriate entries in the AUTOEXEC.BAT file. While Windows 95 itself does not need a CONFIG.SYS or AUTOEXEC.BAT file, compatibility is maintained with existing software or environments that may require one or both of these files.

No MS-DOS?

Unlike Windows 3.1, Windows 95 is not dependent on real-mode operating system components for its interaction with the file system. However, the Windows 95 boot sequence does begin by loading real-mode operating system components that are compatible with MS-DOS. During the boot sequence, support for loading any real-mode drivers and TSRs that are identified in a CONFIG.SYS or AUTOEXEC.BAT file is processed. Because these drivers explicitly look for or use MS-DOS application support, the real-mode operating system components of Windows 95 help maintain compatibility with software that users already have on their system. After the real-mode drivers are loaded, Windows 95 begins loading the protect-mode operating system components. In some cases where a protect-mode Windows–based driver is provided, Windows 95 actually removes real-mode drivers from memory. More information about this subject is given later.

32-Bit Versus 16-Bit Components

To provide a good balance between delivering compatibility with existing applications and drivers, decreasing the size of the operating system working set, and offering improved system performance over Windows 3.1, Windows 95 uses a combination of 32-bit and 16-bit code. In general, 32-bit code is provided in Windows 95 to maximize the performance of the system, while 16-bit code balances the requirements for reducing the size of the system and maintaining compatibility with existing applications and drivers. System reliability is also improved without a cost in terms of compatibility or increased size.

The design of Windows 95 deploys 32-bit code wherever it significantly improves performance without sacrificing application compatibility. Existing 16-bit code is retained where it is required to maintain compatibility, or where 32-bit code would increase memory requirements without significantly improving performance. All of the I/O subsystems and device drivers in Windows 95, such as networking and file systems, are fully 32-bit, as are all the memory management and scheduling components (the kernel and virtual memory manager). Figure 26 depicts the relative distribution of 32-bit code versus 16-bit code present in Windows 95 for system-level services.

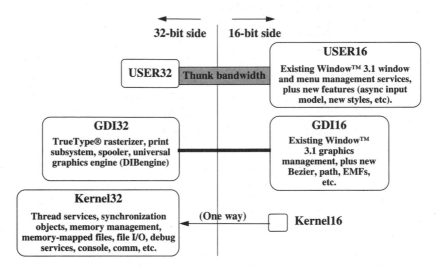

Figure 26. The relative code distribution in Windows 95

As shown in the figure, the lowest-level services provided by the operating system kernel are provided as 32-bit code. Most of the remaining 16-bit code consists of hand-tuned assembly language, delivering performance that rivals some 32-bit code used by other operating systems available on the market today. Many functions provided by the Graphics Device Interface (GDI) have been moved to 32-bit code, including the spooler and printing subsystem, the font rasterizer, and the drawing operations performed by the graphics DIB engine. Much of the window management code (User) remains 16-bit to retain application compatibility.

In addition, Windows 95 improves upon the MS-DOS and Windows 3.1 environments by implementing many device drivers as 32-bit protected-mode code. Virtual device drivers in Windows 95 assume the functionality provided by many real-mode MS-DOS–based device drivers, eliminating the need to load them in MS-DOS. This technique results in a minimal conventional-memory footprint, improved performance, and improved reliability and stability of the system over MS-DOS–based device drivers.

Virtual Device Drivers

A virtual device driver is a 32-bit, protected-mode driver that manages a system resource, such as a hardware device or installed software, so that more than one application can use the resource at the same time. To understand the improvements available in Windows 95 over the combination of MS-DOS and Windows 3.1, it helps to have a basic understanding of what virtual device drivers (VxDs) are and the role they play in the Windows 95 environment.

The term *VxD* refers to a general virtual device driver, with *x* representing the type of device driver. For example, VDD is a virtual device driver for a display device, a VTD is a virtual device driver for a timer device, a VPD is a virtual device driver for a printer device, and so on. Windows uses virtual devices to support multitasking for MS-DOS–based applications, virtualizing the different hardware components on the system to make it appear to each MS-DOS virtual machine (VM) that it is executing on its own computer. Virtual devices work in conjunction with Windows to process interrupts and carry out I/O operations for a given application without disrupting how other applications run.

Virtual device drivers support all hardware devices for a typical computer, including the programmable interrupt controller (PIC), timer, direct-memory-access (DMA) device, disk controller, serial ports, parallel ports, keyboard device, math coprocessor, and display adapter. A virtual device driver can contain the device-specific code needed to carry out operations on the device. A virtual device driver is required for any hardware device that has settable operating modes or retains data over any period of time. In other words, if the state of the hardware device can be disrupted by switching between multiple applications, the device must have a corresponding virtual device. The virtual device keeps track of the state of the device for each application and ensures that the device is in the correct state whenever an application continues.

Although most virtual devices manage hardware, some manage only installed software, such as an MS-DOS device driver or a terminate-and-stay-resident (TSR) program. Such virtual devices often contain code that either emulates the software or ensures that the software uses only data applicable to the currently running application. ROM BIOS, MS-DOS, MS-DOS device drivers, and TSRs provide device-specific routines and operating system functions that applications use to indirectly access the hardware devices. Virtual device drivers are sometimes used to improve the performance of installed software—for example, the 80386 and compatible microprocessors can run the 32-bit protected-mode code of a virtual device more efficiently than the 16-bit real-mode code of an MS-DOS device driver or TSR. In addition, performance is enhanced by eliminating ring transitions that result in executing 32-bit applications that access 16-bit real-mode services, because with virtual device drivers, the system can stay in protected-mode.

Windows 95 benefits from providing more device driver support implemented as a series of VxDs in the Windows environment, instead of using the device drivers previously available as real-mode MS-DOS device drivers. Functionality that was previously supported as MS-DOS device drivers but is now supported as VxDs in Windows 95 includes the following components:

- MS-DOS FAT file system
- SmartDrive
- CD-ROM file system
- Network card drivers and network transport protocols
- Network client redirector and network peer server
- Mouse driver
- MS-DOS SHARE.EXE TSR
- Disk device drivers including support for SCSI devices
- DriveSpace (and DoubleSpace) disk compression

In summary, in Windows 95 VxDs provide the following advantages:

- Improved performance as a result of a 32-bit code path and the elimination or reduction of the need to switch between real and protected mode

- Reduced conventional memory footprint by providing device driver and TSR functionality as protected-mode components that reside in extended memory

- Improved system stability and reliability compared to MS-DOS device driver counterparts

Virtual device drivers in Windows 95 can be identified by .VXD extensions, and virtual device drivers from Windows 3.1 can be identified by .386 extensions.

The System Architecture Layout in Windows 95

Figure 27 illustrates the layout of the base system architecture for Windows 95. Components of the system are divided between Ring 0 and Ring 3 code, offering different levels of system protection. The Ring 3 code is protected from other running processes by protection services provided by the Intel processor architecture. The Ring 0 code consists of low-level operating system services such as the file system and the virtual machine manager.

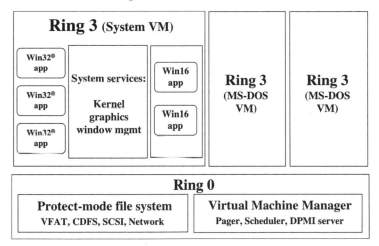

Figure 27. The integrated architecture of Windows 95, which supports running MS-DOS–based, Win16–based, and Win32–based applications

Figure 27 also depicts the way that MS-DOS–based, Win16–based, and Win32–based applications run in the system. The following section discusses the provisions that the system makes for running these applications.

Support for Win16–Based Applications

Win16–based (16-bit) applications run together within a unified address space and run in a cooperatively multitasking manner, as they do under Windows 3.1. Win16–based applications benefit from the preemptive multitasking of other system components, including the 32-bit print and communications subsystem and the improvements made in system robustness and protection from the system kernel in Windows 95.

Based on customer needs, resource needs, and market needs, three goals drove the architectural design of Win16–based application support: compatibility, size, and performance. Functionality adjustments, such as preemptively running Win16–based applications together in the Win16 subsystem or running Win16–based applications in separate VMs, were considered, but each of the options considered failed to meet the three design goals. The following discussion provides some insight into the architecture of Windows 95 as far as running Win16–based applications in a fast, stable, and reliable way is concerned.

Compatibility

First and foremost, Windows 95 needs to run existing Win16–based applications without modification. This factor is extremely important to existing users who want to take advantage of the new functionality offered in Windows 95, such as 32-bit networking, but don't want to have to wait until new Windows 95–enabled applications are available on the market.

Windows 95 builds upon the Windows 3.1 platform to provide support for running existing Win16–based applications and using existing Windows–based device drivers, while providing support for the next generation of 32-bit applications and components. Windows 95 extends the Windows 3.1 architecture in areas that have little or no impact on compatibility, as well as enhances the architecture to deliver a faster, more powerful 32-bit operating system.

Size

While many newer computer purchases are Intel 80486–based computers with 4 MB or 8 MB (or more) of memory, a high percentage of 80386DX–based computers with 4 MB of memory running Windows 3.1 are still in use. To support the needs of the market, Windows 95 must run on a base platform of an Intel 80386DX–based computer with 4 MB of RAM and provide access to its new features and functionality without requiring an upgrade of existing hardware or the addition of more RAM.

To meet its goals, Windows 95 is designed to occupy a working set of components no larger than Windows 3.1, thereby ensuring that any Win16–based application running at a perceived speed on a 4 MB or 8 MB (or greater) computer runs at the same (or higher) speed under Windows 95 without suffering any performance degradation. To meet the size goals of Windows 95, Win16–based applications run within a unified address space, resulting in little overhead beyond that required by Windows 3.1 to support the running of Windows–based applications. Running in a unified address space allows Windows 95 not only to fit on a 4 MB computer, but also to perform well. The architecture of Windows 95 includes innovative design features, such as dynamically loadable VxDs, to decrease the working set of components and memory requirements used by the operating system.

Meeting the size design goal (as well as meeting the compatibility goal) precluded the strategies of running Win16–based applications in a separate VM (by running a separate copy of Windows 3.1 on top of the operating system, which would involve paying a several megabyte "memory tax" for each application) as OS/2 does, or of emulating Windows 3.1 on top of the Win32 subsystem (which would also involve paying a "memory tax" for running Win16–based applications) as Windows NT does.

Running Win16–based applications in separate VMs is very expensive memory-wise. This strategy would require separate GDI, USER, and KERNEL code in each VM that is created, increasing the working set by as much as 2 MB for each Win16–based application that is running (as is the case with OS/2 for Windows). On a computer with 16 MB or more, this increase may not appear significant. However, bearing in mind the existing installed base of computers, running Win16–based applications in their own separate VMs in 4 MB of memory is impossible, and running them in 8 MB with the level of performance observed and expected under Windows 3.1 is very difficult.

Performance

Users expect their existing Win16–based applications to run as fast as or faster than they do under Windows 3.1. Both Win16–based applications and MS-DOS–based applications benefit from the 32-bit architecture of Windows 95, including the increased use of 32-bit device driver components and 32-bit subsystems.

Win16–based applications run within a unified address space and interact with the system much as they do under Windows 3.1. Running Win16–based applications in separate VMs requires either mapping Win16 system components in each address space, as Windows NT does, or providing a separate copy of each system component in each address space, as OS/2 for Windows does. The additional memory overhead required for Win16 system components in each VM to run a Win16–based application has a negative impact on system performance.

Windows 95 balances the issue of system protection and robustness with the desire for better system performance and improves on the system robustness of Windows 3.1. The improvements in this area are briefly discussed in the next section and are described in greater detail in Chapter 5, "Robustness."

Protection

The support for running Win16–based applications provides protection of the system from other running MS-DOS–based applications or Win32–based applications. Unlike

Windows 3.1, an errant Win16–based application cannot easily bring down the system or other running processes on the system. While Win32–based applications benefit the most from system memory protection, the robustness improvements in Windows 95 result in a more stable and reliable operating environment than Windows 3.1.

Win16–based applications run within a unified address space and cooperatively multitask as they do under Windows 3.1. The improvements made to overall system-wide robustness greatly enhance the system's ability to recover from an errant application, and improved cleanup of the system lessens the likelihood of application errors. General protection faults (GPFs) under Windows 3.1 are most commonly caused by an application overwriting its own memory segments, rather than by an application overwriting memory belonging to another application. Windows 3.1 did not recover gracefully when a Windows–based application crashed or hung. When a GPF caused the system to halt an application, the system commonly left allocated resources in memory, causing the system to degenerate.

Because of improved protection in Windows 95, an errant Win16–based application cannot easily bring down either the system as a whole or other running MS-DOS or Win32–based applications. At most, it can impact other running Win16–based applications.

Other protection improvements include the use of separate message queues for each running Win32–based application. The use of a separate message queue for the Win16 address space and for each running Win32–based application provides better recovery of the system and doesn't halt the system if a Win16–based application hangs.

Robustness Improvements

System robustness when running Win16–based applications under Windows 95 is greatly improved over Windows 3.1. Windows 95 now tracks resources allocated by Win16–based applications and uses the information to clean up the system after an application exits or ends abnormally, thus freeing up unused resources for use by the rest of the system.

Robustness improvements are discussed in Chapter 5, "Robustness."

Support for MS-DOS–Based Applications

Windows 95 includes many improvements over Windows 3.1 for running MS-DOS–based applications. As with Windows 3.1, each MS-DOS–based application runs in its own VM. A VM takes advantage of the Intel 80386 (and higher) architecture, which allows multiple 8086-compatible sessions to run on the CPU and thereby allows existing MS-DOS applications to run preemptively with the rest of the system. As with Windows 3.1, the use of virtual device drivers provides common regulated access to hardware resources, causing each application running in a VM to think that it is running on its own individual computer and allowing applications not designed to multitask to run concurrently with other applications.

Windows 95 provides a flexible environment for running MS-DOS–based applications. In Windows 3.1, users sometimes needed to exit Windows to run MS DOS–based applications that were either ill-behaved or required direct access to system resources. MS-DOS–based application compatibility is improved in Windows 95 to the point that almost all MS-DOS–based applications should run under Windows 95.

A detailed discussion of the improvements made to the support for running MS-DOS–based applications within the Windows environment is provided in Chapter 6, "Support for Running MS-DOS–based Applications."

Protection

In Windows, VMs are fully protected from one another, as well as from other applications running on the system. This protection prevents errant MS-DOS–based applications from overwriting memory occupied or used by system components or other applications. If an MS-DOS–based application attempts to access memory outside of its address space, the system notifies the user and terminates the MS-DOS–based application.

Robustness Improvements

System robustness is greatly improved when running MS-DOS–based applications in Windows 95. Robustness is discussed in Chapter 5, "Robustness."

Support for Win32–Based Applications

Win32–based applications can fully exploit and benefit significantly from the design of the Windows 95 architecture. In addition, each Win32–based application runs in its own fully protected, private address space. This strategy prevents Win32–based applications from crashing each other, from crashing running MS-DOS–based applications, from crashing running Win16–based applications, or from crashing the Windows 95 system as a whole.

Win32–based applications feature the following benefits over Win16–based applications in Windows 95 and over Windows 3.1:

- Preemptive multitasking
- Separate message queues
- Flat address space
- Compatibility with Windows NT
- Long filename support

- Memory protection
- Robustness improvements

Preemptive Multitasking

Unlike the cooperative multitasking used by Win16–based applications under Windows 3.1, 32-bit Win32–based applications are preemptively multitasked in Windows 95. The operating system kernel is responsible for scheduling the time allotted for running applications in the system, and support for preemptive multitasking results in smoother concurrent processing and prevents any one application from utilizing all system resources without permitting other tasks to run.

Win32–based applications can optionally implement threads to improve the granularity at which they multitask within the system. The use of threads by an application improves the interaction with the user and results in smoother multitasking operation.

Separate Message Queues

Under Windows 3.1, the system uses the point when an application checks the system message queue as the mechanism to pass control to another task, allowing that task to run in a cooperative manner. If an application doesn't check the message queue on a regular basis, or if the application hangs and thus prevents other applications from checking the message queue, the system keeps the other tasks in the system suspended until the errant application ends.

Each Win32–based application has its own message queue and is thus not affected by the behavior of other running tasks on their own message queues. If a Win16–based application hangs, or if another running Win32–based application crashes, a Win32–based application continues to run preemptively and can still receive incoming messages or event notifications.

Message queues are discussed in more detail in Chapter 5, "Robustness."

Flat Address Space

Win32–based applications benefit from improved performance and simpler construct because they can access memory in a linear fashion, rather than being limited to the segmented memory architecture used by MS-DOS and Windows 3.1. To provide a means of accessing high amounts of memory using a 16-bit addressing model, the Intel CPU architecture provides support for accessing 64K chunks of memory, called *segments*, at a time. Applications and the operating system suffer a performance penalty under this architecture because of the manipulations required by the processor for mapping memory references from the segment/offset combination to the physical memory structure.

The use of a flat address space by the 32-bit components in Windows 95 and by Win32–based applications allows application and device driver developers to write software without the limitations or design issues inherent in the segmented memory architecture used by MS-DOS and Windows 3.1.

Compatibility with Windows NT

Win32–based applications that exploit Win32 APIs common to Windows 95 and Windows NT can run without modification on either platform on Intel–based computers. The commonality of the Win32 API provides a consistent programmatic interface and allows application developers to leverage a single development effort to deliver software that runs on multiple platforms. It also provides scaleability of applications and broadens the base of platforms available for running ISV or custom applications with minimal additional effort.

Application developers are encouraged to develop applications either under Windows 95 or under Windows NT and to test compatibility on both platforms.

Long Filename Support

Win32–based applications that call the file I/O functions supported by the Win32 API benefit from the ability to support and manipulate filenames of up to 255 characters with no additional development effort. To ease the burden of the application developer, the Win32 APIs and common dialog support handle the work of manipulating long filenames, and the file system provides compatibility with MS-DOS and other systems by automatically maintaining the traditional 8.3 filename.

Memory Protection

Each Win32–based application runs in its own private address and is protected by the system from other applications or processes that are running in the system. Unlike errant Win16–based applications under Windows 3.1, errant Win32–based applications under Windows 95 end only themselves, instead of bringing down the entire system if they attempt to access memory belonging to another application.

The use of separate message queues for Win32–based applications also ensures that the system continues to run if an application hangs or stops responding to messages or events.

Robustness Improvements

Win32–based applications benefit from the highest level of system robustness supported under Windows 95. Resources allocated for each Win32–based application are tracked on a per-thread basis and are automatically freed when the application ends. If an application hangs, users can perform a *local reboot* operation to end the hung application without affecting other running tasks, and the system then cleans up properly.

Detailed information about robustness enhancements is given in Chapter 5, "Robustness."

32-Bit File System Architecture

The file system in Windows 95 has been redesigned to support the characteristics and needs of the multitasking nature of its kernel. The changes present in Windows 95 provide many benefits to users and have the following results:

- **Improved ease of use.** Ease of use is improved by the support of long filenames because users no longer need to reference files by the MS-DOS 8.3 filename structure. Instead they can use up to 255 characters to identify their documents. Ease of use is also improved by hiding the filename extensions.

- **Improved performance.** As in Windows for Workgroups 3.11, file I/O performance is improved dramatically over Windows 3.1 by featuring 32-bit protected-mode code for reading information from and writing information to the file system, reading from and writing to the disk device, and intelligent 32-bit caching mechanisms (a full 32-bit code path is available from the file system to the disk device).

- **Improved system stability and reliability.** File system components implemented as 32-bit protected-mode device drivers offer improved system stability and reliability over their MS-DOS device driver counterparts because they can remain in protected mode for code execution and because they leverage existing driver technology first implemented in Windows NT and also available in Windows for Workgroups 3.11.

Architecture Overview

Windows 95 features a layered file system architecture that supports multiple file systems and provides a protected-mode path from the application to the media device, resulting in improved file and disk I/O performance over Windows 3.1. The following features are included in the new file system architecture:

- Win32 API support
- Long filename support
- 32-bit FAT file system
- 32-bit CD-ROM file system
- Dynamic system cache for file and network I/O
- Open architecture for future system support
- Disk device driver compatibility with Windows NT

Figure 28 depicts the file system architecture used by Windows 95.

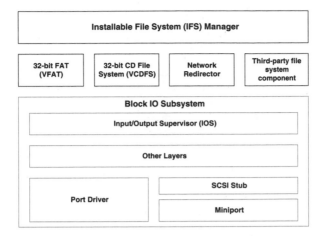

Figure 28. The file system architecture

The file system architecture in Windows 95 is made up of the following components:

- **Installable File System (IFS) Manager.** The IFS Manager is responsible for arbitrating access to different file system components.

- **File system drivers.** The file system drivers layer includes access to file allocation table (FAT)–based disk devices, CD-ROM file systems, and redirected network device support.

- **Block I/O subsystem.** The block I/O subsystem is responsible for interacting with the physical disk device.

Components of each of these layers are examined in the next three sections.

The Installable File System Manager

Under MS-DOS and Windows 3.1, the MS-DOS Int 21h interrupt is responsible for providing access to the file system to manipulate file information on a disk device. To support redirected disk devices, such as a network drive or a CD-ROM drive, other system components, such as the network redirector, would hook the Int 21h function so that it could examine a file system request to determine whether it should handle the request or the base file system should. Although this mechanism provided the ability to add additional device drivers, some add-on components were ill-behaved and interfered with other installed drivers.

Another problem with the MS-DOS–based file system was the difficulty in supporting the loading of multiple network redirectors to provide concurrent access to different network types. Windows for Workgroups provided support for running the Microsoft network redirector at the same time as an additional network redirector, such as Novell NetWare, Banyan VINES, or SUN PC-NFS. However, support for running more than two network redirectors at the same time was not provided.

The key to friendly access to disk and redirected devices in Windows 95 is the Installable File System (IFS) Manager. The IFS Manager is responsible for arbitrating access to file system devices, as well as other file system device components.

File System Drivers

Windows 95 includes support for the following file systems:

- 32-bit file allocation table (VFAT) driver

- 32-bit CD-ROM file system (CDFS) driver

- 32-bit network redirector for connectivity to Microsoft network servers, such as Windows NT Server, along with a 32-bit network redirector to connect to Novell NetWare servers

In addition, third parties will use the IFS Manager APIs to provide a clean way of concurrently supporting multiple device types and adding additional disk device support and network redirector support.

The 32-Bit Protected-Mode FAT File System

The 32-bit VFAT driver provides a 32-bit protected-mode code path for manipulating the file system stored on a disk. It is also re-entrant and multithreaded, providing smoother multitasking performance. The 32-bit file access driver is improved over that provided originally with Windows for Workgroups 3.11 and is compatible with more MS-DOS-device drivers and hard disk controllers.

Benefits of the 32-bit file access driver over MS-DOS–based driver solutions include the following:

- Dramatically improved performance and real-mode disk caching
- No conventional memory used (replacement for real-mode SmartDrive)
- Better multitasking when accessing information on disk with no blocking
- Dynamic cache support

Under MS-DOS and Windows 3.1, manipulation of the FAT and writing to or reading from the disk is handled by the Int 21h MS-DOS function and is 16-bit real-mode code. Being able to manipulate the disk file system from protected mode removes or reduces the need to transition to real mode in order to write information to the disk through MS-DOS, which results in a performance gain for file I/O access.

The 32-bit VFAT driver interacts with the block I/O subsystem to provide 32-bit disk access to more device types than are supported by Windows 3.1. Support is also provided for mapping to existing real-mode disk drivers that may be in use on a user's system. The combination of the 32-bit file access and 32-bit disk access drivers results in significantly improved disk and file I/O performance.

The 32-Bit Cache

The 32-bit VFAT works in conjunction with a 32-bit protected-mode cache (VCACHE) driver and replaces and improves on the 16-bit real-mode SmartDrive disk cache software provided with MS-DOS and Windows 3.1. The VCACHE driver features a more intelligent algorithm for caching information read from or written to a disk drive than SmartDrive, and results in improved performance when reading information from cache. The VCACHE driver is also responsible for managing the cache pool for the CD-ROM File System (CDFS) and the provided 32-bit network redirectors.

Another big improvement VCACHE provides over SmartDrive is that the memory pool used for the cache is dynamic and is based on the amount of available free system memory. Users no longer need to statically allocate a block of memory to set aside as a disk cache because the system automatically allocates or deallocates memory used for the cache based on system use. Because of intelligent cache use, the performance of the system also scales better than with Windows 3.1 or Windows for Workgroups 3.11.

The 32-Bit Protected-Mode CD-ROM File System

The 32-bit protected-mode CD-ROM file system (CDFS) implemented in Windows 95 provides improved CD-ROM access performance over the real-mode MSCDEX driver in Windows 3.1 and is a full 32-bit ISO 9660 CD file system. The CDFS driver replaces the 16-bit real-mode MSCDEX driver and features 32-bit protected-mode caching of CD-ROM data. The CDFS driver cache is dynamic and shares the cache memory pool with the 32-bit VFAT driver, requiring no configuration or static allocation on the part of the user.

Benefits of the new 32-bit CDFS driver include the following:

- No conventional memory used (replaces real-mode MSCDEX)

- Improved performance over MS-DOS–based MSCDEX and real-mode cache

- Better multitasking when accessing CD-ROM information, with no blocking

- Dynamic cache support to provide a better balance between providing memory to run applications versus memory to serve as a disk cache

If MSCDEX is specified in the AUTOEXEC.BAT, the 32-bit CDFS driver takes over the role played by the MSCDEX driver and communicates with the CD-ROM device. The use of MSCDEX is no longer necessary under Windows 95.

Users of CD-ROM multimedia applications benefit greatly from the new 32-bit CDFS. Their multimedia applications run smoother and information is read from the CD-ROM quicker, providing improved performance.

The Block I/O Subsystem

The block I/O subsystem in Windows 95 improves upon the 32-bit disk access fast-disk device architecture in Windows 3.1 and therefore improves performance for the entire file system and a broader array of device support.

As shown in Figure 29, the components of the block I/O subsystem include the high-level I/O Supervisor (IOS) layer, which provides an interface to the block I/O subsystem for the higher layer components; the port driver, which represents a monolithic disk device driver; the SCSI layer, which provides a standard interface and driver layer to provide device-independent control code for SCSI devices; and the SCSI mini-port driver, which contains the device-dependent control code responsible for interacting with individual SCSI controllers.

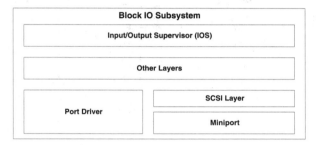

Figure 29. The architecture of the block I/O subsystem

The block I/O subsystem provides the following support in Windows 95:

- A fully Plug and Play–enabled architecture

- Support for mini-port drivers that are binary compatible with Windows NT

- Support for Windows 3.1 fast disk drivers for backward compatibility

- Protected-mode drivers that take over real-mode MS-DOS device drivers when safe to do so

- The ability to support existing MS-DOS real-mode disk device drivers for compatibility

The following sections examine the different areas that make up the block I/O subsystem. The explanations are provided to facilitate an understanding of the components, bearing in mind that the configuration of the disk device driver layers is isolated from the user.

The I/O Supervisor

The I/O Supervisor (IOS) provides services to file systems and drivers. The IOS is responsible for the queuing of file service requests and for routing the requests to the appropriate file system driver. The IOS also provides asynchronous notification of file system events to installed drivers.

The Port Driver

The port driver is a monolithic 32-bit protected-mode driver that communicates with a specific disk device, such as a hard disk controller. This driver is specifically for use with Windows 95 and resembles the 32-bit disk access (fast disk) driver used in Windows 3.1, such as the WDCTRL driver used for Western Digital compatible hard disk controllers. In Windows 95, the driver that communicates with IDE/ESDI hard disk controllers and floppy disk controllers is implemented as a port driver. A port driver provides the same functionality as the combination of the SCSI manager and the mini-port driver.

The SCSI Layer

The SCSI layer applies a 32-bit protected-mode universal driver model architecture to communication with SCSI devices. The SCSI layer provides all the high-level functionality that is common to SCSI-like devices and then uses a mini-port driver to handle device-specific I/O calls. The SCSI Manager is part of this system and provides compatibility support for using Windows NT mini-port drivers.

The Mini-Port Driver

The mini-port driver model used in Windows 95 simplifies the task of writing device drivers for disk device hardware vendors. Because the SCSI Stub provides the high-level functionality for communicating with SCSI devices, disk device hardware vendors need to create only a mini-port driver that is tailored to their own disk device. The mini-port driver for Windows 95 is 32-bit protected-mode code and is binary compatible with Windows NT mini-port drivers, another factor that simplifies the task of writing device drivers. Binary compatibility with NT also results in a more stable and reliable device driver because hardware vendors need to maintain only one code base for device support. Users of Windows 95 also benefit because many mini-port drivers are already available for Windows NT.

Support for IDE, ESDI, and SCSI Controllers

Through the use of either a port driver or a mini-port driver, support for a broad array of disk devices will be available for Windows 95, including popular IDE, ESDI, and SCSI disk controllers. Users won't have to decide whether to use a port driver or a mini-port driver because the driver is provided by the hardware vendor and configuration of the driver is handled by the Windows 95 system.

The Real-Mode Mapper

To provide binary compatibility with real-mode MS-DOS–based disk device drivers for which a protected-mode counterpart does not exist in Windows 95, the block I/O subsystem provides a mapping layer to allow the protected-mode file system to communicate with a real-mode driver as if it were a protected-mode component. The layers above and including this real-mode mapper (RMM) are protected-mode code, and the real-mode mapper translates file I/O requests from protected mode to real mode so that the MS-DOS device driver can perform the desired read or write operation from or to the disk device. An example of when the real-mode mapper would come into play is when real-mode disk-compression software is running and a protected-mode disk-compression driver is not available.

Long Filename Support

The use of long filenames of up to 255 characters in Windows 95 overcomes the sometimes cryptic 8.3 MS-DOS filename convention and allows more user-friendly filenames. MS-DOS 8.3 filenames are maintained and tracked by the system to provide compatibility with existing Win16–based and MS-DOS–based applications that manipulate only 8.3 filenames, but as users migrate to Win32–based applications, the use of 8.3 filename conventions is hidden from the user.

Long filenames are supported by extending the MS-DOS FAT file system and using bits and fields that were previously reserved by the operating system to add special directory entries that maintain long filename information. Extending the MS-DOS FAT layout, rather than creating a new format, allows users to install and use Windows 95 on existing disk formats without having to change their disk structure or reformat their drives. This implementation provides ease of use and allows future growth while maintaining backward compatibility with existing applications.

Because Windows 95 simply extends the FAT structure, long filenames are supported on diskettes as well as hard disks. If a file on a diskette that has a long filename is viewed on a computer that is not running Windows 95, only the 8.3 filename representation is seen.

Figure 30 shows a disk directory with long filenames and their corresponding 8.3 filename mappings on a computer running Windows 95.

```
       Volume in drive C is MY HARDDISK
        Volume Serial Number is 1B47-7161
        Directory of C:\LONGFILE

       . <DIR> 05-11-94 10:34a .
       .. <DIR> 05-11-94 10:34a ..
       4THQUART XLS 147 05-11-94 12:25a 4th Quarter Analysis.xls
       TEXTFILE TXT 147 05-11-94 12:25a TEXTFILE.TXT
```

(continued)

Figure 30. (*continued*)

```
THISISMY DOC 147 05-11-94 12:25a this is my long filename.doc
1994FINA DOC 147 05-11-94 10:35a 1994 Financial Projections.doc
 4 file(s) 588 bytes
 2 dir(s) 48,009,216 bytes free
```

Figure 30. A directory listed from the command prompt, showing both 8.3 and long filenames

Support for Existing Disk Management Utilities

For existing disk management utilities to recognize and preserve long filenames, utility vendors need to revise their software products. Microsoft is working closely with utilities vendors and is documenting long filename support and its implementation as an extension to the FAT format as part of the Windows 95 Software Development Kit (SDK).

Existing MS-DOS–based disk management utilities that manipulate the FAT format, including disk defragmenters, disk bit editors, and some tape backup software, may not recognize long filenames as used by Windows 95 and may destroy long filename entries in the FAT format. However, no data is lost if the long filename entry is destroyed because the corresponding system-defined 8.3 filename is preserved.

Hidden File Extensions

Like Windows 3.1, Windows 95 uses file extensions to associate a given file type with an application. However, to make it easier to manipulate files, file extensions are hidden from users in the Windows 95 shell and in the Windows Explorer, and instead, icons are used in the UI in Windows 95 to differentiate the documents associated with different applications. Information about file type associations is stored in the Registry, and the associations are used to map a given file with the icon that represents the document type. (For compatibility reasons, Windows 95 must track filename extensions for use with existing MS-DOS and Win16–based applications.)

In addition to hiding filename extensions in the Windows 95 shell and the Windows Explorer, application developers can hide filenames from users in their applications. Mechanisms for hiding filenames are documented in the Windows 95 SDK. A good Windows 95 application makes use of these mechanisms for handling files to be consistent with the rest of the Windows 95 environment.

Additional File Date/Time Attributes

To further enhance the file system, Windows 95 maintains additional date/time attributes for files that MS-DOS does not track. Windows 95 tracks the date/time when a new file was created, the date/time when a file was modified, and the date when a file was last opened. These file attributes are displayed in the file's property sheet, as shown in Figure 31 on the following page.

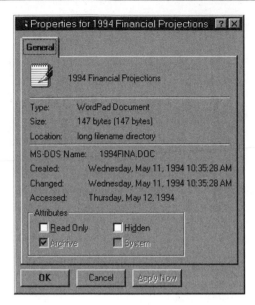

Figure 31. The properties for a file, showing the new file date/time attributes

Utilities vendors can take advantage of this additional date/time information to provide enhanced backup utilities—for example, to use a better mechanism when determining whether a given file has changed.

Coordinated Universal Time Format

MS-DOS has traditionally used the local time of the computer as the time stamp for the directory entry of a file, and continues to use local time for files stored on the local system. However, Windows 95 supports the use of the coordinated universal time (UTC) format for accessing or creating information on network file servers. This format provides the superior, more universal tracking of time information required by networks that operate across time zones.

Exclusive Access for Disk Management Tools

Disk management utilities, such as disk defragmenters, sector editors, and disk-compression utilities, don't get along well with Windows 3.1. File system programs, such as CHKDSK and DEFRAG, require exclusive access to the file system to minimize the disk access complexities that are present in a multitasking environment where disk I/O occurs. For example, without exclusive access to the disk, data corruption might occur if a user requests that a disk operation move information on the disk at the same time that another task is accessing that information or writing other information to disk. However, Windows 3.1 and MS-DOS do not provide a means of controlling access to the disk, so users have been forced to exit Windows and enter MS-DOS to run disk management utilities.

The file system in Windows 95 has been enhanced to support the use of Windows–based disk management utilities by permitting exclusive access to a disk device. Exclusive disk access is handled as part of the file system through a new API mechanism and can be used by utilities vendors to write Windows–based disk management utilities. Microsoft is encouraging third-party utilities vendors to use this API mechanism to move existing MS-DOS–based utilities to Windows, and is also using it to deliver disk management utilities as part of Windows 95.

For example, this mechanism is used by the Disk Defragmenter (Optimizer) utility delivered as part of Windows 95. Unlike the disk defragment utility used under the combination of MS-DOS and Windows 3.1, the Disk Defragmenter in Windows 95 can be run from the Windows 95 shell and can even be run in the background while users continue to work on their systems.

DriveSpace Disk Compression

Windows 95 provides built-in support for DriveSpace disk compression. Compatible with DoubleSpace and DriveSpace disk compression provided with MS-DOS, Windows 95 provides base compression in the form of a 32-bit virtual device driver that delivers improved performance over previously available real-mode compression drivers and frees conventional memory for use by MS-DOS–based applications. Users of MS-DOS–based DoubleSpace and DriveSpace don't need to change their existing compressed volume file (CVF) and thus don't need to take any special actions when they install Windows 95.

As shown in Figure 32, the DriveSpace disk compression tool provided with Windows 95 is GUI-based and provides the ability to compress a physical hard drive or removable floppy drive. The Compress a Drive dialog box, shown in Figure 33 on the following page, graphically depicts the amount of free space available before compression and the estimated space available after compression.

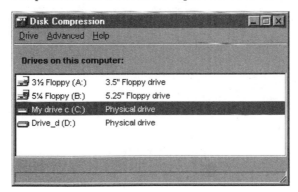

Figure 32. The DriveSpace disk compression tool

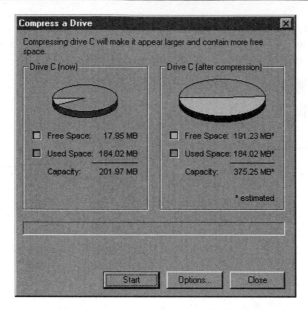

Figure 33. The Compress a Drive dialog box, which graphically displays free space

System Capacity Improvements

Windows 95 provides better system capacity for running MS-DOS and Win16–based applications than Windows 3.1. A number of internal enhancements to the base system prevent internal system resources from being exhausted as quickly as was possible when running multiple Windows–based applications under Windows 3.1.

Many of the artificial limitations present in Windows 3.1 were due to its architecture or internal data structures, which were in turn largely due to the fact that Windows 3.1 had to run on an Intel 80286–based computer. These limitations have for the most part been overcome in Windows 95, to the benefit of users as well as ISVs and other developers.

System Resource Limitation Improvements

Many users have encountered *Out of Memory* error messages when running multiple Windows–based applications under Windows 3.1, even though the system still reports several megabytes of available free memory. Typically these messages were displayed because the system could not allocate an internal memory resource in a Windows API function call due to lack of available space in a region of memory called a *heap*.

Windows 3.1 maintains heaps for system components called GDI and USER. Each heap is 64 KB in size and is used for storing GDI or memory *object* information allocated when an application calls a Windows API function. The amount of space available in the combination of these two heaps is identified as the percentage of system resources that are free and is displayed in the About dialog box in Program Manager and other Windows applications, as shown in Figure 34.

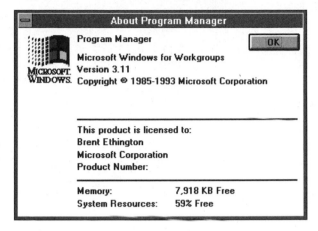

Figure 34. The About dialog box in Program Manager in Windows 3.1, showing free system resources

The percentage of free system resources displayed in the About dialog box is calculated using an internal algorithm to represent the aggregate percentage of free memory in the GDI and USER heaps. When the free system resources percentage gets too low, users commonly see an *Out of Memory* error message, even though the amount of free memory shown in the About dialog box is still quite high. This error can result from low memory in either the GDI or USER heap (or both).

To help reduce the system resource limitation, a number of the data structures stored in the 16-bit GDI and USER heaps in Windows 3.1 have been moved out of these heaps and stored in 32-bit heaps, providing more room for the remaining data elements to be created. As a result, system resources decrease less rapidly in Windows 95 than they did in Windows 3.1.

For compatibility, not all objects were removed from the 16-bit GDI or USER heap and placed in a 32-bit heap. For example, some Windows–based applications manipulate the contents of the GDI heap directly, bypassing the published API mechanisms for doing so, because their developers think direct manipulation increases performance. However, because these applications bypass the Windows API mechanisms, moving their data from the existing heap structures and placing them in 32-bit heaps would cause these applications to fail because of memory access violations.

Win16–based and Win32–based applications use the same GDI and USER heaps. The impact of removing selected items from the heaps was closely examined and objects were selected based on the biggest improvement that could be achieved while affecting the fewest number of applications. For example, the GDI heap can quickly become full because of the creation of memory-intensive region objects that are used by applications for creating complex images and by the printing subsystem for generating complex output. Region objects were removed from the 64 KB 16-bit GDI heap and placed in a 32-bit heap, benefiting graphic-intensive applications and providing for the creation of more smaller objects by the system. Windows 95 improves the system capacity for the USER heap by moving menu and window handles to the 32-bit USER heap. Instead of the total limit of 200 for these data structures in Windows 3.1, Windows 95 allows 32,767 menu handles and an additional 32,767 window handles *per process* rather than system-wide.

In addition to moving information from the GDI and USER heaps, robustness improvements in Windows 95 that facilitate system cleanup of unfreed resources also relieve system resource limitations. When Windows 95 determines that the owner and other ended processes no longer need the resources in memory, Windows 95 cleans up and deallocates leftover data structures. The robustness improvements in Windows 95 are discussed in Chapter 5, "Robustness."

Better Memory Management

Windows 95 improves addressibility to provide better access to physical memory, as well as improves upon the swapfile implementation provided in Windows 3.1 to support virtual memory supplementation of physical memory.

Linear Memory Addressing for Win32–Based Applications

To support a 16-bit operating environment, the Intel processor architecture uses a mechanism, called *segments*, to reference memory by using a 16-bit segment address and a 16-bit offset address within the segment. A segment is 64 KB in size, and applications and the operating system pay a performance penalty when they access information across segments. For 32-bit operating system functionality and Win32–based applications, Windows 95 addresses this issue by using the 32-bit capabilities of the Intel 80386 (and above) processor architecture to support a flat, linear memory mode. A linear addressing model simplifies the development process for application developers, removes the performance penalties imposed by the segmented memory architecture, and provides access to a virtual address space that permits the addressing of up to 4 GB (4 gigabytes, or 4 billion bytes) of memory. Windows 95 uses the flat memory model internally for 32-bit components and virtual device drivers.

Compatibility with the Windows NT Memory Model

Windows 95 uses the same memory model architecture as Windows NT, providing high-end operating system functionality for the mainstream system. Windows 95 allows full use of the 4 GB of addressable memory space to support even the largest desktop application. The operating system provides a 2 GB memory range for applications and reserves a 2 GB range for itself.

Virtual Memory Support (Swapfile) Improvements

Windows 95 addresses problems and limitations imposed in Windows 3.1 by its virtual memory swapfile implementation. With Windows 3.1, users were faced with a myriad of choices and configuration options for setting up a swapfile to support virtual memory. They had to decide whether to use a temporary swapfile or a permanent swapfile, how much memory to allocate to the swapfile, and whether to use 32-bit disk access to access the swapfile. A temporary swapfile did not need to be contiguous, and Windows would dynamically allocate hard disk space when it was started and free up the space when it was terminated. A permanent swapfile provided the best performance, but it had to be contiguous, had to be set up on a physical hard disk, and was statically specified by the user and not freed up when the user exited Windows.

The swapfile implementation in Windows 95 simplifies the configuration task for the user and, because of improved virtual memory algorithms and access methods, combines the best of a temporary swapfile and a permanent swapfile. The swapfile in Windows 95 is dynamic and can shrink or grow based on the operations performed on the system. The swapfile can occupy a fragmented region of the hard disk and it can be located on a compressed disk volume.

Windows 95 uses intelligent system defaults for the configuration of virtual memory, relieving the user of the task of changing virtual memory settings. Figure 35 shows the simplified virtual memory configuration settings.

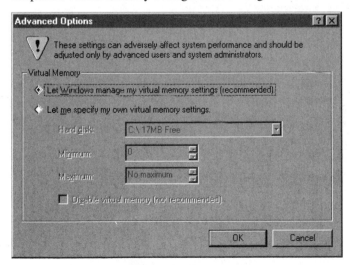

Figure 35. The simplified virtual memory settings

The Registry: A Centralized Configuration Store

Windows 95 uses a mechanism called the *Registry* to serve as the central configuration store for user, application, and computer-specific information. The Registry solves problems associated with the .INI files used in Windows 3.1 and is a hierarchical database that stores system-wide information in a single location, making it easy to manage and support.

Solutions to .INI Problems

Windows 3.1 uses initialization (.INI) files to store system-specific or application-specific information about the state or configuration of the system. For example, the WIN.INI file stores state information about the appearance or customization of the Windows environment; the SYSTEM.INI file stores system-specific information on the hardware and device-driver configuration of the system; and various .INI files, such as WINFILE.INI, MSMAIL.INI, CLOCK.INI, CONTROL.INI, and PROGMAN.INI, store application-specific information about the default state of an application.

Problems with .INI files under Windows 3.1 for configuration management include the following:

* Information is stored in several different locations, including CONFIG.SYS, AUTOEXEC.BAT, WIN.INI, SYSTEM.INI, PROTOCOL.INI, private .INI files, and private .GRP files.

* .INI files are text-based and limited in total size to 64KB, and APIs allow for get/write operations only.

* Information stored in .INI files is non-hierarchical and supports only two levels of information: key names broken up by section headings.

* Many .INI files contain a myriad of switches and entries that are complicated to configure or are used only by operating system components.

* .INI files provide no mechanism for storing user-specific information, thus making it difficult for multiple users to share a single computer.

* Configuration information in .INI files is local to each system, and because no API mechanisms are available for remotely managing configuration, managing multiple systems is difficult.

To solve these problems, the Registry was designed with the following goals in mind:

* Simplify the support burden.
* Centralize configuration information.

- Provide a means to store user, application, and computer-specific information.
- Provide local and remote access to configuration information.

The Registry is structured as a database of keys in which each key can contain a value or other keys (subkeys). As shown in Figure 36, the Registry uses a hierarchical structure to store text or binary value information and maintains all of the configuration parameters normally stored in the Windows system .INI files such as WIN.INI, SYSTEM.INI, and PROTOCOL.INI. Although similar in some ways to the Registration Database used in Windows 3.1, which served as a central repository for file associations and OLE registration information, the Registry in Windows 95 extends the Registration Database structure to support keys that can have more than one value and also support data of different types.

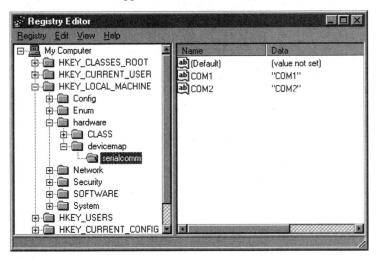

Figure 36. The hierarchy of the Registry, as displayed by the Registry Editor

The Registry is made up of several .DAT files that contain system-specific information (SYSTEM.DAT) or user-specific information (USER.DAT). System-specific information, such as the static reference to loading virtual device drivers, is moved as appropriate from the SYSTEM.INI file to the Registry.

System Switch Simplification

Another improvement in Windows 95 over the Windows 3.1 use of .INI files is related to system switch simplification. Windows 3.1 supports several hundred different configuration switches that can be specified in system .INI files, including WIN.INI and SYSTEM.INI. With intelligent enhancements made to the system and better dynamic configuration properties, Windows 95 has reduced the number of entries normally associated with .INI files. These reductions didn't result from simply moving .INI entries to the Registry but by examining and justifying the presence of each and every one.

No .INI Files?

Like CONFIG.SYS and AUTOEXEC.BAT, WIN.INI and SYSTEM.INI and application-specific .INI files still exist for compatibility reasons. The Win16 APIs for manipulating .INI files still manipulate .INI files, but developers of Win32–based applications are encouraged to use the Registry APIs to consolidate application-specific information.

Many existing Win16–based applications expect to find and manipulate the WIN.INI and SYSTEM.INI files to add entries or load unique device drivers, so Windows 95 examines .INI files during the boot process. For example, the [386Enh] section of SYSTEM.INI is checked for virtual device drivers.

Role in Plug and Play

One of the primary roles of the Registry in Windows 95 is to serve as a central repository for hardware-specific information for use by the Plug and Play system components. Windows 95 maintains information about hardware components and devices that have been identified through an enumeration process in the hierarchical structure of the Registry. When new devices are installed, the system checks the existing configuration in the Registry to determine which hardware resources—for example, IRQs, I/O addresses, DMA channels, and so on—are not being used, so that the new device can be properly configured without conflicting with a device already installed in the system.

Remote Access to Registry Information

Another advantage of the Registry for Win32–based applications is that many of the Win32 Registry APIs use the remote procedure call (RPC) mechanism in Windows 95 to provide remote access to Registry information across a network. As a result, desktop management applications can be written to aid in the management and support of Windows–based computers, and the contents of the Registry on a given PC can be queried over a network. Industry management mechanisms, such as SNMP or DMI, can easily be integrated into Windows 95, simplifying the management and support burden of an MIS organization. For more information about manageability and remote administration, see Chapter 9, "Networking."

Better Font Support

Font support in Windows 95 has been enhanced to provide better integration with the UI and has been optimized for the 32-bit environment. It also provides capabilities such as font smoothing for fonts that have not previously been offered as part of a mainstream operating system.

The 32-Bit TrueType Rasterizer

The rasterizer component for rendering and generating TrueType fonts is enhanced in Windows 95. The rasterizer is written as a 32-bit component, and delivers better fidelity from the mathematical representation to the generated bitmap, as well as better performance for rendering TrueType fonts.

In addition to performance enhancements, the new 32-bit rasterizer provides support for generating complicated glyphs—for example, Han—and results in a faster initial boot time in Windows 95 than in Windows 3.1 when many fonts are installed.

CHAPTER 5

Robustness

Windows 95 improves on the robustness of Windows 3.1 to provide great support for running MS-DOS–based, Win16–based, and Win32–based applications, and to provide a high level of system protection from errant applications.

Windows 3.1 provided a number of mechanisms to support a more robust and stable environment over Windows 3.0, including the following:

- **Better resource clean-up.** When an MS-DOS–based or Windows–based application crashed, users could continue running in a way that allowed them to save their work.

- **Local reboot.** Users could shut down an application that hung.

- **Parameter validation for API calls.** The system could catch many common application errors and fail the API call, rather than allow bad data to be passed to an API.

Just as the improvements in Windows 3.1 provided a more robust and stable environment than Windows 3.0, the improvements in Windows 95 provide an even better environment.

System-Wide Robustness Improvements

System-wide improvements resulting in a more robust operating system environment than Windows 3.1 include:

- Better local reboot
- Virtual device driver thread clean-up when a process ends
- Per-thread state tracking
- Virtual device driver parameter validation

Better Local Reboot

The capability whereby users can end an application or VM that hangs is called a *local reboot*. With Windows 3.1, users could perform a local reboot by pressing the three-key CTRL+ALT+DEL combination. Users could pretty easily end errant VMs with a local reboot request, but a local reboot request for a Windows–based application often didn't end the errant Windows–based process or brought the entire system down.

Windows 95 greatly improves the local reboot support by providing a means to end an MS-DOS–based application running in a VM, a Win16–based application, or a Win32–based application without bringing down the entire system. Moreover, the process of cleaning up the system after a local reboot is now more complete than for Windows 3.1. (This process is described later in this chapter.)

In Windows 3.1, when a user requests a local reboot, the system may identify the active application as the application that has the focus of the local reboot request, or it may report back that there is no application in a hung or inactive state. In Windows 95, the system displays the Close Program dialog box, which identifies the tasks that are running and the state that the system perceives each one to be in, as shown in Figure 37. This level of detail affords the user much more flexibility and control over the local reboot than with Windows 3.1.

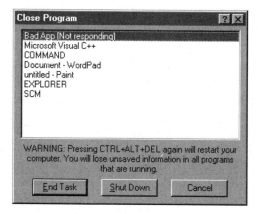

Figure 37. The Close Program dialog box

Applications are identified as "not responding" when they haven't checked the message queue for a period of time. Although some applications don't check the message queue while performing computationally intensive operations, well-behaved applications check the message queue frequently. In Windows 95, as in Windows 3.1, Win16–based applications must check the message queue to relinquish control to other running tasks.

Try It!

Perform a Local Reboot

1. With a couple of applications running, press CTRL+ALT+DEL. You are presented with a list of active applications. Applications that are hung are identified as *Not responding*.

2. Terminate one of the tasks by clicking *End Task*.

Virtual Device Driver Thread Clean-Up

Local reboot support is also aided by improved VxD thread clean-up when a given process ends. With Windows 3.1, the system often couldn't recover either if it was running real-mode code, such as BIOS routines, when an application ended abnormally, or if the user requested a local reboot to end a seemingly-hung application. For example, if an operation (such as a network operation in real-mode, a disk I/O, or an asynchronous application request) ended abnormally because of another application-based error, Windows 3.1 sometimes couldn't clean up properly to free allocated resources and sometimes couldn't even return control to the user.

Windows 95 improves system clean-up by providing each system VxD with the ability to track the resources it allocates on a per-thread basis. Because most computer system functionality and support is handled in Windows 95 by VxDs rather than by real-mode code or BIOS routines, Windows 95 can recover from errors or situations that, under Windows 3.1, would require that the computer be rebooted.

When Windows 95 ends a given thread (because the user exited the application, a local reboot was requested, or the application ended abnormally), each VxD receives notification that the thread is ended. This notification allows the VxD to safely cancel any operations it is waiting to finish and frees any resources that the VxD previously allocated for the thread or application. Because the system tracks each VM, Win16–based application, and Win32 thread as a separate per-thread instance, the system can clean up properly at each of these levels, without affecting the integrity of the system.

Per-Thread State Tracking

To aid in system clean-up, resource tracking in Windows 95 is much better than in Windows 3.1. In addition to tracking resources on a per-thread basis by system VxDs, resources such as memory blocks, memory handles, graphics objects, and other system items are allocated and also tracked by system components on a per-thread basis. Tracking these resources on a per-thread basis allows the system to clean up safely when a given thread ends, either normally—at the user's request—or abnormally. Resources are identified and tracked by both a thread ID and the major Windows version number that is stored in the .EXE header of the application.

For a discussion of how the thread ID and the Windows version number are used to facilitate clean-up of the system and recovery of allocated resources for Win16–based and Win32–based applications, see the robustness sections for Win16–based and Win32–based applications later in this chapter.

Virtual Device Driver Parameter Validation

Virtual device drivers are an integral part of the Windows 95 operating system and have a more important role than in Windows 3.1, because many operating system components are implemented as VxDs. To help provide a more stable and reliable operating system, Windows 95 provides support for parameter validation of virtual device drivers, which was not available for Windows 3.1. The debug version of Windows 95 system files provided as part of the Windows 95 SDK and Windows 95 DDK can be used by VxD developers to debug their VxDs during the course of development, ensuring that their VxDs are stable and robust.

In addition to improving system-wide robustness, Windows 95 provides improved robustness for running MS-DOS–based, Win16–based, and Win32–based applications, which also ensures that Windows 95 is a more stable and reliable environment than Windows 3.1.

Robustness for MS-DOS–Based Applications

Because of improved support, users can run MS-DOS–based applications under Windows 95 that they could not run under Windows 3.1. Several improvements that provide great robustness for running MS-DOS–based applications are described in the next two sections.

Virtual Machines Protection Improvements

Each MS-DOS–based application runs in a separate VM and is configured by default to execute preemptively and run in the background when another application is active. Each VM is protected from other tasks running in the system, so an errant Win16–based or Win32–based application can't crash a running MS-DOS–based application, and vice versa.

Under Windows 3.1, each VM inherited the attributes and environment configuration from the global System VM. Each VM was protected from other VMs, preventing errant MS-DOS–based applications from accessing memory or overwriting system code and thus possibly bringing the system down. However, the VMs did not completely prevent an MS-DOS–based application from overwriting MS-DOS system code, because MS-DOS–based applications had full access to all memory locations in the first megabyte of addressable memory space (the real-mode memory range).

Windows 95 provides a higher level of memory protection for running MS-DOS–based applications by preventing the applications from overwriting the MS-DOS system area in real mode. If users want the highest level of system protection, they can configure their MS-DOS–based applications to run with general memory protection enabled. (This mode is not enabled by default because of the overhead required to validate memory access requests.) In addition, parameter validation of Int 21h operations on pointers is performed, thereby increasing the robustness of the system.

Better Clean-Up When a Virtual Machine Ends

When a VM ends in Windows 3.1, some resources, such as DPMI memory, are not released properly. When a VM ends in Windows 95—either normally because the user exited the application or VM or requested a local reboot, or abnormally because the application hung—the system frees all resources allocated to the VM. These resources include not only those allocated and maintained by the system VxDs, but also those allocated for the VM by the Virtual Machine Manager, including any DPMI and XMS memory that the VM requested.

Robustness for Win16–Based Applications

Windows 95 provides improved support for running Win16–based applications. It also provides robust support for Win16–based applications, plus compatibility with existing Windows–based applications, while keeping memory requirements low. The next two sections describe improvements for Win16–based applications running under Windows 95.

Per-Thread State Tracking

With Windows 3.1, when a Windows–based application ended, the resources that had been used by the application were not released by the system. Some Windows–based applications took this behavior into account and didn't free certain resources, so that their allocated resources could be accessed by other in-memory Windows–based applications or by system components such as DLLs.

Changing the way the system behaves when a Win16–based application ends—for example, immediately freeing up all the resources allocated to the application—might have resulted in the breaking of existing applications. To facilitate resource tracking under Windows 95, each Win16–based application runs as a separate thread in the Win16 address space. When a Win16–based application ends, Windows 95 doesn't immediately release the resources allocated to the application but holds them until the last Win16–based application has ended. (Windows 95 determines that no more Win16–based applications are running by associating the Windows version number of the application with the thread ID for the running process.) When the last Win16–based application has ended and it is safe to free all resources allocated to Win16–based applications, Windows 95 begins releasing the resources.

Parameter Validation for Win16 APIs

Windows 3.0 was perceived by some users as unstable because Unrecoverable Application Errors (UAEs) were common when working with Windows–based applications. Most of this instability was in fact caused by Windows–based applications that passed invalid parameters to Windows API functions. The APIs in turn attempted to process this bad data and usually attempted to access an invalid area of memory. For example, when an application inadvertently passed a NULL pointer to a Windows API function and the function tried to access memory at the reference, a UAE or "general protection fault" would be generated.

Windows 95 provides parameter validations for all Win16–based APIs and checks incoming data to API functions to ensure that the data is valid. For example, functions that reference memory are checked for NULL pointers, and functions that operate on data within a range of values are checked to ensure that the data is within the proper range. If invalid data is found, an appropriate error number is returned to the application, and it is then up to the application to catch the error condition and handle it accordingly.

The Windows 95 SDK provides debug system components to help software developers debug their applications. The debug components provide extensive error reporting for parameter validation to assist developers in tracking common problems related to invalid parameters during the course of development.

Robustness for Win32–Based Applications

Although better robustness for running MS-DOS–based and Win16–based applications is provided by Windows 95 than by Windows 3.1, even greater support for robustness is available for running Win32–based applications. Win32–based applications also benefit from preemptive multitasking, a linear (rather than segmented) address space, and support for a feature-rich API set.

Robustness support for Win32–based applications includes the following:

- A private address space for each running Win32–based application, segregating and protecting one application from others that are running concurrently

- Win32 APIs that support parameter validation and provide a stable and reliable environment

- Resource tracking by thread and the immediate freeing of resources when the thread ends

- Separate message queues for each running Win32–based application, ensuring that a hung Win32–based application does not suspend the entire system

A Private Address Space for Each Win32–Based Application

Each Win32–based application runs in its own private address space so that its resources are protected at the system level from other applications running in the system. This strategy also prevents other applications from inadvertently overwriting the memory area of a given Win32–based application and prevents that Win32–based application from inadvertently overwriting the memory area of another application or of the system as a whole.

Parameter Validation for Win32 APIs

As with Win16–based applications, Windows 95 provides parameter validation for Win32 APIs used by Win32–based applications. The Windows 95 SDK helps software developers debug errors resulting from attempts to pass invalid parameters to Windows APIs. For additional information about parameter validation for Win16 APIs, see the discussion of robustness for Win16–based applications presented earlier in this chapter.

Per-Thread Resource Tracking

Windows 95 tracks the resources allocated to Win32–based applications by thread. Unlike resources allocated to Win16–based applications, resources allocated to Win32–based applications are automatically released when a thread ends processing. This immediate freeing of system resources ensures that the resources are available for use by other running tasks.

Resources are cleaned up properly when threads either end execution on their own—for example, if the application developer inadvertently failed to free allocated resources—or when the user requests a local reboot that ends a given Win32–based application thread or process. Unlike Win16–based applications designed to run under Windows 3.1, Win32–based applications free up their allocated resources immediately when a separate thread or the application itself ends.

Separate Message Queues for Win32–Based Applications

The Windows environment performs tasks based on the receipt of messages sent by system components. Each message is generated based on an action, or *event*, that occurs on the system. For example, when a user presses a key on the keyboard and releases it or moves the mouse, a message is generated by the system and passed to the active application to inform it of the event that occurred. Windows–based applications call specific Windows API functions to extract event messages from message queues and perform operations on the messages—for example, accept an incoming character typed on the keyboard, or move the mouse cursor to another place on the screen.

Under Windows 3.1, a single message queue was used by the entire system. Win16–based applications cooperatively examined the queue and extracted messages addressed to them. This single-queue scheme posed some problems. For example, if a Win16–based application hung and prevented other applications from checking the message queue, the message queue would become full and accepted no new messages. Other Win16–based applications were then suspended until control was relinquished to them and they were able to check for event messages.

Windows 95 solves the problems inherent with the single message queue in Windows 3.1 by providing separate message queues for each running Win32–based application. As shown in Figure 38, the system takes messages from the input message queue and passes them to the appropriate Win32–based application or to the Win16 Subsystem if the message is destined for a Win16–based application. If a Win32–based application hangs and no longer accepts and processes its incoming messages, other running Win16 and Win32–based applications are not affected.

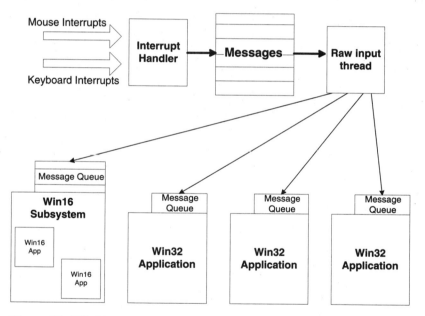

Figure 38. Win32–based applications use separate message queues for increased robustness

If a Win32–based application ends or the user requests a local reboot for a Win32–based application, having separate message queues improves the robustness of the operating system by making it easier to clean up and free the system resources used by the application. It also provides greater reliability and recoverability if an application hangs.

Local Reboot Effectiveness

Because of robustness improvements for Win32–based applications, including the use of a private address spaces, separate message queues, and resource tracking by thread, users should be able request a local reboot to end almost all ill-behaved Win32–based applications without affecting the integrity of the Windows system or other running applications.

When Windows 95 ends a Win32–based application, its resources are immediately deallocated and cleaned up by the system. Because Win32–based applications run in their individually allocated environments, this method is even more robust than the method for reallocation of Win16–based application resources. For more details of the robustness of Win16-based applications, see the appropriate section earlier in this chapter.

Structured Exception Handling

An *exception* is an event that occurs during the execution of a program and requires the execution of software outside the normal flow of control. Hardware exceptions can result from the execution of certain instruction sequences, such as division by zero or an attempt to access an invalid memory address. A software routine can also explicitly initiate an exception.

The Win32 API supports a mechanism called *structured exception handling* for handling hardware-generated and software-generated exceptions. Structured exception handling gives programmers complete control over the handling of exceptions. The Win32 API also supports termination handling, which enables programmers to ensure that whenever a guarded body of code is executed, a specific block of termination code is also executed. The termination code is execute regardless of how the flow of control leaves the guarded body. For example, a termination handler can guarantee that clean-up tasks are performed even if an exception or some other error occurs while the guarded body of code is being executed. Structured exception and termination handling is an integral part of the Win32 system, and it enables a very robust implementation of system software.

Windows 95 provides structured exception and termination handling for Win32–based applications. By using this functionality, applications can identify and rectify error conditions that might occur outside their realm of control, providing a more robust computing environment.

CHAPTER 6

Support for Running MS-DOS–Based Applications

Support for MS-DOS–based applications, device drivers, and TSRs is maintained in Windows 95. In fact, Windows 95 offers better compatibility for running MS-DOS–based applications than Windows 3.1 does, including applications that are hardware-intensive, such as games.

Like Windows 3.1, Windows 95 allows users to launch an MS-DOS command prompt as an MS-DOS VM. The functionality supported in an MS-DOS VM is the same as that available under the latest version of MS-DOS, allowing users to run the same intrinsic commands and utilities.

Windows 95 delivers great support for running MS-DOS–based applications and enables even applications that would not run under Windows 3.1 to run properly. This support allows MS-DOS–based applications to coexist peacefully with the rest of the Windows 95 environment.

Summary of Improvements over Windows 3.1

Improvements made to the system provide the following benefits for running MS-DOS–based applications in the Windows 95 environment:

- Zero conventional memory footprint for protected-mode components

- Improved compatibility for running MS-DOS-based applications

- Improved robustness for MS-DOS–based applications

- Better support for running MS-DOS–based games, including in a window

- Support for running existing MS-DOS–based applications without exiting Windows 95 or running MS-DOS externally

- Consolidated attributes for customizing the properties of MS-DOS–based applications

- The availability of the Toolbar when running an MS-DOS–based application in a window, providing quick access to features and the functionality for manipulating the window environment

- A user-scaleable MS-DOS window through the use of TrueType fonts

- The ability to gracefully end an MS-DOS–based application without exiting the application

- The ability to specify local VM environment settings on a per-application basis through the use of a separate batch file

- Support for new MS-DOS commands, providing tighter integration between the MS-DOS command line and the Windows environment

Zero Conventional Memory Footprint Components

Windows 95 helps make the maximum amount of conventional memory available for running existing MS-DOS–based applications. Some MS-DOS–based applications did not run under Windows 3.1 because by the time MS-DOS–based device drivers, MS-DOS–based TSRs, MS-DOS–based networking components, and Windows 3.1 were loaded, not enough conventional memory was available. Windows 95 replaces many of the 16-bit real-mode components with 32-bit protected-mode counterparts to provide the same functionality while improving overall system performance and using no conventional memory.

32-bit virtual device drivers are provided to replace their 16-bit real-mode counterparts for functions such as those listed in the table on the facing page.

The memory savings that results from using 32-bit protected-mode components can be quite dramatic. For example, if a PC were configured with the NetWare NetX client software and used a SCSI CD-ROM drive, SMARTDrive, the MS-DOS mouse driver, and DriveSpace disk compression, the conventional memory savings that would result from using Windows 95 would be *over* 262 KB!

Functions Carried Out by 32-Bit Device Drivers in Windows 95		
Description	**File(s)**	**Conventional Memory Saved**
Microsoft Network client software	NET.EXE (full) PROTMAN NETBEUI EXP16.DOS (MAC)	95 KB 3 KB 35 KB 8 KB
Novell NetWare client software	LSL EXP16ODI (MLID) IPXODI.COM NETBIOS.EXE NETX.EXE VLM.EXE	5 KB 9 KB 16 KB 30 KB 48 KB 47 KB
MS-DOS extended file sharing and locking support	SHARE.EXE	17 KB
Adaptec SCSI driver	ASPI4DOS.SYS	5 KB
Adaptec CD-ROM driver	ASPICD.SYS	11 KB
Microsoft CD-ROM Extensions	MSCDEX.EXE	39 KB
SmartDrive disk caching software	SMARTDRV.EXE	28 KB
Microsoft Mouse driver	MOUSE.COM	17 KB
Microsoft DriveSpace disk compression driver	MOUSE.COM	37 KB

Try It!

Test Conventional Memory Savings

1. Install Windows 95 on a PC with a configuration similar to one that now runs Windows 3.1. For example, use PCs with SCSI drivers, network drivers, and system support files, such as SMARTDRV, MSCDEX, or SHARE.

2. With MS-DOS–based device drivers and TSRs loaded on both machines, type *mem /c* at a command prompt command under Windows 3.1 and under Windows 95. Notice the memory savings under Windows 95 for the same configuration.

Compatibility Improvements

For a number of reasons, some MS-DOS–based applications wouldn't run properly under Windows 3.1. For example, some MS-DOS–based applications required that lots of free conventional memory be available and thus were prevented from running in an MS-DOS VM by large real-mode components, such as network drivers or device drivers. Other MS-DOS–based applications wouldn't run under Windows 3.1 because they required direct access to the computer hardware and conflicted with Windows internal drivers or other device drivers.

The MS-DOS support goal of Windows 95 is to be able to run the "clean" MS-DOS–based applications that ran under Windows 3.1 *and* the "bad" MS-DOS–based applications that tried to take over the hardware or required machine resources unavailable under Windows 3.1.

Many MS-DOS–based games assume that they are the only application running on the system and access and manipulate the underlying hardware directly, thus preventing them from being run in an MS-DOS VM under Windows 3.1. Games are the most notorious class of MS-DOS–based applications that don't get along well with Windows 3.1. Some of these applications write to video memory directly, manipulate hardware support resources such as clock timers, and take over hardware resources such as sound cards.

A number of strategies have been used to provide better support for running MS-DOS–based applications that interact with the hardware, including better virtualization of computer resources such as timers and sound devices. In addition, the use of 32-bit protected-mode device drivers benefits MS-DOS–based applications by providing more free conventional memory than was available under Windows 3.1, so that memory-intensive applications run properly.

Different MS-DOS–based applications require varying levels of support from both the computer hardware and from the operating system. For example, some MS-DOS–based games require close to 100 percent use of the CPU to perform properly, and other MS-DOS–based applications modify interrupt addresses and other low-level hardware settings. Windows 95 provides several different levels of support for running MS-DOS–based applications. These levels of support take into account that different applications interact with the hardware in different ways, and that some behave well, whereas others expect exclusive access to the PC system and hardware. By default, MS-DOS–based applications are preemptively multitasked with other tasks running on the system and can run either full-screen or in a window. (CPU-intensive MS-DOS–based applications may not perform well in a window but can be run in full-screen mode to get the best response level.)

Single MS-DOS Application Mode

To provide support for the most intrusive set of MS-DOS–based applications that work only under MS-DOS and require 100 percent access to the system components and system resources, Windows 95 provides a mechanism that is the equivalent of running an MS-DOS–based application from real-mode MS-DOS. This mechanism, called *single MS-DOS application mode*, provides an "escape hatch" for applications that run only under MS-DOS. In this mode, Windows 95 removes itself from memory (except for a small stub) and provides the MS-DOS–based application with full access to all the resources in the computer. Relatively few MS-DOS–based applications need to run in single MS-DOS application mode because of the improved compatibility support provided by Windows 95.

To run an MS-DOS–based application in this mode, the user sets the Single MS-DOS Application Mode property on the Program tab of the MS-DOS property sheet for the application. To create a unique environment tailored to an application's needs and system requirements, the user can also specify a CONFIG.SYS or AUTOEXEC.BAT file to run for the application. When the user runs an MS-DOS–based application in this mode, Windows 95 asks whether running tasks can be ended. With the user's approval, Windows 95 ends all running tasks, loads a real-mode copy of MS-DOS, and launches the specified application. This process is like exiting Windows 3.1 and then running the specified MS-DOS–based application under MS-DOS. When the user exits the MS-DOS–based application, Windows 95 restarts and returns the user to the Windows 95 shell. This solution is much more elegant than requiring users to dual-boot between different operating systems in order to run desired applications.

Try It!

Run an MS-DOS–Based Application

1. Identify an MS-DOS–based application that you know does not run under Windows 3.1, and run it under Windows 95. Does it work?

2. Identify an MS-DOS–based application that you know runs under Windows 3.1 full-screen but not in a window, and run it under Windows 95 in a window. Does it work?

Support for Graphic-Intensive MS-DOS–Based Applications

Windows 95 improves the support for running graphic-intensive MS-DOS–based applications in the Windows environment. MS-DOS–based applications that use VGA graphic video modes can now be run in a window; they no long have to be run in full-screen mode as with Windows 3.1. Users can still choose to run graphic-intensive MS-DOS–based applications in full-screen mode for the best level of performance.

Memory Protection

To support a higher level of memory protection for running MS-DOS–based applications, Windows 95 includes on the Program property sheet a global memory protection attribute that allows the MS-DOS system area to be protected from errant MS-DOS–based applications. When the global memory protection attribute is set, the MS-DOS system area sections are read-protected so that applications can't write to this memory area and corrupt MS-DOS support and MS-DOS–based device drivers. In addition to system area protection, enhanced parameter validation is performed for file I/O requests issued through the MS-DOS Int 21h function, providing a higher degree of safety.

This option is not enabled by default for all MS-DOS–based applications because of the additional overhead associated with providing improved parameter and memory address checking. Users can set this flag if they constantly have difficulty running a specific MS-DOS–based application.

Better Defaults for Running MS-DOS–Based Applications

By default, Windows 3.1 ran MS-DOS–based applications full screen and disabled the ability of MS-DOS–based applications to run in the background. To change this default behavior for a specific MS-DOS–based application, users had to use the PIF Editor (PIFEDIT) application to modify or create a program information file (PIF) for the application.

By default, Windows 95 runs MS-DOS–based applications in a window and enables the background-execution setting, allowing the application to continue to run when it is not the active application. This change in default behavior provides better integration of running MS-DOS–based applications and Windows–based applications without requiring users to change or customize the state of the system.

Consolidated Customization of MS-DOS–Based Application Properties

Each MS-DOS–based application has different characteristics and mechanisms for using machine resources such as memory, video, and keyboard access. Both Windows 95 and Windows 3.1 understand how to run Windows–based applications because requests for system services are handled through the use of the Windows API. However, MS-DOS–based applications include only minimal information about their requirements in the format of their .EXE headers. To provide additional information about their requirements to the Windows environment, PIFs are used to specify the necessary configuration settings.

Under Windows 3.1, the PIF Editor application, shown in Figure 39, was used to create or change properties associated with running MS-DOS–based applications. Problems associated with the PIF Editor and the PIF creation process included difficulty in accessing the PIF Editor and PIF settings, the lack of association for new users between PIF properties and the MS-DOS–based application, the lack of a single location for storing PIF files (other than placing them all in the Windows directory), and less-than-intelligent defaults for running MS-DOS–based applications.

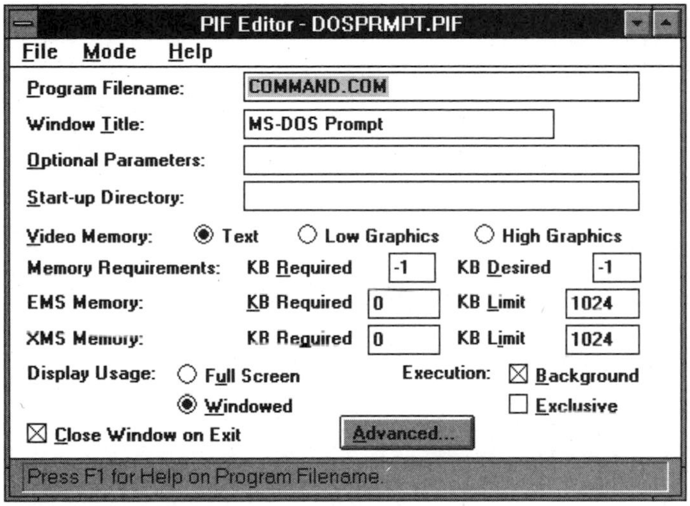

Figure 39. The PIF Editor in Windows 3.1

Windows 95 enhances the ability to define properties for running MS-DOS–based applications by consolidating PIF files into a single location (the PIF directory where Windows 95 is installed), providing easy access to property information for an application (right-clicking the application's icon or window), and providing better organization of properties (through the use of a tabbed property sheet, shown in Figure 40 on the next page). By means of these improvements, Windows 95 provides greater flexibility and control for running MS-DOS–based applications.

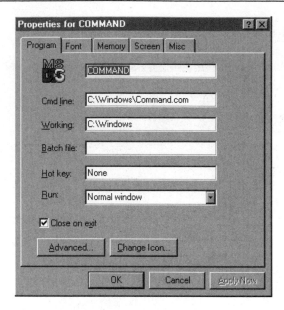

Figure 40. The property sheet for configuring an MS-DOS–based application

Try It!

View the Property Sheet for an MS-DOS–Based Application

1. Right-click the icon for an MS-DOS–based application, and choose *Properties*.

2. Right-click the title bar of an active MS-DOS–based application, and choose *Properties*.

Toolbars in MS-DOS Windows

In addition to providing compatibility enhancements to better support the running of MS-DOS–based applications, Windows 95 makes using MS-DOS–based applications in the Windows environment even easier than Windows 3.1. Many Windows–based applications provide one or more toolbars for quickly accessing common features and functionality, Windows 95 extends this simple but powerful feature to provide easy access to the functionality associated with an MS-DOS–based application, as shown in Figure 41.

Figure 41. A toolbar in a windowed MS-DOS dialog box

Optionally, users can enable the display of a toolbar in the window of a running MS-DOS–based application to provide the user with quick access to the following functionality:

- Simpler access to cut, copy, and paste operations for integrating text or graphic MS-DOS–based applications with Windows–based applications

- Easy switching from windowed to full-screen mode

- Quick access to property sheets associated with the MS-DOS–based application

- Access to MS-DOS VM tasking properties, such as exclusive or foreground processing attributes

- Easier access to font options for displaying text in a windowed MS-DOS VM

Scaleable MS-DOS Windows

Windows 95 supports the use of a TrueType font in a windowed MS-DOS VM, which allows users to scale the MS-DOS window to any size. When the font size is set to Auto, the contents of the MS-DOS window are sized automatically to display the entire window within the user-specified area. Figure 42 on the next page shows the size of the MS-DOS command prompt window being made smaller.

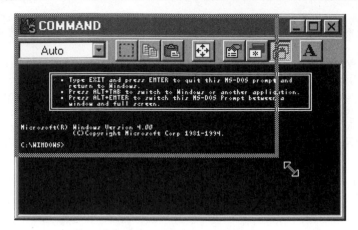

Figure 42. Because of TrueType font support, the contents of this MS-DOS window will be scaled to fit the smaller size of the window so that they are still displayed in their entirety.

Try It!

Scale an MS-DOS Window

1. Open an MS-DOS VM window, click the *Font* tab on the property sheet, and check that the font size is set to *Auto*.

2. Point to the scale region in the lower-right corner of the window, change the size of the window, and notice how the window's contents are rescaled. (This functionality is more noticeable when performed at higher resolutions.)

Ending MS-DOS–Based Applications Gracefully

Windows 95 provides support for gracefully closing an MS-DOS VM through a property sheet setting that is available on an application-by-application basis. When this setting is enabled, users can close the MS-DOS–based application just as they would a Windows–based application—by clicking the Close Window button.

In addition to gracefully ending an MS-DOS–based application, robustness improvements made to the Windows 95 system ensure that system clean-up is completed properly and that all allocated resources are freed. As a result, memory used by an MS-DOS–based application running under Windows 95 is deallocated properly and made available for use by other applications (unlike under Windows 3.1, which didn't properly free DPMI memory).

Local Virtual Machine Environment Settings

When Windows 3.1 started, it used the MS-DOS environment specified before it started as the default state for each subsequently created MS-DOS VM. Any TSRs or other memory resident software that was loaded before Windows started was replicated across all MS-DOS VMs, whether the VM needed it or not. With Windows 3.1, users could not run a batch file to set the VM environment before starting a given MS-DOS–based application. (Actually, users could run a batch file under Windows 3.1, but when the batch file finished processing the command statements, the MS-DOS VM was closed.)

Under Windows 95, a batch file can be optionally specified for a given MS-DOS–based application, allowing customization of the VM on a local basis before running the MS-DOS–based application. The batch file is specified on the Program tab of the MS-DOS–based application's property sheet, as shown in Figure 43. Using a batch file allows MS-DOS environment variables to be set or customized for individual MS-DOS–based applications and for TSRs to be loaded in the local VM only. This mechanism is like having different AUTOEXEC.BAT files for different MS-DOS–based applications.

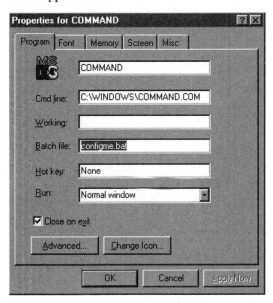

Figure 43. Specifying a batch file on the Program tab of the MS-DOS–based application property sheet

Support for Accessing Network Resources with UNC Pathnames

Windows 95 makes accessing network resources from the MS-DOS command prompt easier by supporting the use of universal naming conventions (UNC). UNC provides a standard naming scheme for referencing network servers and shared directories. It uses the following syntax:

*servername**sharename*[*pathname*]

The Windows 95 shell allows users to browse and connect to network servers without mapping a drive letter to the network resource. Windows 95 supports the same functionality at an MS-DOS command prompt and allows the user to do the following:

- View the contents of shared directories on network servers from both Microsoft Network servers and Novell NetWare servers by typing *dir* *servername**sharename*[*pathname*]

- Copy files from the contents of shared directories on network servers from both Microsoft Network servers and Novell NetWare servers by typing *copy* *servername**sharename**pathname**file destination*

- Run applications from shared directories on network servers for both Microsoft Network servers and Novell NetWare servers by typing *servername**sharename**pathname**filename*

New MS-DOS Prompt Commands

The MS-DOS command processor and utilities have been enhanced to provide better integration between MS-DOS functionality and the Windows environment. Commands that manipulate files have been extended to support long filenames, and some new commands have been added to Windows 95 to provide access to new capabilities supported by the system.

For example, the **start** command, which has the following syntax:

start *<application name>* | *<document name>*

allows users to start an MS-DOS or Windows–based application from the command prompt in one of the following ways:

- Start an application by specifying the name of a document to open, and Windows 95 launches the application associated with the given file type. For example, typing *start myfile.xls* starts the application associated with the specified file, if there is a valid association.

- Start an MS-DOS–based application in a different MS-DOS VM instead of the current one.

- Start a Windows–based application from an MS-DOS command prompt. Typing the name of a Windows–based application is essentially the same as typing *start <application>*.

Try It!

Launch an Application from the MS-DOS Command Prompt

1. Type *start /?* to see the options available.

2. Type *start edit* to start the MS-DOS Edit application in another VM.

3. Type *start /m clock* to start the Clock Windows–based application in minimized form.

Support for Long Filenames

Many MS-DOS intrinsic commands and utilities have been extended to support the use of long filenames. For example, the following commands are among those that have been extended to support long filenames:

- The **dir** command has been extended to show long filenames in the directory structure, along with the corresponding 8.3 filename. Also, the **dir** command now supports a verbose mode so that users can display additional file details by typing *dir /v*.

- The **copy** command has been extended to allow mixing of long and short filenames in copy operations. For example, typing *copy myfile.txt "this is my file"* creates a new file with a long filename.

C H A P T E R   7

Plug and Play

Configuring PC hardware and operating systems has become a significant problem in the PC industry, resulting in customer dissatisfaction and increased support costs, which in turn impacts PC market growth. A broad-based group of PC industry members is tackling this problem by developing an open and extensible framework architecture called *Plug and Play*. The Plug and Play specifications describe hardware and software changes to the PC and its peripherals that free PC users from manually configuring hardware resources. Microsoft Corporation, Compaq Computer Corporation, and Intel Corporation cooperatively launched the effort to create the Plug and Play architecture and have been key contributors and leaders in developing and implementing the Plug and Play specifications. Furthermore, Plug and Play is an industry-wide effort, with the specifications governed by the Plug and Play Association, an independent organization of leading PC and peripheral manufacturers.

Windows 95 is the operating system that ties Plug and Play components together. It makes PCs easier to use by providing the following operating system services:

- Help in device detection for installing and configuring devices

- Event notification for informing other system components and applications of dynamic changes to the system state

- Tight integration among device drivers, system components, and the user interface to make the operating system easier to use, configure, and manage

Plug and Play in Windows 95 not only offers functionality to make it easy to use Plug and Play PCs, but also makes it easier to configure and manage existing (legacy) PC hardware.

The Problem with Today's PCs

For users who are not trained technicians, installing and configuring devices on PCs can be a daunting task. Most users have neither the time nor the inclination to learn about such arcane subjects as IRQ lines, DMA channels, SCSI termination, or monitor timings. However, if users want to add devices to their PCs or take advantage of the features of new devices, they must know about these subjects because most existing PC systems offer no alternative. When potential PC users hear about problems that current users encounter in these areas, their viewpoint that PCs are complex, intimidating, and difficult to use is reinforced.

Although the availability of add-on devices is an advantage of the PC, the fact that the typical PC contains devices made by numerous vendors tends to compound hardware and software configuration problems. The hardware, operating system, and applications don't know about other PC components, and the hardware can't tell when conflicts exist between different devices trying to share the same system resource. The main problems associated with today's PC hardware and operating systems can be summarized as follows:

- **Adding devices to a PC can be a painful process.** A lack of coordination between hardware and software components leads to conflicts between devices vying for valuable system resources, such as IRQs, DMA addresses, and I/O addresses. Information about the configuration of a PC is not easily accessible, leading to confusion and an increased burden on users and technical support resources to solve conflicts and other device errors.

- **Software has no idea what's in the system.** Today's operating systems support only rudimentary mechanisms for allowing applications to determine the configuration of a PC. Information about basic properties—the type of CPU, the amount of memory configured, and possibly information about base devices, such as communication ports—is usually all that's available. No consistent mechanisms exist for obtaining detailed information about connected peripherals, and no support is available for receiving system notification that may be associated with dynamic configuration of system resources, such as the addition or removal of a device on-the-fly.

- **Evolution of the PC platform is stalled because of compatibility problems.** Many different bus standards are used in PCs today, including ISA, EISA, Micro Channel, PCMCIA, serial ports, parallel ports, and ECP. Creating a new bus standard or device architecture while maintaining compatibility with the existing architectures is a difficult task. Plug and Play provides a framework on which to design and implement new PC architectures, providing a common and consistent way for devices to interact and coexist, using a bus-independent design.

Higher Flexibility Requirements for Mobile Computers

The big problem facing the current PC architecture is trying to support the higher flexibility requirements for mobile computers. Mobile computers are used in a number of environments by on-the-road users, and the technology aimed at mobile computing professionals is growing by leaps and bounds. The configuration scenario shared by mobile computer users is different from that of desktop computer users. The mobile environment is much more dynamic and demands higher flexibility from the computing platform in the following ways:

- **Flexible configuration support.** Mobile users need flexible configuration support whether in the office and on the road. Users plug their mobile PCs into a docking station when in the office and run them in an undocked state while on the road. When it is docked, a mobile PC might be connected to a network so that it can access shared corporate resources. When it is undocked, the PC might need to be reconfigured, perhaps to support network connectivity through a dial-up process rather than a local, physical connection.

- **Support for hot-docking or hot-plugging of devices.** The advent and popularity of PCMCIA poses some dilemmas for the operating system and application programs. A main issue is how best to provide support for dynamic configuration when a device is added or removed from the system. For example, what should the operating system or application do in response to the addition of a PCMCIA card that provides access to SCSI devices, provides additional hard disk storage, or adds modem connectivity to the PC? Any of these hardware changes might affect the way software behaves on the system, so the operating system needs to support a mechanism for notifying applications that their system configuration state might change and that they will need to take appropriate action. For example, if a Plug-and-Play-aware word processing application is used to open a document on a PCMCIA hard disk drive and the user then decides to remove that hard disk, the word processing application would save and close the document before the hard disk is removed.

The Plug and Play Solution

Through automatic installation of drivers and seamless configuration, the Plug and Play architecture transforms the PC from a complex, difficult to configure piece of hardware into more of an "appliance." A key benefit of Plug and Play is that it helps create and support a platform that turns the PC into a more mobile and dynamic environment.

The Plug and Play architecture is an open, flexible, and cost-effective framework for designing Plug and Play products. The group of leading vendors who developed Plug and Play obtained reviews for their design proposals from hundreds of companies in the industry. As a result, Plug and Play works on many types of bus architectures— ISA, EISA, PCMCIA, VESA local bus (VL-bus), PCI local bus, and so on—and I/O port connections and can be extended to future designs.

Three major benefits of the Plug and Play architecture are as follows:

- **Reduced support costs for end-users, MIS organizations, and industry hardware and software vendors.** Reducing the complexities of installing and configuring devices and peripherals has a material benefit for both users and MIS organizations. As many as half of all support calls currently received by operating system and device manufacturers are related to installation and configuration of devices. For businesses, reducing the high cost of supporting PCs increases the use of PCs in the workplace and focuses information systems personnel on using computer technology to solve business problems. Both Plug and Play PCs and legacy PCs store hardware and software configuration in the Registry for centralized access, so support benefits can be achieved on existing hardware.

- **Easy installation and configuration of add-on devices, with little or no user intervention.** Windows 95 stores all information about the hardware and resource configuration of peripheral devices, such as IRQs, I/O addresses, DMA channels, and memory addresses, in the Registry. On Plug and Play PCs, resource allocation is automatically arbitrated by the system, and frcc rcsources are used to configure the hardware device. On legacy PCs, the information stored in the centralized Registry is used to notify users of potential resource conflicts when configuring peripherals. The known resource information is also used to perform device detection.

  On Plug and Play PCs, users can easily install or connect Plug and Play devices to the system, letting the system automatically allocate hardware resources with no user intervention. For example, a desktop PC can easily be turned into a multimedia playback system by simply plugging in a CD-ROM and sound card. The user plugs in the components, turns on the PC, and "plays" a video clip.

  On legacy PCs, users get help when installing new devices. For example, if a user is installing a new device that requires an IRQ setting and a legacy network card that uses IRQ 5 is already installed, the system tells the user that a device is already using IRQ 5 and that a different IRQ setting should be chosen. Even on legacy PCs, Plug and Play means that device conflicts are a thing of the past.

- **Designing PC systems with new features.** The best way to understand the potential of new features made possible by Plug and Play is by means of examples such as the following:

  - With warm-docking capabilities, a businessperson can remove a portable PC from its docking station while the PC is still running and go to a meeting. The portable PC automatically reconfigures itself to accommodate the absence of the network card and large disk drive.

- An infrared (IR)-enabled subnotebook automatically recognizes, installs, and configures an IR-enabled printer when the user walks into the printer room.

Plug and Play Support in Windows 95

The Plug and Play specifications are designed to be implementation-independent and are not tied to a specific operating system. It is up to the operating system developer to define the level of support the system provides. Windows 95 was designed and built with Plug and Play support in mind and therefore every component provides a very rich implementation of Plug and Play functionality. With Windows 95, configuration of hardware resources is greatly simplified over legacy configuration techniques: It just works.

Plug and Play in Windows 95 makes PCs even easier to use and supports both existing market requirements and future PC growth to deliver the following:

- **Compatibility with legacy hardware.** With over 140 million MS-DOS–based and Windows–based PCs used throughout the world, providing compatibility with legacy hardware was a requirement. Compatibility with existing hardware ensures that neither Windows 95 nor the new Plug and Play peripherals require the purchase of completely new hardware.

- **Automatic installation and configuration of Plug and Play devices.** With Plug and Play, initial PC configuration is automatic. Users no longer need to configure their systems and make system-resource assignments, such as those for IRQs, I/O ports, and DMA addresses. These assignments are handled by the BIOS and operating system, thus avoiding configuration conflicts. Installation and configuration of add-on devices and peripherals is also automatic.

- **A dynamic operating environment that supports mobile computing environments.** This functionality brings out the real power of the Plug and Play architecture and sets Windows 95 apart from other operating system implementations of Plug and Play. Dynamic Plug and Play properties in Windows 95 include support for the following:

  - Hot-docking and undocking of mobile computers to change the state of the system dynamically

  - Hot-plugging and unplugging of Plug and Play devices on the fly

  - "Dynaload drivers," which are loaded by the operating system for devices that are present and removed from memory when the device is no longer available

- Unified messaging mechanism for dynamically notifying other operating system components and applications about changes to the state of the system

Users of Windows 95 can reconfigure their PCs on the fly and have the changes take effect immediately, without rebooting.

- **A universal driver model that simplifies device driver development.** To simplify the development of device drivers for independent hardware vendor (IHV) hardware devices, Windows 95 incorporates the use of a universal driver model in various components of the system. Whereas Windows 3.1 supported a universal driver model only for printer drivers, Windows 95 provides this support for several other areas, including communications drivers, display adapter drivers, mouse drivers, and disk device drivers. The universal driver model ensures that IHVs can easily write peripheral drivers, thus increasing the number of Plug and Play devices available on the market.

- **An open and extensible architecture that supports new technologies.** The Plug and Play implementation in Windows 95 is flexible and extensible enough to support future technologies as they emerge on the market. The Plug and Play Initiative will spur the creation of new and innovative technologies, and Windows 95 will support them.

- **The availability of configuration information for simplified systems management.** The sharing of configuration information not only helps users solve configuration problems, but also helps MIS organizations support and manage PCs within corporate environments, which may have hundreds or thousands of PCs. Through the use of the Registry, configuration information is easily available to the system and to applications, both locally and remotely.

The following sections of this chapter give additional information about the Plug and Play capabilities of Windows 95.

The Benefits of Plug and Play with Windows 95

Plug and Play is of enormous benefit to users. No longer do they need to manually set jumpers and switches to redirect IRQs, DMA channels, or I/O port addresses. This benefit saves users' time and also saves OEMs and IHVs the expense of supporting large numbers of user service calls related to these configurations.

Plug and Play is designed so that adding a device, either permanently or temporarily, requires nothing more than taking it out of the box and plugging it in. Because the PC seamlessly adjusts to the new configuration, the following benefits are achieved:

- **Users need not concern themselves with the inner workings of Plug and Play—it just works.** The Plug and Play specifications define how the various hardware devices, software drivers, and operating system components interact. As far as the user is concerned, the PC simply works. Plug and Play reduces the time users spend on technical problems and increases their productivity and satisfaction with PCs.

- **Users can install Plug and Play devices in legacy PCs.** Components that use the Plug and Play architecture can accommodate the lack of device-reporting mechanisms in non–Plug and Play devices. Information about these devices is stored centrally in the Registry, and devices that cannot be reconfigured by the software receive first priority when resources are allocated.

- **Users can more easily manage and support PC configurations.** Many procedures, such as setting IRQ lines, figuring out the right jumper settings, and installing the correct device drivers, were once done manually, but are now performed by the Plug and Play PC system. Problems users encountered with non-Plug and Play PCs generated a tremendous support burden. Customer frustration with the configuration process reduced the demand for add-on and upgrade products. For businesses, the high cost of supporting PCs inhibited increased use of PCs in the workplace and diverted information systems personnel from focusing on using computer technology to solve business problems.

Hardware Design Guide for Microsoft Windows 95

Intended for PC manufacturers, peripheral vendors, and readers interested in learning the technical details of Plug and Play, the *Hardware Design Guide for Microsoft Windows 95* from Microsoft Press contains the official Microsoft guidelines and recommendations for developing—and developing for—a *PC 95* computer. This comprehensive discussion of the Plug and Play specification explores the *PC 95* concept in detail; examines the rationale for improving on the present standards; and outlines the design criteria for Plug and Play systems, devices, buses, and peripherals. It also covers the technical details of the *PC 95*, including internal and external peripherals, the BIOS used in the *PC 95*, and the new services performed by the BIOS as the go-between for the Plug and Play operating system and the system hardware.

You can find or order the *Hardware Design Guide for Microsoft Windows 95* wherever better computer books are sold, or you can order it directly from Microsoft Press at 1-800-MSPRESS (in Canada call 1-800-667-1115). Outside of the U.S. and Canada, contact your local computer book retailer or the Microsoft subsidiary in your area.

The Device Manager

To properly manage resources, such as IRQs, I/O addresses, and DMA addresses, on PCs, Windows 95 tracks devices, and the resources allocated to them, in the Registry. This information is maintained for both Plug and Play devices and legacy devices. The Device Manager, accessible by opening the System icon in the Control Panel, provides a graphical representation of devices configured in Windows 95 and allows properties used by these devices to be viewed and, as appropriate, changed. Although users normally have no need to modify entries from within the Device Manager, the information is useful for identifying which devices Windows 95 knows about for a particular PC configuration.

Figure 44 shows a sample Device Manager property sheet identifying different devices configured in Windows 95. The *View devices by connection* option on the Device Manager property sheet displays the devices configured in the system in a hierarchy, with the associated adapter or controller card. For example, if this option were selected, the CD-ROM device would be listed under the SCSI controller adapter heading, identifying the connection and associated device.

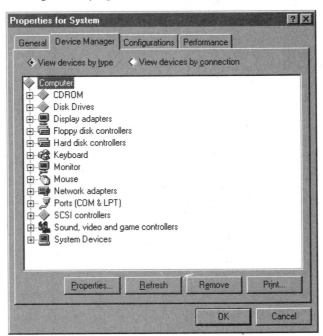

Figure 44. The Device Manager property sheet

In addition to showing devices configured in Windows 95, the Device Manager also shows the resources allocated to the configured devices. Resources used by devices such as memory ranges, I/O addresses, DMA addresses, and IRQs can be viewed on the View Resources tab of the property sheet for the computer configuration. Figure 45 shows the resources for a sample computer configuration.

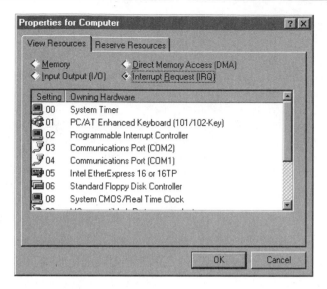

Figure 45. Viewing resources in the Device Manager

The power of Plug and Play derives from the fact that Windows 95 is aware of the resources available on the computer, of the resources allocated by the computer, and of the required resources being reported by each Plug and Play device. By means of the resource configuration information maintained in the Registry, Windows 95 is able to automatically identify and resolve device resource conflicts for Plug and Play devices. For legacy devices, the tracking of resources in Windows 95 helps users and support organizations quickly and easily identify conflicting resources and devices because these conflicts are highlighted in the Device Manager.

C H A P T E R   8

Device Support

Microsoft Windows 95 features improved support for hardware devices and peripherals including disk devices, video display adapters, mice, modems, and printers. With Windows 3.1, device drivers were, for the most part, monolithic and complex for device manufacturers to develop. However, Windows 3.1 simplified printer driver development by using a mini-driver architecture, which provides printer device-independent code in a universal driver written by Microsoft, and device-dependent code for direct communication with the printer written by the IHV. The mini-driver architecture increased the stability of driver support for the printer and decreased the amount of time needed for printer manufacturers to develop driver support for a new printer. In Windows 95, the mini-driver architecture is now available for other types of drivers, and although IHVs can still write monolithic drivers, use of the mini-driver model is recommended because of the advantages it provides.

Device Driver Philosophy

The device driver philosophy of Windows 95 is based upon a mini-driver/mini-port layered model that provides the following benefits:

- **Leverages IHVs' hardware knowledge.** IHVs know their hardware. They understand the various I/O mechanisms that their hardware supports, and they know the commands that their hardware device will respond to. The mini-driver model allows IHVs to implement the device-dependent portion of the code used to interact with their hardware device.

- **Leverages Microsoft's Windows knowledge.** Microsoft developed the universal driver code, which is the layer of code that sits between the API layer of device interaction (as used by other Windows components) and the device-dependent code that controls the device. The development team that wrote the Windows components above the API layer understands the mechanisms available from the operating system for interacting with the code. This model leverages Microsoft's knowledge of the operating system with the IHVs' knowledge of their hardware.

- **Increases system stability and reliability.** Because the universal driver is the mechanism through which the Windows components communicate with the device, this driver receives a high level of scrutiny and debugging. Through extensive use and testing, the universal driver code is made stable and reliable. Because IHVs no longer have to write the code that would be considered device-independent (as they did when they wrote monolithic drivers), the code required for driver-dependent functions for interacting with the hardware device is minimized. The complexity of the necessary code is reduced and the driver development process is simplified. A less complex driver is presumably more stable and reliable than a traditional monolithic driver.

- **Increases forward compatibility.** Forward compatibility is ensured by allowing the device-independent code to continue to evolve and by encapsulating the device-dependent code in a mini-driver. If an IHV develops new functionality in a hardware device, the mini-driver model also simplifies modifications to the driver. The IHV doesn't need to completely rewrite the entire device driver; the new functionality can simply be added to the mini-driver (if even necessary).

- **Supports OEM/IHV innovation.** The mini-driver model provides mechanisms for IHVs to add special device functionality support beyond what would be considered the base set of required functionality. The mini-driver model doesn't require IHVs to sacrifice any flexibility to simplify the driver development process.

Windows 95 uses the mini-driver/mini-port layered model for components throughout the operating system, including printers, display devices, modems, communication devices, and mice.

Disk Device Support

In addition to providing compatibility with existing MS-DOS–based and Windows–based disk device drivers, Windows 95 provides better disk device support than is available under Windows 3.1. Windows 95 features a new block I/O subsystem that provides broader 32-bit disk device support as well as improved disk I/O performance. In addition, disk mini-port device drivers written for use with Windows 95 are compatible with Windows NT, and vice versa.

Windows 95 also enhances the disk device support provided in MS-DOS and Windows 3.1 to provide improved support in the following areas:

- **Support for large media using logical block addressing.** Extensions to the Int 13h disk controller support are provided in the protected-mode disk handler drivers to support disks with cylinder numbers greater than 1024. (Windows 3.1 did not provide support for hard drives with more than 1024 cylinders in the 32-bit disk access drivers.)

- **Better support for removable media.** Windows 95 provides better support for removable media devices and allows the system to lock or unlock the device to prevent the media from being removed prematurely. Windows 95 also provides an eject mechanism for devices that support it, so that users can use software control to eject media from a device—for example, new floppy drives that support software-based media ejection.

Support for IDE Drives and Controllers

Windows 95 provides improved support for IDE drive configurations. The enhanced support includes the following:

- **Support for large IDE disk drives.** Some new IDE drives support a logical block addressing (LBA) scheme that allows them to exceed the 1/2 gigabyte (528 MB) size limitation. Support for IDE disk drives as large as 137 GB is provided by the Windows 95 operating system. This support was provided in real-mode before Windows 95, but is provided in a protected-mode disk driver by Windows 95.

- **Support for an alternate IDE controller.** Windows 95 allows the use of two IDE controllers in a PC, or the combination of an IDE controller in a laptop and an alternate controller in a laptop docking station—available, for example, in some Compaq laptop/docking station combination products. This support was provided in real-mode before Windows 95, but is provided in a protected-mode disk driver by Windows 95.

- **Support for IDE-based CD-ROM drives.** The majority of disk devices in personal computers use an IDE-based hard disk controller. Adding a CD-ROM drive typically requires adding an additional controller card to provide either SCSI or a proprietary interface for connecting to the CD-ROM drive. A new crop of inexpensive CD-ROM drives that connect to IDE-compatible disk controllers are emerging onto the market, and Windows 95 recognizes and supports these devices.

Support for SCSI Devices and Controllers

Windows 95 provides great support for SCSI disk devices, which was not available in Windows 3.1. The following support is available for SCSI devices:

- **Broad support for popular SCSI controllers.** Windows 95 includes 32-bit disk device drivers for popular SCSI controllers from manufacturers such as Adaptec, Future Domain, Trantor, and UltraStor, providing great support right out of the box.

- **Compatibility with Windows NT mini-port drivers.** Windows 95 supports the use of Windows NT mini-port SCSI drivers without modification or recompiling. Compatibility with Windows NT–based mini-port drivers ensures broad device support for disk devices under Windows 95, while simplifying driver development efforts for hardware manufacturers.

- **ASPI/CAM compatibility for MS-DOS–based applications and drivers.** Support for the Advanced SCSI Programming Interface (ASPI) and Common Access Method (CAM), which allow application and driver developers to submit I/O requests to SCSI devices, is provided in Windows 95. As a result, existing MS-DOS–based applications and drivers that use the ASPI or CAM specification work properly under Windows 95.

- **16-bit and 32-bit ASPI for Windows–based clients and applications.** In addition to MS-DOS–based compatibility with ASPI, Windows 95 includes 16-bit and 32-bit drivers to support Windows–based ASPI clients and applications.

Support for ESDI Controllers

In addition to supporting IDE and SCSI disk devices, Windows 95 provides 32-bit disk driver support for ESDI controllers.

The High-Speed Floppy Disk Driver

As with hard disk controller support, Windows 95 provides protected-mode support for communicating with floppy disk controllers. Windows 95 provides Int 13h hard disk controller support as 32-bit device drivers, resulting in improved performance, stability, and robustness of the system. Windows 95 provides floppy disk controller support as a 32-bit device driver, resulting in improved performance for file I/O to floppy disk drives, plus improved system reliability.

Users can now effectively format a diskette or copy files to/from a diskette while performing other tasks.

Try It!

Test Floppy Disk and Multitasking Performance

1. Perform common tasks under Windows 95 while you are formatting a floppy disk or copying files to a diskette. For example, try navigating through the shell or launching another application.

2. Perform the same tasks under Windows 3.1 to compare the different multitasking behavior.

Display Adapter and Monitor Support

Video display adapter and monitor support in Windows 95 is another area that has received a lot of attention during the design phases of Windows 95.

Summary of Improvements over Windows 3.1

Windows 95 addresses many of the problems inherent in Windows 3.1 display drivers and provides enhanced functionality and easier setup and configuration. Benefits of the new display driver support in Windows 95 include the following:

- More stable and reliable video display adapter drivers

- Support for many more video cards provided by drivers in Windows 95

- A mini-driver architecture that makes it easier for IHVs to write video display drivers

- Support for new features, including the ability to change video resolution on the fly without restarting Windows 95 (important for hot-docking and warm-docking support)

- Video driver support for mobile computer docking and undocking, providing the functionality to autoswitch between the video card in the portable computer and the video card in the base unit

- Consistent and unified installation and configuration of display drivers and of display properties, such as colors, wallpaper patterns, and screen savers

- Image Color Matching support for device-independent color usage, which Microsoft worked in conjunction with Kodak to offer

- Support for new generations of hardware and device functionality, such as Energy Star Monitors conforming to the VESA Display Power Management Signaling (DPMS) specification, and detection of monitor properties, such as the maximum resolution supported when used in conjunction with monitors that support the VESA Display Data Channel (DDC) specification

Driver Stability and Reliability Improvements

By using a mini-driver architecture for video display adapter drivers, Windows 95 improves support for the range of products offered by IHVs and provides more stable and reliable drivers. Windows 95 provides a universal driver to support device-independent code and functionality normally handled by a monolithic video display driver, and supports device-dependent code in a display mini-driver. The mini-driver uses the Windows 95 graphics device-independent bitmap (DIB) engine, providing a better mechanism for manipulating memory bitmaps, including improved performance.

Because mini-drivers are simpler than monolithic display drivers, they are easier to write and to debug. Extensive testing on a less complex driver results in better stability and reliability in the overall operating system.

Furthermore, to ensure broad display adapter device support in Windows 95, Microsoft developed many display drivers with the cooperation of all major display controller IHVs. Microsoft also worked closely with IHVs to write additional display drivers, and assisted IHVs with optimizing their display drivers and performance-tuning them to enhance the speed at which information is displayed by the driver. This development effort results in improved graphic performance over Windows 3.1 and over native Windows 3.1 display drivers.

The use of the mini-driver architecture for display drivers in Windows 95 leverages Microsoft's development experience in writing fast, reliable graphics code with the IHVs' engineering experience, allowing IHVs to concentrate on delivering high-performance hardware accelerated display adapters.

Video Display Performance Improvements

Not only are the video display adapters in Windows 95 more stable and reliable, but the display drivers should also benefit from improved performance. The mini-driver architecture for display drivers in Windows 95 is centered around a new 32-bit DIB engine that features 386/486 optimized code for fast, robust drawing for high-resolution and frame buffer-based display adapters. The use of a universal driver to provide the device-independent display adapter support, instead of requiring each IHV to redesign this code, allows base functionality to be optimized and thus benefits all mini-driver display drivers.

For example, graphics performance at 256 colors is dramatically improved on unaccelerated Super VGA graphics controllers such as the Tseng Labs ET4000, which has received benchmark results over 90 percent faster than Windows 3.1. Windows 95 includes drivers for nearly all popular graphics accelerators and has benchmarked faster than Windows 3.1 on the following models/chipsets:

- ATI Ultra (mach8), Ultra Pro (mach32), Ultra Pro Turbo (mach64)
- Cirrus Logic 5426/28/29/34
- Compaq QVision
- S3 911/924/801/805/928
- Tseng Labs ET4000 W32i
- Western Digital 90C31/33
- IBM XGA, XGA/2

Support for More Video Display Adapters Than Windows 3.1

Setup in Windows 95 includes support for automatically detecting the video display adapter installed in the PC and installing the appropriate Windows 95 display driver. Although Windows 95 supports the use of display device drivers written for use with Windows 3.1, Microsoft is working closely with IHVs to provide Windows 95–specific display drivers that take advantage of new features and functionality available in Windows 95. For example, efforts are ongoing to assist third parties in implementing extensions to support Plug and Play detection and on-the-fly resolution changes, and in redesigning display drivers to leverage the mini-driver model.

Robustness Improvements

The video drivers provided with Windows 95 are stringently tested to ensure greater reliability and stability than drivers for Windows 3.1.

In addition to better-quality video drivers, Windows 95 includes mechanisms to ensure that bad or incompatible video drivers cannot prevent users from accessing the system. Under Windows 3.1, a bad video driver would commonly result in returning users back to an MS-DOS command prompt with no explanation about the failure. Under Windows 95, if a video driver fails to load or initialize when the system starts, Windows 95 defaults to the generic VGA video driver. Given that driver configuration is handled through a graphical interface, users can then at least get into Windows 95 to fix the system.

New Control Panel Enhancements and Customization Properties

Windows 95 consolidates display properties into a common Display icon in the Control Panel, allowing easy customization of the colors, wallpaper, screen saver, and display adapter settings from a single location. Access to display properties is as easy as selecting Control Panel from the Start button's Settings menu or by right-clicking the desktop to display the appropriate property sheet, which is shown in Figure 46.

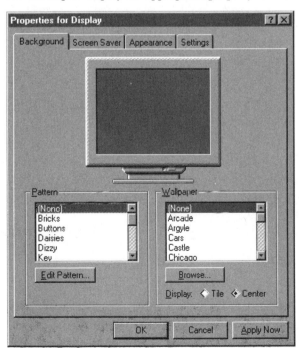

Figure 46. The property sheet for the display

Through the new consolidated display properties, users can now do the following:

- See the appearance of display changes modeled on screen before the changes are applied. This capability has been referred to as *What You See Before You Get It* (WYSBYGI).

- Change background settings to select patterns or wallpaper for the desktop.

- Select a screen saver to be activated after the computer is idle for a specified amount of time.

- Change window appearance properties for displaying text in title bars or menus, such as the font, font style (including bold or italic), and font size, providing more flexibility and levels of customization than Windows 3.1.

- Change the display settings, such as the number of colors to use with the display driver, or change the size of the desktop area on the fly (if the display driver and display adapter supports this functionality).

The consolidation of display properties is another example of how Windows 95 makes using and customizing the environment easier for users.

Image Color Matching Support

Windows 95 provides image color matching (ICM) support for mapping colors displayed on screen and colors generated on output devices to provide consistency. For more information, see the discussion of ICM support in Chapter 11, "Printing."

Energy Star Monitor Support

Energy Star is an effort inspired by the Environmental Protection Agency (EPA) to develop computer hardware and peripherals that conserve power when in idle states. This idea is similar to the standby mode commonly implemented in laptop computers to save power.

In a PC system, the video display monitor is typically one of the power-hungry components. Manufacturers of newer display monitors have incorporated energy-saving features into their monitors based on the VESA Display Power Management Signaling (DPMS) specification. Based on signals from a video display adapter, software can place the monitor in standby mode or even turn it off completely, thus reducing the power it uses when inactive.

Users typically display screen savers to prevent burn-in of a monitor image. Windows 95 extends this screen saver mechanism to provide a time-delay setting that allows the user to put the display monitor in a low-power standby mode, as well as a delay setting for turning the monitor off completely. Figure 47 shows the delay settings that enable this capability.

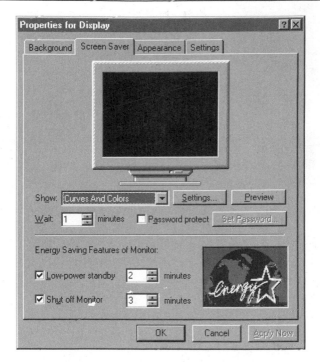

Figure 47. The screen saver settings for monitor energy-saving features

For example, a user may want to set options to display a specific screen saver after 5 minutes of inactivity, to set the PC to standby after the screen saver has displayed for 10 minutes, and to turn off the monitor after 15 minutes of standby.

To take advantage of the Energy Star power-consumption mechanisms, users need both a monitor that meets the DPMS/Energy Star specifications and a video card that meets the VESA DPMS specifications. The video display driver must support the extensions necessary to control the monitor device. Several manufacturers are presently shipping monitors designed to support the Energy Star goals.

Try It!

Change the Display Settings

1. Open the *Control Panel* and click the *Display* icon. The display property sheet appears.

2. Change the desktop background.

3. Select a screen saver.

4. Change the display appearance.

5. Switch video resolutions on the fly (if supported by your video display adapter and monitor).

Mouse and Pointing Device Support

As with other device drivers, the mini-driver architecture of Windows 95 simplifies mouse driver development and improves virtualization in a protected-mode mouse driver to better support MS-DOS–based applications in the Windows environment.

Summary of Improvements over Windows 3.1

Mouse support in Windows 95 results in the following improvements over Windows 3.1:

- Provides smooth, reliable input support through the use of protected-mode drivers

- Supports more devices by making it easier for IHVs to write drivers, and supports a mini-driver architecture model

- By supporting Plug and Play, makes mouse and pointing devices easy to install and use

- Implements mouse driver functionality in a single driver and eliminates the need to use MS-DOS–based mouse drivers, which increases robustness and saves conventional memory

- Supports connecting a mouse *after* Windows 95 has started. Mobile computer users who forget to connect a mouse before turning on the computer can connect a mouse without restarting the computer

Windows Mouse Driver Improvements

Windows 3.1 provided support for using the system mouse in an MS-DOS–based application running in a window, but using a mouse in an MS-DOS–based application running full screen required that an MS-DOS–based mouse driver be loaded before starting Windows.

Windows 95 provides mouse support as a protected-mode VxD and eliminates the need to load an MS-DOS–based mouse driver. Better virtualization of mouse interrupt services allows protected-mode Windows–based mouse drivers to provide mouse support for Windows–based applications, for MS-DOS–based applications running in a window, and for MS-DOS–based applications running in full-screen mode. The improvements in this area result in a zero conventional memory footprint for mouse support in the Windows 95 environment.

In addition to better mouse services, Windows 95 improves the device support to allow the use of serial ports COM1 through COM4 for connecting a mouse or other pointing device.

Mouse Control Panel Enhancements

Windows 3.1 provided rudimentary support for configuring a mouse as part of the Mouse option in the Control Panel and also provided more flexible mouse settings in a separate driver-specific applet. Windows 95 consolidates mouse configuration and customization support into a single Control Panel icon and uses a tabbed property sheet, shown in Figure 48, to provide easy access to all the possible settings, such as the setting for the behavior of the mouse buttons and for the behavior of the mouse pointer.

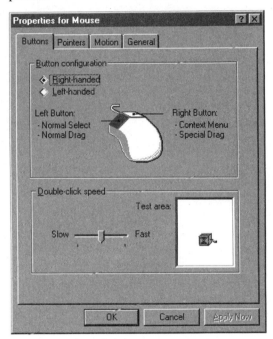

Figure 48. The mouse property sheet

Try It!

Use a Single Mouse Driver

1. Remove the real-mode mouse driver from your CONFIG.SYS or AUTOEXEC.BAT and after restarting your PC, run an MS-DOS–based application that supports the use of a mouse.

2. Open an application, such as MS-DOS Edit, and use it both in a window and full screen. Notice that the mouse is available in both modes.

3. Type *mem /c* at the MS-DOS prompt and verify that the mouse driver is not loaded in real-mode.

CHAPTER 9

Networking

Windows–based desktops are being connected to corporate networks at a steadily increasing rate. As a result, demands for better network integration, improved network and system management capabilities, and better network performance and reliability are growing as more business-critical functions rely on the PC network. Because of these demands, companies are faced with increased costs to run PC networks and are investing in tools and staff to meet the challenge of day-to-day network management.

Windows 95 is constructed to address the needs of corporate network administrators with a well-integrated, high-performance, manageable 32-bit network architecture. Windows 95 is also designed to address the needs of the Windows user by making access to and control of the network consistent, and by making network browsing and printing much easier through the many enhancements in the UI. In addition, Windows 95 is designed to address users' mobility needs by enabling remote access to the network from portable PCs.

Given the size of customers' current investments in both Windows and their PC network infrastructures, one overriding goal for networking in Windows 95 is compatibility. Compatibility involves ensuring continued support for existing real-mode components, as well as making the new 32-bit protected-mode components in Windows 95 compatible with existing 16-bit MS-DOS–based applications and device drivers and existing 16-bit Windows–based applications and DLLs.

This chapter introduces the 32-bit, protected-mode networking architecture built into Windows 95 and shows how it provides well-integrated network support, manageability, improved performance, user-level network security, and dial-up access to the network.

Summary of Improvements over Windows 3.1 and Windows for Workgroups 3.11

The primary improvements in networking for Windows 95 include the following:

- A robust, open, high-performance 32-bit network architecture, with 32-bit network client software, 32-bit file and printer sharing software, 32-bit network protocols, and 32-bit network card drivers

- Support for using multiple redirectors, multiple protocols, and multiple network card device drivers simultaneously to facilitate integrating the desktop into a heterogeneous network environment

- Support for industry standard connectivity and systems management solutions, including TCP/IP, IPX, SNMP, and DMI

- Great integration with Novell NetWare, including high-performance, 32-bit protected-mode NetWare–compatible client software for connecting to NetWare 3.x and 4.x servers, and peer sharing for NetWare environments

- Great integration with Windows NT Server to support a powerful client/server solution

- Built-in support for systems management, including the ability to remotely administer, monitor, and view the configuration of PCs over the network

- Improved dial-up network access support, providing remote access to Microsoft Network servers, Novell NetWare servers, and UNIX servers. Support for remote protocols such as PPP and SLIP is provided.

- Improved network printing, making it easier for users to connect and configure printers in network environments

Easier Networking with Windows 95

The Microsoft Network support provides full interoperability with other Windows 95 PCs, and PCs running Windows for Workgroups, Windows NT, Windows NT Server, LAN Manager, and any other Microsoft-compatible servers. Windows 95 includes support for both client access and peer services capabilities on a Microsoft Network. Additionally, other network servers and services are provided by third parties—for example, Artisoft, Banyan, DEC, Novell, and SunSelect provide Windows 95 support for their respective network servers.

This section summarizes the key features and concepts in Windows 95 that make networking much easier to implement and use.

Great Novell NetWare Integration

Windows 95 has built-in support for two networks: the Microsoft and Novell NetWare networks. (Built-in support for Novell NetWare is new with Windows 95.) Installation of support for one or both networks is as simple as clicking the Setup program for Windows 95 or the Network icon in the Control Panel. Both the Client for Microsoft Networks and the Microsoft Client for NetWare Networks are implemented as high-performance, high-reliability 32-bit protected-mode components.

Microsoft Client for NetWare Networks

The Microsoft Client for NetWare Networks in Windows 95 provides interoperability for NetWare 3.x and 4.x servers. Systems running Windows 95 can use all NetWare server services, browse NetWare servers, connect to servers, and queue print jobs either using the UI in Windows 95 or using Novell's NetWare command line utilities. The Microsoft Client for NetWare Networks in Windows 95 even run "TSR clean" NetWare logon scripts. In addition, Windows 95 provides continued support for Novell NetWare real-mode components, thereby supporting both the NetWare 3.x NetX shell and the NetWare 4.x VLM shell.

File and Printer Sharing Services for NetWare Networks

Windows 95 also provides NetWare–compatible peer services for file and printer sharing. These services feature user-level security by implementing a "pass through" security link to an existing Novell NetWare server to leverage the existing user database. Windows 95 doesn't introduce a new security scheme; rather, it fully leverages the existing user-level security built into NetWare's bindery.

The "Well-Connected Client" Operating System

Today's networks are heterogeneous and becoming even more connected. Companies are linking their Windows PCs to multiple PC network servers, mainframe and mini-computer host systems, UNIX machines, and a variety of services like the Internet. The desktop operating system must meet this challenge and provide support for often very disparate connectivity needs on the network. Today's desktop operating systems do not provide the necessary support for running multiple network clients simultaneously. Windows 95 has been explicitly designed with multiple network support as a key design goal.

Because integrated networking support is a key focus of the design of Windows 95, it's much easier to install and manage support for a single network or even multiple networks simultaneously using Windows 95. Building upon the support in Windows for Workgroups 3.11, which was capable of supporting up to two networks, Windows 95 can simultaneously support up to ten 32-bit, protected-mode network clients using its Network Provider Interface. This interface defines a set of APIs used by Windows 95 to access the network for tasks such as logging onto the server, browsing servers, connecting to servers, printing, and so on.

Installing network provider support is simple; it's done via the Network Setup icon in the Control Panel or from the Network Setup dialog box when first installing Windows 95. A Windows 95 desktop can run client support for NetWare, Windows NT Server, Banyan, DEC PathWorks and Sun NFS simultaneously.

PC users in a network environment that includes Apple Macintosh computers can use Windows 95 to exchange documents and share information with Macintosh users when Macintosh–compatible file services are used with Windows NT Server or Novell NetWare to connect to the common file server. (Long filename support in Windows 95 further simplifies the integration of the two systems.)

Internet Information with a Mouse Click

With Windows 95, you have easy access to the Internet, whether you dial into a commercial Internet provider or you gain access via your corporate network over TCP/IP. Windows 95 provides all the "plumbing" you need to tap into the information on the worldwide Internet network. Built-in support for TCP/IP, dial-up protocols, such as Point to Point Protocol (PPP) and Serial Line Internet Protocol (SLIP), and Windows Socket services make connecting to the Internet and the information highway just a mouse-click away.

TCP/IP, the protocol used on the Internet, is implemented in Windows 95 as a fast, robust, 32-bit Windows–based TCP/IP stack. This implementation does not have the conventional memory footprint common with MS-DOS–based drivers or TSRs.

Dial-up protocol support gives users flexibility in choosing the Internet access provider they want to dial into. Connection can be via a standard asynchronous modem or an ISDN connection.

Support for Windows Socket services allows use of any of the large collection of third-party and public-domain Internet utilities, such as Mosaic, WinWAIS, and WinGopher, to easily connect to the Internet and access the thousands of worldwide information servers.

Additionally, Windows 95 includes telnet and ftp to help users take advantage of the Internet. Windows 95 also supports sending and receiving e-mail messages over the Internet through the use of a provided mail driver that integrates with the Microsoft Exchange client, the universal inbox in Windows 95. For more information about Internet mail support in Windows 95, see Chapter 14, "Microsoft Exchange: E-Mail, Faxes, and More."

"Point and Click" Networking

For users, running even one network client can be confusing and running multiple network clients is nearly unmanageable. Each server has its own set of unique client-side utilities and commands that are often difficult to remember and use. When the desktop PC has support for multiple networks loaded, the user is faced with at least twice the number of commands and utilities to remember and may have to remember multiple passwords to access network resources.

The easy-to-use Network Neighborhood in Windows 95 makes it easier for users to perform common network operations on disparate servers. First, the network manager can establish one password to log a user onto the appropriate Windows 95 PC and network resources. These services could, for example, include e-mail, group scheduling applications, dial-in support, or database access. Additionally, common network actions, such as browsing servers, managing connections, and printing, are all performed identically through the UI in Windows 95, regardless of the type of server Windows 95 is connected to. As a result, users can locate, connect, and start print jobs on a NetWare print server as easily as they can with a printer attached to a Windows NT Server. All the common network actions can be accomplished visually, using the mouse to navigate through the network resources, the connections, and so on. Users aren't required to memorize any new network commands. For both the Client for Microsoft Networks and Microsoft Client for Novell NetWare Networks, users can run the corresponding command line utilities as well. This ongoing backward compatibility is necessary to support batch files that are currently in use and to ease the transition to the Windows 95 environment.

The Network Neighborhood also helps to manage the complexity of the network by showing it from the user's perspective—that is, it shows only what the user is interested in seeing. When the user initially opens the Network Neighborhood, the window contains only the servers the user has logged onto or the servers the user most frequently connects to, unless the user has explicitly customized the network view by dragging and dropping the server into the Network Neighborhood. This context-sensitive view of the network reduces the number of network resources the user initially encounters to a more manageable number of objects. For Windows NT domains and NetWare 3.x and 4.x, the network context presented is the "login server" and any other connected servers.

For a more in-depth discussion of the Network Neighborhood and the UI, see Chapter 3, "The Windows 95 User Interface."

Easier Mobile Network Support

Two features in Windows 95 make connecting to a network easier for mobile PC users: Plug and Play and Dial-Up Networking.

- **Plug and Play.** Plug and Play in Windows 95 solves several problems that face mobile PC users. Mobile users no longer have to maintain multiple configurations, such as desktop and portable configurations. Windows 95 recognizes when they add or remove peripherals, such as when they remove a network card and add a modem for dial-up network access. Because Windows 95 supports hot and warm docking, users no longer have to reboot their systems each time they make a change to the configuration. In addition, Windows 95 has built-in Card and Socket services that allow for hot removal and insertion of PCMCIA cards, including network cards.

   Network Plug and Play support in Windows 95 also includes application-level support. An application that is network-aware understands whether or not the network is available. If the network adapter is removed, the application automatically put itself into "offline" mode to allow the user to continue to work, or it shuts down gracefully.

- **Dial-Up Networking.** Maintaining data access to their corporate network while working in a remote location is another challenge for mobile users. Currently, several solutions for dialing into the corporate network exist, but most of these solutions are not well integrated with Windows, requiring a different set of tools. The Dial-Up Networking client in Windows 95 provides modular support for multiple dial-up providers, including Windows NT RAS servers and NetWare. It also supports several protocols, including NetBEUI, IPX/SPX, and TCP/IP via PPP and SLIP. Support for dial-up can also be offered by third parties—for example, Shiva has implemented Windows 95 support using the modular architecture of the Dial-Up Networking client in Windows 95.

Windows 95 Client: Designed for Manageability

Many corporations have rapidly growing networks that in some cases run worldwide. Keeping the networks and the ever increasing number of systems connected to the networks running at peak performance is a challenge for both end-users and network managers. Corporations are beginning to deploy network and desktop management tools to help them meet this challenge.

Windows 95 has built-in network and system management instrumentation to enable current and future management tools to remotely monitor, query, and configure Windows 95 PCs. Using these tools, network managers can quickly inventory the software and hardware used on their networks. Working from a Windows 95 PC, network managers can remotely diagnose and reconfigure Windows 95 systems, as well as remotely monitor system and network performance on a Windows 95 PC. The following key components make Windows 95 very manageable:

- **The SNMP agent.** Windows 95 incorporates an agent that implements the Simple Network Management Protocol (SNMP). This agent complies with the Internet Engineering Task Force (IETF) SNMP specification, responding to queries and sending notifications of events that take place on the PC to an SNMP console. The

SNMP console allows a network manager to remotely monitor and manage the Windows 95 PC. Events can be managed from a central SNMP management console.

- **The SNMP MIB, MIB-II.** The SNMP MIB describes what information about the system is available to the SNMP console. Windows 95 includes the MIB-II, which describes the Microsoft TCP/IP protocol and allows information about the protocol stack to be communicated back to the management console. For example, the management console can query the MIB-II for the IP address, the name of the user at this IP address, or IP routing information.

- **The DMI agent.** DMI applications provide cross-platform desktop management capabilities. Version One of the DMI specification was finalized this spring, and Microsoft, as a founding member of the DMTF, will follow the specification's ongoing evolution. Soon after its release, Windows 95 will offer a DMI agent, with support for the agent built on top of the Registry.

- **Registry-based system management.** Central to the operation of Windows 95 is the Registry. Similar in design to the Registry in Windows NT, the Registry in Windows 95 replaces the many .INI files previously used by Windows and Windows–based applications. The Registry contains information used by Windows 95 that describes the hardware configuration of the PC, preferences defined by the user, and application specific information. The Registry is a database containing keys and values. For example, HKEY_USER_NAME is the key for the user's name, and the name "Fred Smith" is the value associated with this key. A special category of keys, called *dynamic keys*, are memory resident and can contain frequently changing data updated by system components, device drivers, or applications. For example, the number of packets sent per second could be registered by the network adapter device driver.

  The Registry consists of three components: SYSTEM.DAT, which describes the PC configuration and computer-specific application information; USER.DAT, which defines user preferences and user-specific application information; and POLICY.POL, which defines "system policies" relating to either of the other two components. Each component is a file that resides on the PC or on a network server. The Registry is remotely accessible via an RPC-based interface. The Win32 Registry APIs are used to access the Registry, both locally and remotely.

Management Tools for Windows 95

Several tools for Windows 95 make managing the system or the network much easier. These tools include the following:

- **The Registry Editor.** Allows local or remote editing of the Registry in Windows 95.

- **The System Policy Editor.** Used by network managers to set per-user or per-group "policy" overrides on Registry entries. It creates the POLICY.POL component of the Registry. This tool (the Windows for Workgroups' admincfg tool) contains a superset of those settings.

- **The Performance Monitor.** Allows local or remote viewing of the performance of the various I/O components of a local system or remote PC. For example, the file system, the network components, or data from the network card can be monitored. The data is updated dynamically using the Registry's dynamic keys.

- **NetWatcher.** Allows local or remote viewing and management of the network connections of peer services in Windows 95.

Easier to Set Up and Install

PC and network managers faced several challenges when installing Windows in the past. Some network managers installed Windows on the network server for later installation onto users' PCs or to run Windows from the server. In the case of later installation, network managers had to decide on an approach for a number of variables: making the process appear transparent to the user; rolling out Windows using a "push" or "hands-free" installation; using specific settings for different categories of users; and updating these configurations when either Windows, Windows applications, or device driver updates were available. In the case of running Windows from the server, network managers had to manage variables such as having local swapping files and some local .INIs and applications; allowing user-level configurations; supporting disparate hardware configurations; and handling the roving user on the network.

Windows 95 addresses several elements of these problems with an improved Setup utility and the Registry. The new Setup streamlines the installation of Windows 95 on a network server for both later installation onto users' PCs and running Windows 95 from the server. In fact, the Windows 95 Setup utility has a scripting feature, making it possible to implement "hands-free" installation of Windows 95 from a network server to client PCs.

Running Windows 95 from a server becomes much simpler largely because of its Registry. The Registry is a centralized database of all hardware, software, and user information that is easy to maintain remotely on the server. This simple mechanism contrasts sharply with the state of configuration under Windows 3.1, with CONFIG.SYS, AUTOEXEC.BAT, and a myriad of .INI files for Windows and Windows–based applications. Moreover, the separation of hardware configuration and user profiles in the Registry means that if users move around on the network, their preferences follow them from PC to PC, regardless of the hardware configuration they're currently working on.

Network Architecture in Windows 95

The Network architecture in Windows 95 radically improves on the level of network support and integration that existed in Windows 3.1. The key design points of the networking architecture in Windows 95 are the following:

- **Fast, 32-bit VxDs.** The networking components in Windows 95 are built as 32-bit virtual device drivers, which have no conventional memory footprint, and are loaded dynamically when needed by the system. In addition, because the operating system and the device drivers are all running in protected mode and overhead for mode switching and virtualization between protected and real-mode operation is no longer incurred, network I/O performance is 50 to 200 percent faster than under Windows 3.1.

- **Reliability.** Because the networking components in Windows 95 run in protected mode and are designed to a well-defined set of interfaces, they are more reliable than real-mode network components. Real-mode network components may conflict in memory or attempt to exclusively chain the same set of interrupts, which commonly leads to system hangs or error conditions. These errors don't occur with protected-mode network components because Windows 95 arbitrates the hardware resource allocation.

- **Modular, open design.** The network architecture in Windows 95 is highly modular and includes a new Network Provider Interface (NPI), an Installable File System (IFS) interface, and a version of Network Driver Interface Specification (NDIS) version 3.1 that has been enhanced for Plug and Play support. The specifications for all three interfaces are available to third-party network vendors.

- **Multiple network support.** Windows 95 is designed to accept multiple network providers, multiple network redirectors written to the IFS interface, and multiple NDIS drivers as needed. As a result, client support for Microsoft Networks and Novell NetWare can be run simultaneously. Windows 95 is capable of concurrently supporting up to ten 32-bit, protected-mode network clients and one real-mode network client.

- **Multiple protocol support.** One of the NDIS components in Windows 95, the Protocol Manager, supports the loading of multiple transport protocols. The Protocol Manager enables Microsoft and third parties to independently write protocol stacks that coexist well for Windows 95. Windows 95 includes built-in support for IPX/SPX, TCP/IP, and NetBEUI.

- **Plug and Play.** All of the networking components in Windows 95 are designed for dynamic Plug and Play operation. For example, when a PCMCIA network card is inserted, the NDIS 3.1 network card driver is automatically loaded, and the network is available. When either the PCMCIA network card or the network cable is removed, Windows 95 doesn't hang as many real-mode networks do, but instead notifies any applications using the network that the network is no longer available and continues to run.

Figure 49 shows the general layout of the network architecture built into Windows 95. The following sections in this chapter describe key aspects of this architecture, including the NPI, the IFS, and NDIS 3.1.

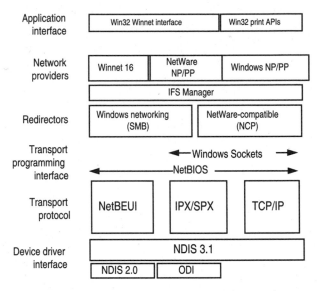

Figure 49. The layered network architecture of Windows 95

Network Provider Interface: Concurrent Support for Multiple Network Servers

Windows 95 has an open, modular Network Provider Interface to allow support for multiple networks to be installed in Windows 95 simultaneously. The NPI enables Microsoft or any third party network provider to integrate various network services seamlessly into Windows 95. The NPI has the following key benefits:

- The open interface allows network vendors to supply tightly integrated support for their network servers for Windows.

- All supported networks are identically accessed and managed through the Windows 95 Network Neighborhood UI.

The NPI abstracts the network services for the Windows 95 UI components, as well as the various Windows 95 network and desktop management components. The NPI consists of two parts: the network provider API and the network providers. The network provider API is a single, well-defined set of APIs used by Windows 95 to request network services, such as those for browsing servers, connecting to and disconnecting from servers, and queuing a print job. These requests are then passed to the network providers. The network provider layer sits below the API layer and provides the network services requested by components of Windows 95. Conceptually, this model is similar to the design of the various device driver interfaces of Windows 95—a well-defined set of interfaces used by the operating system to request services, and the services themselves, which are provided by a device driver that is often written by a third party.

The most obvious abstraction of the various network services provided by the NPI is the Windows 95 system login. Each network provider can provide a unique logon dialog box to suit the needs of the network server's security model. For example, the logon dialog box shown in Figure 50 is for logging onto a Windows NT Server domain:

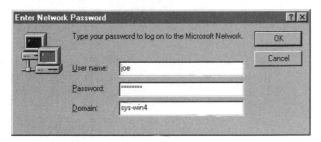

Figure 50. The network logon dialog box for the Windows NT Server domain

The dialog box for logging onto a Novell NetWare 3.*x* server, shown in Figure 51, offers additional information to allow users to log on as GUEST. This dialog box is invoked when a user first accesses a NetWare server.

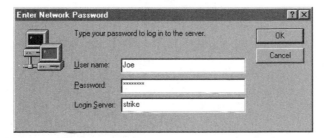

Figure 51. The network logon dialog box for Novell NetWare 3.*x* or 4.*x*

When the logon information from the dialog box has been validated against the requested server, the password is passed back to Windows 95, which can then use the password as the "password control" and unlock any linked system or network resources. In this fashion, Windows 95 can accommodate the various ways that network servers provide their services, while offering the user a very consistent interface.

Another example of support from the network provider that is visible to users occurs when they specify server name strings. For example, Microsoft–compatible networks use the Universal Naming Convention, which takes this form:

*server-name**share-name*

However, NetWare servers are specified in this form:

server-name/volume-name:directory-name

The respective network providers correctly parse the syntax of their server name strings, so users who are accustomed to using the NetWare server syntax can type name strings in that form wherever strings are required by the Windows 95 UI to access NetWare server resources.

Installable File System: Support for Multiple Network Redirectors

The Installable File System interface built into Windows 95 is a well-defined set of APIs that are used to implement all file systems in the operating system, including the VFAT (32-bit FAT) and CD-ROM file systems. The IFS implementation in Windows 95 is functionally similar to the IFS implementations in Windows for Workgroups and Windows NT. For networking, the IFS is used to implement network redirectors. The IFS interfaces are documented for use by vendors of network servers when implementing their redirectors for Windows 95. The IFS offers the following key benefits for network redirectors for Windows 95:

- **Multiple redirector support.** The IFS interface was designed for multiple redirectors.

- **Increased reliability.** The IFS model arbitrates resource requests, removing the source of many real-mode redirector conflicts.

- **Improved performance.** Network redirectors benefit from the unified IFS cache, which makes client side network redirector caching available.

The IFS consists of a set of file system APIs and loadable file system drivers (FSDs). Multiple FSDs can be resident in the system simultaneously. The FSDs provide the logic necessary for the file system to provide a consistent view of devices and arbitrates access, update, and control of devices of very different physical media types. For network redirectors, the FSDs provide mechanisms to locate, open, read, write and delete files, as well as services such as named pipes and mailslots.

To illustrate the flow of control, take as an example opening a file that is actually a link to a file on a server from a Windows 95 desktop. The user double-clicks the icon. The Windows 95 shell parses the link and determines that the file is a network object. The shell passes the filename to the NPI, which if necessary reestablishes the network connection to the server on which the object resides. The NPI then calls the network redirector to open the file on the file server. The network redirector translates the file request into a request formatted for the specified network file server, transmits the request to the server via its link through the NDIS layer, and returns to the NPI and the shell a handle to the open file.

The Microsoft–supplied redirectors for the Client for Microsoft Networks and the Microsoft Client for NetWare are both implemented as IFS FSDs.

NDIS 3.1: Multiple Protocol Support

Network Driver Interface Specification version 3.1 is a superset of the NDIS 3.0 functionality that exists for Windows NT and Windows for Workgroups 3.11. NDIS 3.1 has enhancements for Windows 95 in the following key areas:

- **Plug and Play enhancements to the Protocol Manager and Media Access Control (MAC) layer.** These enhancements enable network drivers to be dynamically loaded and unloaded.

- **A new NDIS mini-driver model.** The mini-drivers for use with Windows 95 are binary compatible with the mini-driver implementation used in Windows NT 3.5.

The primary changes to the NDIS model were extensions for Plug and Play support, and upgrading an NDIS 3.0 driver to NDIS 3.1 is very straight-forward—for example, in some cases Microsoft engineers have taken only one hour to update an NDIS driver's source code. However, instead of making this type of upgrade, vendors can instead choose to provide a mini-driver. The mini-driver model dramatically decreases the amount of code that a network adapter vendor must write, and NDIS mini-drivers developed for Windows 95 and Windows NT are binary compatible.

Conceptually, the mini-driver model is similar to the driver models implemented for printers, disk drivers, and display drivers. Essentially the mini-driver divides the existing NDIS Media Access Control (MAC) layer into two halves. The mini-driver half implements only the code that is specific to the network adapter card, including specific implementation details, such as establishing communications with the card, turning electrical isolation on and off (if implemented) for Plug and Play, doing media detection, and enabling any value-added features the card may contain. The mini-driver is wedded to the NDIS wrapper, which implements the other half of the MAC functionality. This NDIS wrapper contains the code that is "common" to all NDIS drivers. (NDIS 3.1 mini-drivers are roughly 40 percent smaller than existing NDIS 3.0 MACs because in earlier versions of NDIS, each MAC carried this redundant code.)

An NDIS 3.1 stack is composed of three components: the protocol, the MAC or mini-port, and the mini-port wrapper. NDIS contains the Protocol Manager, which loads and unloads the protocol. This manager can manage multiple protocols loaded simultaneously. Immediately below the protocol is either the MAC or the mini-driver, if a mini-driver is used. Multiple MACs or mini-drivers can be loaded in systems in which multiple network adapter cards are loaded. Finally, the mini-port wrapper layer below the mini-port does a mapping of Windows NT Hardware Abstraction Layer (HAL) layer APIs for I/O. This mini-port wrapper layer is very thin because Windows 95 can always assume that it's being run on an Intel architecture.

Novell NetWare Integration

Windows 95 provides a complete, Microsoft–supplied Microsoft Client for NetWare Networks for Windows. This client can be installed as the default network support for Windows 95, or it can coexist with the Client for Microsoft Networks, as shown in Figure 52. The Microsoft Client for NetWare Networks for Windows 95 provides interoperability with NetWare 3.*x* and 4.*x* servers.

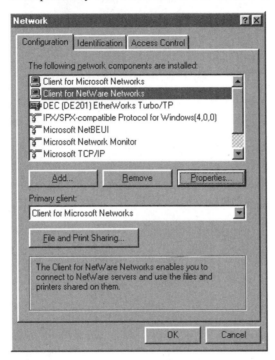

Figure 52. The Control Panel's Network tool, showing the Client for Microsoft Networks and the Microsoft Client for NetWare Networks running simultaneously

Windows 95 can also run on top of the existing Novell NetWare 3.*x* or 4.*x* clients, the NETX or VLM shells. This support is intended to help customers make the transition from their real-mode network to the fully 32-bit protected-mode network implementation in Windows 95, using smaller steps if necessary.

The 32-Bit Microsoft Client for NetWare Networks

The Microsoft Client for NetWare Networks has the following key features:

- High performance—up to 200 percent faster for some network operations compared with Windows 3.1 with the NetWare VLM shell installed

- Robust and reliable client support

- Zero conventional memory footprint

- An auto-reconnect feature

- Packet burst protocol support

- Client side caching

- Plug and Play awareness

- Full integration with the UI in Windows 95

- Full interoperability with Novell NetWare 3.*x* and 4.*x* clients and servers

- The ability to run NetWare command line utilities

- Graphical logon to NetWare 3.*x*, or 4.*x* via the NetWare Bindery

- User-level security implemented using "pass-through" to the Bindery

- A NetWare–compatible logon command processor

- Point and Print support

The client is fully implemented as 32-bit virtual device driver components. Designed to run in protected-mode and operate in a multitasking environment, the client is much more robust than real-mode networking components and takes no conventional memory.

The Microsoft Client for NetWare Networks has great performance characteristics. On large block transfers over the network, it is up to 200 percent faster than Windows 3.1 using the VLM shell; in fact, it is up to 200 percent faster than Windows 95 using the VLM shell. For most network operations that are a mix of reading and writing, the Microsoft Client for NetWare Networks is between 50 and 200 percent faster, depending on the mix of network I/O.

The Microsoft Client for NetWare Networks is enabled for Plug and Play. Portable computers that support this capability can be hot-docked or undocked and the networking support is properly loaded and unloaded without hanging the system. (Hot-docking and undocking is the equivalent of connecting and disconnecting the network cable from a Windows 95 PC. Under Windows 95, the system continues to function, whereas in real-mode networks, connecting and disconnecting causes the system to hang.) PCMCIA network cards also function in the same manner.

Logon to Windows 95 is linked to a NetWare Bindery. This link logs users onto both the Windows 95 system and their preferred NetWare server via a single graphical logon process.

As shown in Figure 53, users can specify that the Microsoft Client for NetWare Networks should process NetWare logon scripts. If drive mappings and search drives are specified in a logon script, the same user configuration is implemented under Windows 95, with no changes necessary. The Windows 95 logon processor can also parse conditional statements in NetWare logon scripts. One key difference in logon processing is that because the Windows 95 logon processor operates in protected mode, it cannot load TSRs. Logon scripts that load TSRs must be updated to remove the TSR-loading commands, and the TSRs must be loaded in the 16-bit driver load prior to the protected-mode operation. (In some cases, these TSRs have protected-mode equivalents built into Windows 95, and loading them may not be necessary.)

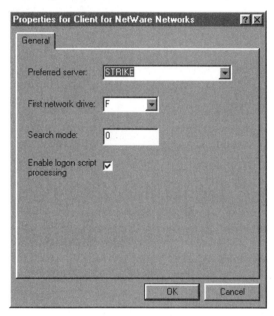

Figure 53. The property sheet for the Microsoft Client for NetWare Networks, showing that a preferred server has been specified and logon scripts have been enabled

The Microsoft Client for NetWare Networks in Windows 95 can also load and run NetWare command line utilities. It supports the MS-DOS level NetWare APIs, and the 16-bit Windows DLLs that NetWare supplies can be run on the Microsoft Client for NetWare.

File and Printer Sharing for NetWare Networks

Windows 95 provides peer services for NetWare clients. During the installation of Windows 95 and via the Network icon in Control Panel, users can install either the NetWare Compatible Peer Services or Microsoft Network Peer Services. The peer services in Windows 95 are meant to work in concert with an existing Novell NetWare server and add complementary sharing services.

The NetWare Compatible Peer Services enable the sharing of local files and printers on the Windows 95 system. For the NetWare Compatible Peer Services to be activated, a Novell NetWare server must be on the network. Without this server, file and printer sharing cannot be enabled because of the pass-through security model. Under this model, user-level security is implemented using the Bindery, the NetWare server's security authority, which passes the validation of users through to the NetWare server. (Unlike with file and printer sharing services for Microsoft Networks, share level security is not supported.)

Before sharing is enabled, a NetWare server must be specified via the Security tool in the Control Panel. The Control Panel's Network tool is then used to specify which server or domain controller is the PC's designated security authority, as shown in Figure 54.

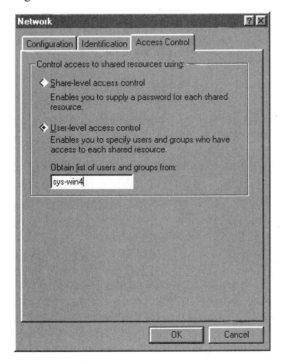

Figure 54. Specifying user-level (pass-through) security from a Windows NT domain named SYS-WIN4

Adding users to the list of those who can share the PC's hard drive is accomplished via an Add Users option on the hard disk's property sheet. Selecting this option displays the dialog box shown in Figure 55 on the next page, where access privileges are specified. The list of users that can share the hard disk is obtained from the security authority specified in the Control Panel's Network tool—SYS-WIN4 in this case.

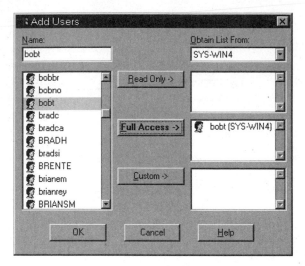

Figure 55. Specifying access privileges for a user through user-level security

When a user attempts to access a shared device on the Windows 95 system, the Windows 95 PC receives the connection request and validates the user name or group membership with the NetWare server. If the name or group membership is valid, the peer services in Windows 95 then check whether the name or group has been granted access rights to the shared resource and grants or denies the connection request accordingly.

The sharing-enabling process illustrates two points:

- User management is all done in the namespace of the existing NetWare server. Windows 95 doesn't add another namespace to administer, and the NetWare server is administered using the tools that are currently in use—for example, tools that the NetWare network manager currently uses, such as SYSCON, are used for user account management for Windows 95 user-level security.

- Only valid user accounts and groups can be shared with NetWare Compatible Peer Services.

Peer services in Windows 95 are remotely administerable via the NetWatcher. The network manager can monitor connections to any resource on any Windows 95 peer services PC on the network, and can disconnect users and remotely change access rights for specific users. By default, remote administration is limited to user accounts with the administrator privilege.

The Microsoft Print Server for NetWare Networks

In Windows 95, the file and printer sharing services for NetWare networks include a Win32–based PSERVER capability, which can despool print jobs from NetWare queues to printers on Windows 95 PCs. Consequently, a NetWare server queue can be serviced by a printer attached to a system running the file and printer sharing services for NetWare. One benefit of this capability is that because print queues can all be managed centrally from the NetWare server, users can print to one queue. If the network includes several systems running Windows 95 with peer services enabled, each system can despool from one queue, increasing overall network-based printer capacity. Alternatively, queues can be designated specifically for printers attached to a system running the file and printer sharing services for NetWare networks.

NetWare 4.*x* Support

The Microsoft Client for NetWare Networks supports a NetWare 4.*x* server if it is running Bindery emulation. The NetWare 4.*x* server is then browsable from the Network Neighborhood like any other NetWare server.

Microsoft is working to provide an updated Microsoft Client for NetWare Networks with support for NDS logon and browsing and will make this client support available for little or no cost when it is complete. Current plans call for this support to be available shortly after Windows 95 is released.

The Microsoft Client for NetWare Networks includes support for both the MS-DOS–based APIs and Windows–based APIs defined by Novell. Both of the 16-bit Novell DLLs for Windows—NWNET.DLL and NWCALLS.DLL—can be run with the Microsoft Client for NetWare Networks, ensuring that any MS-DOS or Windows–based applications and utilities that are NetWare–aware run compatibly with the Microsoft Client for NetWare Networks.

Other NetWare Interoperability

Windows 95 offers these additional interoperability features:

- Full support for Novell command-line utilities (client and server) for NetWare 3.*x*

- Support for booting diskless workstations from NetWare servers

- Floppy boot capability

- Dial-up connectivity to Novell's NetWare Connect server

Microsoft Network Integration

Windows 95 includes a network client that implements support for Microsoft Network functionality. This client allows Windows 95 to connect to Windows for Workgroups, Windows NT Server, and LAN Manager and interoperate with IBM LAN Server, DEC Pathworks, AT&T Starlan, and LAN Manager for UNIX, as well as other SMB-compatible networks.

The 32-Bit Client for Microsoft Networks

Key Client for Microsoft Networks features include the following:

- Robustness
- Zero conventional memory footprint
- An auto-reconnect feature
- Client-side caching
- Plug and Play awareness
- Full integration into the UI in Windows 95
- Protocol independence
- Point and Print for one-click printer setup

The Client for Microsoft Networks is implemented as a collection of 32-bit, protected-mode components. The Network Provider, the Redirector, and NDIS 3.1 drivers are implemented as VxDs, and because the components execute in protected-mode without the overhead of switching to real-mode, they provide great performance. The Network Provider implements client-side caching for an additional performance boost. The client's components have higher reliability than real-mode components, they are designed for operation in a multitasking environment, and they run in kernel Ring 0 context. As a result, they are not affected by errant Windows–based applications as real-mode network components are. And because they run in protected-mode, they have no conventional memory footprint.

The client is enabled for key features of Windows 95, such as long filenames, links, auto-reconnect to servers, Point and Print, and Plug and Play, and it is integrated tightly into the Windows 95 shell via the NPI. The client is protocol-independent, and it can use IPX/SPX (the default installed protocol), TCP/IP, or NetBEUI.

The client provides full interoperability with Windows for Workgroups, Windows NT Server, LAN Manager, and LAN Manager for UNIX. It also provides compatibility with AT&T StarLAN, IBM LAN Server, 3Com 3+Open and 3+Share, and DEC Pathworks.

For compatibility and to help customers implement floppy boot or better manage the transition to Windows 95, a real-mode client for Microsoft Networks is also included. The Microsoft real-mode components can be "unloaded" by the operating system after the protected-mode networking software is loaded.

The 32-Bit Microsoft Network Peer Services

Windows 95 includes enhanced peer services for Microsoft Networks. The peer server in Windows 95 supports the user-level security model when used in conjunction with a Windows NT Server, and the peer services can be linked directly to domain-based user accounts. As a result, network administrators can centrally control access to peer services at the domain controller. This domain controller can be either a Windows NT Server or a LAN Manager domain controller.

User-level security begins with sharing a device on a Windows 95 system. The list of users that appears in the sharing dialog box are provided by the domain controller, so only validated domain users can share the device. After the share is established, user logons are specified for access rights. When a user requests access to a shared Windows 95 resource, the Windows 95 peer services check the user's logon name against the domain controller's list. If the user logon is valid, the peer services then check whether this user has access privileges for this resource. If the user has access privileges, the connection is established.

Like Windows for Workgroups, Windows 95 includes share-level peer services. This level of security associates a password with a shared disk directory or printer. Share-level security can be implemented in a network consisting of only PCs running Windows 95 or in a network that includes other Microsoft Networks–compatible servers.

Peer services in Windows 95 are remotely administerable via the NetWatcher. A network manager can monitor connections to any resource on any Windows 95 peer services PC on the network and can disconnect users and remotely change access rights for specific users. By default, remote administration is limited to user accounts with the administrator privilege.

Network Compatibility

Windows 95 includes built-in support for Microsoft Networks and Novell NetWare Networks. In addition, the Setup program in Windows 95 can correctly install and configure Windows 95 for a variety of existing real-mode networks, including, but not limited to the following:

- 3Com: 3+Open and 3+Share
- Artisoft LANtastic
- Banyan VINES
- Beame and Whiteside's B&W-NFS
- DEC PATHWORKS
- IBM: LAN Server, LAN Program, and PC LAN Program
- Microsoft LAN Manager and MS Net
- Novell NetWare
- SunSelect PC-NFS
- TCS 10net

Protocol Support

Protocols for networking components in Windows 95 are implemented as 32-bit protected-mode components. Windows 95 can support multiple protocols simultaneously. Protocol stacks can be shared among the installed networks. As an example, a single TCP/IP protocol stack can serve the needs of both the Client for Microsoft Networks and the Microsoft Client for NetWare Networks.

All three protocols included with Windows 95 (IPX/SPX, TCP/IP, and NetBEUI) are Plug and Play enabled. As a result, the Windows 95 system continues to run if the network is unavailable, either because a portable computer has been undocked or a PCMCIA network card has been removed. If the network is unavailable, the protocol stacks unload themselves from the system after sending notification to any dependent applications. Plug and Play enabling also means protocols can be loaded automatically. For example, if a portable computer is undocked and attached to an infrared (IR) line-of-sight network, the TCP/IP protocol is unloaded and the appropriate IR protocol is loaded.

The IPX/SPX-Compatible Protocol

The IPX/SPX stack is the new default protocol for Windows 95 and is compatible with the Novell NetWare IPX/SPX implementation. This protocol stack can be used to communicate to either a NetWare server, or a Windows NT Server 3.5. This protocol is routable, and will run compatibly on most network infrastructure (such as bridges, routers, and so on) that are designed for IPX/SPX routing. The IPX/SPX protocol in Windows 95 includes support for "packet burst" which can offer improved network performance.

One enhancement made to the Microsoft IPX/SPX implementation is Windows Sockets programming interface support. The Windows Sockets interface is supported using IPX/SPX as the protocol. Hence, any WinSock applications can run on top of IPX/SPX with Windows 95. Support is provided for only Win32 WinSock applications.

The IPX/SPX implementation in Windows 95 also has support for the NetBIOS programming interface.

The TCP/IP Protocol

The TCP/IP protocol is becoming widely accepted for connectivity to the Internet and as an industry standard for many corporate networks. In Windows 95, TCP/IP is fully implemented as a 32-bit, high-performance VxD that consumes no conventional memory. It includes several of the more commonly used command-line utilities, such as telnet, ftp, arp, ping, route, netstat, nbstat, ipconfig, tftp, rexec, rcp, rsh, and traceroute.

The TCP/IP protocol support in Windows 95 includes the Windows Sockets programming interface and a WinSock DLL. (A 16-bit WinSock is provided for compatibility with existing WinSock applications, and a 32-bit WinSock is provided for Win32–based WinSock applications.)

NetBIOS programming interface support is also supplied with the TCP/IP support.

DHCP Support

Working with other industry leaders, Microsoft has created a *bootp* backward-compatible mechanism for automatic allocation of IP addresses to make implementation of the TCP/IP protocol more manageable. The Dynamic Host Configuration Protocol (DHCP) runs from a Windows NT DHCP server and allows network managers to centrally establish a range of IP addresses per subnet for any Windows 95 TCP/IP client requesting an address. It also allows network managers to centrally establish a "lease time"—how long the allocated IP address is to remain valid. Unlike bootp, the address allocation is dynamic, not preconfigured. In this fashion, it is possible to move from subnet to subnet and always have a valid IP address mask. Windows 95 includes a ipconfig utility that allows a user or administrator to quickly examine the allocated IP address, its lease time, and other useful data about the DHCP allocation, as shown in Figure 56.

```
Windows IP Configuration Version 0.1
     Host Name . . . . . . . :
     DNS Servers . . . . . . :
     DNS Lookup Order. . . . :
     Node Type . . . . . . . : Mixed
     NetBIOS Scope ID. . . . :
     IP Routing Enabled. . . : No
     WINS Proxy Enabled. . . : No
     WINS Resolution For Windows Sockets Applications Enabled : No
     DNS Resolution For Windows Networking Applications Enabled : No

Adapter Address 00-AA-00-18-B0-C4:
     DHCP Enabled. . . . . . : Yes
     IP Address. . . . . . . : 11.105.43.177
     Subnet Mask . . . . . . : 255.255.0.0
     Default Gateway . . . . : 11.105.0.1
     DHCP Server . . . . . . : 11.105.43.157
     Primary WINS Server . . : 11.101.13.53
     Secondary WINS Server . : 11.101.12.198
     Lease Obtained. . . . . : Tue 10th. May 1994 6:44:40 am
     Lease Expires . . . . . : Wed 11th. May 1994 6:44:40 am
```

Figure 56. The output of the ipconfig utility, showing useful data about the DHCP allocation

DHCP support can be specified at installation time or enabled via the Control Panel's Network tool. If DHCP support is disabled, an IP address can be entered in the Microsoft TCP/IP property sheet, as shown in Figure 57 on the next page.

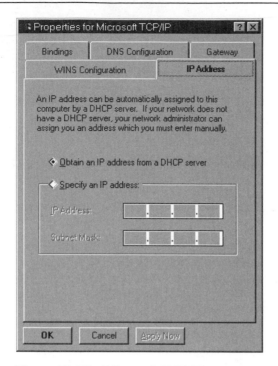

Figure 57. The Microsoft TCP/IP property sheet, showing the DHCP configuration

WINS Support

The TCP/IP protocol stack in Windows 95 lets users choose to install support for either the Windows NT Windows Internet Naming Service (WINS) or the OSF DCE Domain Naming Service (DNS). These naming services provide name resolution by binding the node name and the currently allocated IP address, providing for correct addressing of any requests for resources from a node anywhere on the network. The amount of network traffic needed to locate the node on the network is thus minimized. Windows 95 supports a single DNS server and up to two WINS servers.

The NetBEUI Protocol

Windows 95 includes a NetBEUI protocol stack that is compatible with existing networks using NetBEUI. This stack provides compatibility with Windows for Workgroups, Windows NT Server, LAN Manager, and other networks. A NetBIOS programming interface is also supported.

Network Interprocess Communications Interfaces

Windows 95 includes support for a variety of distributed computing programming interfaces, including the following:

- Client-side named pipes
- Mail slots
- OSF DCE-compliant Remote Procedure Call (RPC)
- Network DDE
- The Windows Sockets interface

Long Filename Support

The network clients in Windows 95 support the use of long filenames. If the Windows 95 system is connected to a network server that supports long filenames, then support for filenames on the server is identical to the local long filename support in Windows 95. (On some servers, the length of filenames and the list of restricted characters may differ from those of Windows 95.) Long filename support is possible on both the Windows NT Server and NetWare servers if the servers are properly configured.

Network Printing

Windows 95 includes a number of enhancements designed to make printing easier over the network, including the following:

- **Point and Print.** A printer driver can be automatically installed when connecting to a printer attached to a Novell NetWare, Windows NT Server, or Windows 95 print server. As a result, Windows 95 printer drivers can be located on a Windows NT Server or Novell NetWare server and automatically installed by their Windows 95 clients.

- **The Microsoft Print Server for NetWare Networks.** For compatibility with NetWare's PSERVER functionality, Windows 95 peer services can despool print jobs from Novell NetWare print queues.

- **Deferred printing.** When a Windows 95 PC is disconnected from the network, print jobs are deferred until the PC is once again attached to the network. Print jobs that have been deferred automatically start when the PC is reconnected.

- **Remote printing management.** Print jobs can be held, canceled, or restarted remotely. In addition, on systems that have ECP ports, information about the print job status can be returned, such as paper tray status, paper jams, or other error conditions.

Network Security

Windows 95 implements a full user logon. The first thing most users encounter after booting their Windows 95 systems is a logon dialog box, which varies depending on the type of network. For example, the Windows NT Server logon dialog box may prompt for a username, password, and domain name. The Novell NetWare 4.x logon dialog box may prompt for a username, password, and preferred server name. When the username and password pair have been validated against the network server's security authority, the Windows 95 UI is displayed.

Network managers can configure the Windows 95 system to allow entry into the UI with no network access if users fail to log on. (This configuration is the default.) As an alternative solution to this problem, network managers can specify guest accounts that have limited network access.

The Windows 95 user logon should not be construed as a mechanism to fully secure PCs. Because the PCs are still vulnerable to a floppy boot, all data stored on their hard disks is potentially available. The underlying file system in Windows 95 is the MS-DOS FAT file system, which has no built-in encryption or other security mechanisms.

Network resources are secured under Windows 95 using the same security mechanisms employed by network servers on corporate networks. The username and password in Windows 95 can be configured to be the same as those used by the network server so as to control network access, provide user-level security for access to shared resources on the local PC, and control the various agents in Windows 95, as well as limit who has remote administration authority on this Windows 95 system. In this fashion, Windows 95 leverages the existing investment in network servers, management tools, utilities and infrastructure. Network managers can manage user accounts centrally on the server, just as they always have. They can also use familiar tools for managing user accounts.

Password Control: Unified Logon

The Password Control in Windows 95 can provide a unified logon for all system components requiring password authentication services, as well as for any applications that choose to use the Password Control services. For example, protected spreadsheets or databases might use the Password Control services.

The Password Control associates the username and password supplied at Windows 95 logon with other authentication-conscious programs or system components. However, for higher security, network managers can choose to associate other passwords with access to vital corporate data or other sensitive network services.

Figure 58 shows the Password Control dialog box, which is accessible from the Control Panel:

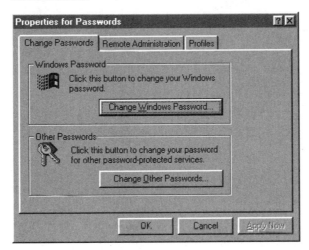

Figure 58. The property sheet for security, showing the Password Control settings

The Password Control provides a mechanism to individually manage components that choose to use the unified password cache. Windows 95 can be configured to use the Windows 95 logon for authentication on a service by service or application by application basis, making it possible to access all resources on the Windows 95 system, as well as on the network, using the Password Control in Windows 95. One example of how the Password Control service is used within Windows 95 is to provide a single logon to both the network and the Microsoft Exchange client, the mail client provided with Windows 95. Then when users log onto their PCs, the password they entered to log onto Windows 95 also automatically logs them onto e-mail. This single logon provides a solution for the problem of password proliferation.

User-Level Security

Windows 95 uses the logon process to provide user-level security for a variety of services beyond network resource access, including the following services that are remotely accessible:

- File and printer sharing
- Dial-up network Access gateway control
- Backup agent
- Network and system management

Pass-Through Security

Pass-through security is implemented in Windows 95 as the mechanism to enable user-level security. Pass-through literally means that Windows 95 passes authentication requests through to a Windows NT Server or NetWare server. Windows 95 does not implement its own unique user-level security mechanism but instead uses the services of an existing server on the network.

File and Printer Sharing

For file and printer sharing using Windows 95 peer services, enabling pass-through security is a two-step process. First, user-level security must be enabled using the Control Panel. Second, the device must be shared and users with access privileges must be specified. Right-clicking the drive C icon in My Computer displays a property sheet that shows what shares already exist and which users have access, and allows new devices to be shared and new users to be added to specific shares. The usernames listed in this property sheet are supplied by either the Windows NT Server domain, the NetWare Bindery, or NDS.

Remote Administration

The Remote Administration function of a Windows 95 PC specifies the users or groups who have authority to manage the Windows 95 system, including the following:

- Dial-up network access gateway control
- Backup agent
- Remote access to the Registry
- Remote NetWatcher access
- Remote system performance monitoring

Remote Administration is controlled via the Network Security tool in the Control Panel. Figure 59 shows Remote Administration enabled. In this case, Remote Administration is limited to the Domain Admins network manager group—any user who is a member of this group can remotely administer this Windows 95 system. Individual users can also be designated as remote administrators—for example, sophisticated users could be given remote administrator access to their systems.

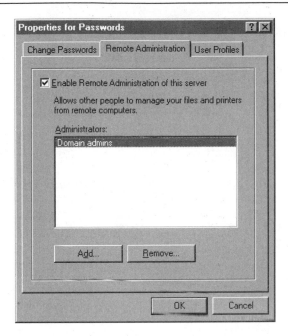

Figure 59. The property sheet for security, showing the Remote Administration settings

Dial-Up Server Remote Access Gateway

Windows 95 includes a single-line, dial-in gateway that allows a Windows 95 PC with peer services enabled to serve as a gateway to the network. The gateway is established via the property sheet shown in Figure 60 on the next page.

Like the Dial-Up Networking client, the Remote Access Gateway supports the following protocols:

- TCP/IP via the Point to Point Protocol (PPP)
- IPX/SPX via PPP
- NetBEUI

The Remote Access Gateway implements pass-through security, so only authenticated users can log onto the Gateway services. After connecting to the Gateway, Dial-Up Networking clients can access any network resource that they have privileges to use, including network server resources and peer services.

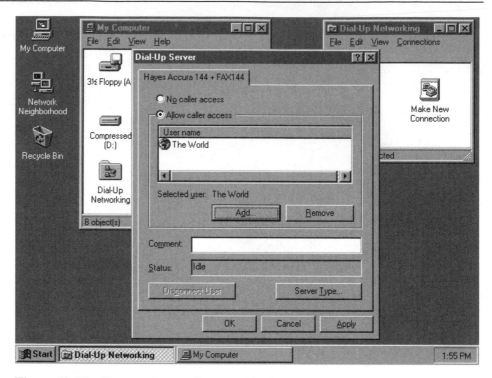

Figure 60. The Remote Access Gateway dial-in property sheet, which shows that dial-in access to the network is available via this Windows 95 PC

C H A P T E R   1 0

Systems Management

Windows 95 is the first version of Windows expressly designed for manageability. The design ensures that management of the Windows 95 PC is accessible both locally and remotely via a privileged network manager. Network security is used to determine administrator-privileged accounts using pass-through security. Windows 95 also provides for PC users to be logically separated from the underlying configuration of their PCs so that the PC and user configurations and privileges can be managed independently. As a result, network managers can allow users to "rove" on the network—that is, log on from virtually any PC on the network and then operate from a desktop that has the correct settings and network privileges. The logical separation also means that a single PC can be shared by multiple users, each with a different desktop configuration and different network privileges.

Given the proliferation of PCs connected to corporate networks, the Windows 95 PC must be able to participate in any network-wide management schemes. Windows 95 is designed to meet various network management criteria by providing built-in support for several of the key network management standards. With this infrastructure built into Windows 95, network management applications will be able to provide tools for network managers to keep PCs and networks running more efficiently and cost effectively.

Open management interfaces are key to the management implementation in Windows 95. Where a standard exists, Windows 95 implements an enabling technology to embrace the standard—for example, an SNMP agent is supplied to enable remote management of Windows 95 PCs via any number of third-party SNMP consoles. Where no standard exists, the management interfaces are documented in the Win32 API set. Microsoft expects that management software will be available for Windows 95 from a wide range of vendors.

The following list outlines the key components of the management infrastructure in Windows 95:

- The Registry
- The Registry Editor

- User Profiles (the user component of the Registry)
- Hardware Profile (the system component of the Registry)
- System Policies (the network and system policy component of the Registry)
- The System Policy Editor
- Remote Administration Security (the remote admin authentication scheme)
- Remote Procedure Call (the mechanism used to remotely administer Windows 95)
- NetWatcher
- The System Monitor (the performance monitor)
- The SNMP Agent
- The DMI Agent
- Tape Backup Agents, such as ARCServe and Arcada MTF

The discussion of the management infrastructure in Windows 95 is organized as follows:

- The Registry
- User Management
- System Management
- Network Management

The Registry

The Registry is the central repository in which Windows 95 stores all its configuration data. The Windows 95 system configuration, the PC hardware configuration, Win32–based applications, and user preferences are all stored in the Registry. For example, any Windows 95 PC hardware configuration change that is made via a Plug and Play device is immediately reflected in a configuration change in the Registry. Because of these characteristics, the Registry serves as the foundation for user, system, and network management in Windows 95.

The Registry essentially replaces the various MS-DOS and Windows 3.11 configuration files, including AUTOEXEC.BAT, CONFIG.SYS, WIN.INI, SYSTEM.INI, and the other applications .INI files. However, for compatibility purposes, instances of CONFIG.SYS, WIN.INI, and SYSTEM.INI files may exist on a Windows 95 PC for backward compatibility with either 16-bit device drivers or 16-bit applications that must run on Windows 95. For example, 16-bit applications will probably continue to create and update their own .INI files.

The Registry concept in Windows 95 is built upon the Registry concept first implemented in Windows NT. The Registry is a single configuration datastore built directly into the operating system. Although it is logically one datastore, physically it consists of three different files to allow maximum network configuration flexibility. Windows 95 uses the Registry to store information in the following three major categories:

- User-specific information, in the form of User Profiles, is contained in the USER.DAT file.

- Hardware or computer-specific settings (the Hardware Profile) are contained in the SYSTEM.DAT file.

- System Policies are designed to provide an override for any settings contained in the other two Registry components. System Policies may contain additional data specific to the network or corporate environment, as established by the network manager. They are contained in the POLICY.POL file. Unlike SYSTEM.DAT and USER.DAT, POLICY.POL is not a mandatory component of a Windows 95 installation.

Together, these three components comprise the Registry. Breaking the Registry into these three logical components provides the following benefits:

- The Registry components can be located in physically different locations. For example, the SYSTEM.DAT component and other Windows 95 system files might be located on the PC's hard disk, and the USER.DAT component might be located in the user's logon directory on a network server. With this configuration, users can log on to various PCs on the network and still have their unique network privileges and desktop configuration, allowing the "roving user" network configuration for Windows 95.

- All of the Registry files and the rest of the system files in Windows 95 can be installed on a network server. This configuration enables Windows 95 to be run on a diskless or remote initial program load (RIPL) workstation, or from a floppy disk boot configuration. With this scenario, Windows 95 can be configured to page to a local hard disk but still load all its system files from a server.

- The Registry and all of the system files can be installed on the local hard disk. With this configuration, multiple users can share a single Windows 95 PC. Each user has a separate logon username, separate user profile, separate privileges, and separate desktop configuration.

- The network manager can administer an entire network's user privileges by having a single, global POLICY.POL file. Or the network manager can establish these policies on a server basis or on a per-user basis. In this fashion, a network manager can centrally enforce a "common desktop configuration" for each end-user type. For example, a data-entry Windows 95 PC can be configured so that only two applications—the data entry application and e-mail—can be run. Additionally, the network manager can specify that data-entry users cannot modify this desktop configuration. In spite of this configuration, the Windows 95 PC can fully participate in the network and is fully configurable if a different user with more network privileges logs onto the same PC.

- Separate privileges can be assigned to users and to a PC. For example, if a user who has sharing privileges logs onto a Windows 95 PC that has no sharing (no peer services), the user cannot access the PC's resources. This feature is useful if certain PCs contain sensitive data that should not be "shareable" to the corporate network.

The Registry contains ordered pairs of keys and their associated values that are manipulated via the Win32 Registry APIs. For example, the Registry might have a Wallpaper key with an associated value of WORK.BMP, meaning that the current desktop background is configured to use the "Work" bitmap.

Additionally, a special category of keys known as *dynamic keys* are either pointers to a memory location or a call-back function. Dynamic keys are a new Registry enhancement in Windows 95. They are used by device drivers or Windows 95 subsystems that want to register a dynamic data type, such as a counter, in the Registry. In the case of network cards, the dynamic keys represent data such as data transfer rates, number of framing errors, packets dropped, and so on. In general, dynamic keys are used for data that is updated frequently and is therefore not well suited for storage in the disk-based Registry. Because the dynamic keys exist in memory, their data can be quickly updated and quickly accessed. The data can be accessed by the system performance tools in Windows 95, which call the Registry for the data they are monitoring.

Arbitrary keys and values can be created either programmatically or by using the Registry Editor (REGEDIT) tool. The APIs for managing the Registry are the Win32 Registry APIs, which can be remotely invoked via the Microsoft RPC (DCE-compliant) support built into Windows 95. Windows 95 includes both the client and server portions of Microsoft RPC, making the Registry manageable remotely from another Windows 95 PC. In this scenario, the network manager's system is the RPC client. It accesses the Registry APIs on the target Windows 95 PC via the RPC server running on the target machine. This RPC access to the Registry is secure, and network managers can limit access to either named privileged users or a group of network managers.

The Registry is also editable using the Registry Editor utility. As shown in Figure 61, the Registry consists of various parallel "trees." The Registry Editor is built upon the RPC support and can edit the local Windows 95 Registry, as well as the Registries on remote Windows 95 PCs. Although the Registry Editor is very powerful, it is fairly rudimentary in design and is intended for use by knowledgeable PC and network support staff or power users. Most end-users will never use the Registry Editor because Registry entries are usually modified via the Control Panel, by applications, or via Plug and Play.

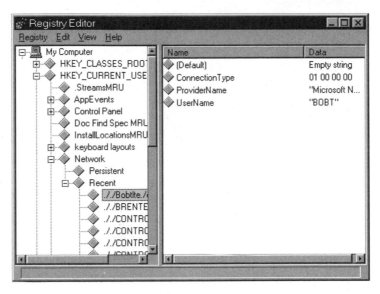

Figure 61. The Registry Editor, showing the settings stored in the Registry, which can be accessed remotely

As Figure 62 illustrates, the Registry is the central datastore that all system management services build upon. Note that all key subsystems are united by the Registry, and "agents" for standard management protocols, such as SNMP, are implemented for Windows 95 using the Registry and Registry services.

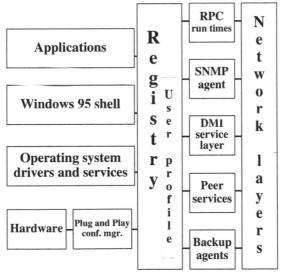

Windows 95 desktop system

Figure 62. The Windows 95 management architecture, showing the central role of the Registry

User Management

Windows 95 is the first version of Windows to implement functionality for management of user-specific configurations and user-specific privileges. User management under Windows 95 is most evident with the introduction of a user logon dialog box that minimally prompts users for their logon names and passwords each time they reboot a Windows 95 PC. This logon dialog box captures the username and password, which can trigger Windows 95 to dramatically reconfigure the desktop and, as needed, limit access to either network resources or sharing capabilities from this Windows 95 PC. Windows 95 can also pass the username and password through to registered applications and network services that use the Windows 95 logon information as a "master key" for granting or denying access.

The user management capabilities in Windows 95 are built upon the following components:

- User Profiles
- System Policies
- Server-Based Security

User Profiles

In Windows 3.11, settings unique to a user were located in many disparate locations, including AUTOEXEC.BAT, CONFIG.SYS, WIN.INI, SYSTEM.INI, and numerous application-specific .INI files. Because this data was often intertwined with the Windows internal configuration data, providing good user management using Windows 3.11 was very difficult. For example, the simple task of allowing multiple users to work on a single PC was not possible with "out-of-the-box" Windows 3.11. Managing multiple user configurations on a network was even more difficult.

Various tools and products attempted to retroactively address the lack of user management capabilities in Windows 3.11. Out of necessity, many companies wrote their own user management tools or used third-party products to help manage multiple users on their networks. Very often, this user namespace did not leverage the existing namespace of the corporate network resident on the network servers. In some cases, the user management software was implemented as a replacement Windows shell, with varying degrees of compatibility with existing Windows–based applications and the underlying network client software.

User management in Windows 95 is integral to the system and is implemented in a feature known as User Profiles. User Profiles are part of the Registry, and they contain system, application, and network data that are unique to individual users of a Windows 95 PC. The User Profile characteristics can be set by the user, by the network manager, or by the help-desk staff. In contrast to Windows 3.11, the User Profiles in Windows 95 are contained within a single file named USER.DAT. By keeping all user-specific data in one file, Windows 95 can provide a means to manage the user of the PC separately from the configuration of the Windows 95 operating system and the PC hardware. This separation also allows the user information to be located in a physically different location than that of the system configuration. It also allows the User Profiles to be updated separately from the rest of the Registry. All settings contained within a User Profile are administerable locally or remotely from another Windows 95 PC. Windows 95 enables centralized user management, and the network manager can user the Registry Editor provided with Windows 95 or a variety of third-party tools to automate management of User Profiles.

The settings contained in User Profiles include the following:

- Windows 95 settings, including desktop layout, background, font selection, colors, shortcuts, display resolution, and so on

- Network settings, including network connections, workgroup, preferred server, shared resources, and so on

- Application settings, including menu and toolbar configurations, fonts, window configuration preferences, and so on

User Profiles can effectively be disabled for Windows 95 PCs with only one user, by disabling the option that gives each user a separate desktop in the property sheet for security, shown in Figure 63.

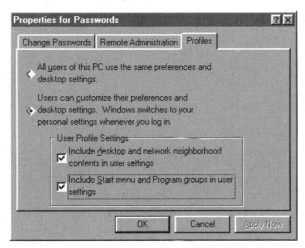

Figure 63. The property sheet for security, showing User Profiles enabled and specifying unique desktops, Taskbar options, and program groups for each user

System Policies

System Policies are designed to give network managers the ability to customize control over Windows 95 for users of differing capabilities or network privilege levels, including control of the user interface, network capabilities, desktop configuration, sharing capabilities, and so on. Like the other two Registry components, System

Policies consist of pairs of keys and values. Unlike the other two Registry components, System Policies are designed to override any settings that may exist in User Profiles or Hardware Profile. System Policies are not necessary to enable a Windows 95 system to boot. They are loaded last and are typically downloaded from a location on the network server defined by the network manager.

System Policies can be used to define a "default" setting for the User Profile or the Hardware Profile, as shown in Figure 64. Default settings for both a default user and a default computer may solve the problem of preconfigured PCs for network managers. New PC hardware comes pre-installed with Windows and, in some cases, with the network hardware and software necessary to connect to the corporate network. Many network managers have a network-wide standard Windows 3.11 that they configure by hand on each PC before the PC is allowed on the corporate network. However, if a PC is delivered directly to an end-user, as is often the case, the network manager doesn't have the opportunity to install the network-wide standard configuration on that PC. Default System Policies can solve this problem. For example, if the network-wide standard Windows configuration consists of a standard set of applications and a standard set of network privileges, such as servers to which connection is allowed, the network manager can preconfigure a default user-based set of System Policies to "enforce" these standards the first time the PC is connected to a network server. Assuming that the user logs on with a valid network logon username, the network privileges made available will be exactly those that the user is entitled to.

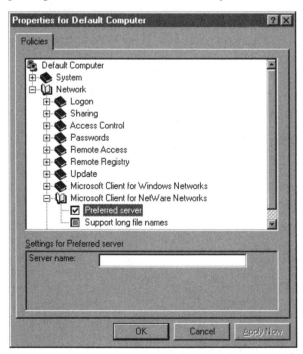

Figure 64. The System Policies properties for a default computer

The range of desktop control offered by System Policies is fairly comprehensive and includes standard network connections and the enabling and disabling of peer sharing capabilities, as well as such controls as password aging. For example, the network manager can define a desktop for a user and then "lock down" this desktop configuration by turning on the attribute that makes the desktop unmodifiable by the user. The network manager can also ensure that the user has access only to approved applications by not allowing the user to run any other programs. This restriction prevents the user from running programs from the command line or from the UI browsers and thus prevents installation of additional software. Another example of the way System Policies might be used is to disable elements of the Control Panel for users who have the habit of reconfiguring their PCs and as a result, are perennially "help-desk intensive."

System Policies for Users

Windows 95 supports a set of System Policies integrated with various system components for controlling the Windows 95 environment on a per-user basis. The following areas and System Policies can be controlled for users:

- **Control Panel.** Within this category of options, network managers can set policies to prevent the user from accessing Control Panel features. Policies include:

    - Restricting access to the Control Panel's Display settings, Network settings, Printers settings, System settings, and Security settings

- **Desktop.** Policies can prevent users from modifying desktop features. Policies include:

    - Specifying a wallpaper and color scheme to be used

- **Network.** The network policies provide restrictions to file and printer sharing. Policies include:

    - Disabling file sharing and printer sharing controls

- **Shell.** The shell (UI) policies can be used to customize folders and other elements of the desktop and to restrict changes to the UI. Policies include:

    - Customizing the user's Programs folder, Desktop items, Startup folder, Network Neighborhood, and Start menu

    Restrictions include:

    - Removing the Run and Find commands from the Start menu

    - Removing folders and the Taskbar from Settings on the Start menu

    - Hiding drives in My Computer and hiding the Network Neighborhood

    - Removing Entire Network from the Network Neighborhood

- Hiding all items on the desktop

- Disabling the Shut Down command, which prevents changed settings from being saved at exit

- **System.** These policies restrict the use of Registry editing tools, applications, and MS-DOS–based applications. Policies include:

    - Restricting the use of Registry editing tools

    - Running only selected Windows–based applications

    - Disabling the ability to run an MS-DOS command prompt and single MS-DOS application mode

System Policies for Computers

Windows 95 supports a set of System Policies integrated with various system components for controlling the Windows 95 environment on a per-computer basis. The following areas and System Policies can be controlled for computers:

- **System.** These policy settings relate to the computer configuration. Policies include:

    - Identifying the network path for Windows Setup

    - Enabling User Profile support

    - Identifying items to be run each time the computer starts or to be run only once when the computer first starts

- **Network.** These policy settings relate to the network configuration of the computer. Policies include:

    - Controlling logon settings

    - Disabling file and printer sharing

    - Activating user-level security

    - Controlling password settings

    - Disabling remote dial-up access

- Controlling remote access to the Registry

- Defining properties for remote policy updates

- Defining settings for the Client for Microsoft Networks and the Microsoft Client for NetWare Networks

- Setting attributes for the SNMP service

Registry Tools

The primary user management tools in Windows 95 are the Registry Editor and the System Policy Editor. For most other types of user administration, network managers use the same user accounts tools on their PC servers that they used before Windows 95.

Registry Editor

The Registry Editor allows network managers to directly read and write values that are contained in the User Profiles and the Hardware Profile in the Registry. Using this tool, network managers can read current settings, modify them, create new keys and values, or delete current keys and values in the Registry.

The Registry Editor can edit remote Registries using the RPC-enabled Win32 Registry APIs built into Windows 95. In the case of a User Profile residing on a network server, the network manager simply connects to the network server and opens the file using normal file I/O—no RPC connection is needed between the Windows 95 client and the network server.

System Policy Editor

The System Policy Editor, shown in Figure 65 on the following page, generates the System Policies file, POLICY.POL. This tool allows network managers to specify specific network policies or user configurations for Windows 95. The tool is extensible by third parties; the ADF format is a text file that can be extended by network tool vendors or by network managers as needed. The System Policy Editor works via local file I/O and is not RPC-enabled. Because the System Policies file is located centrally on a network server, typically one copy is needed per server. All the network manager needs to do is connect to the network server and edit the System Policies file.

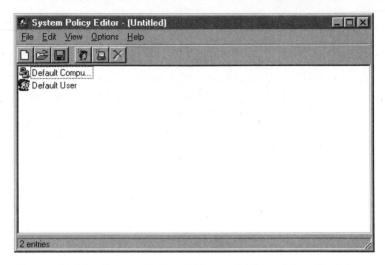

Figure 65. The System Policy Editor, which enables administrators to define policies on a per-user basis

The Role of the Server in Systems Management

In user management, the server plays a central role. All user namespace management is performed on the network server, so the native user-level security mechanism built into the network server is used by Windows 95 for user logon authentication and pass-through security. Windows 95 has no built-in user-level security mechanism of its own. As a consequence, network managers can use the familiar server administration tools to manage user accounts for Windows 95.

The second role of the server in user management in Windows 95 is to contain copies of User Profiles and System Policies. Typically, User Profiles are stored in user directories that are read/write enabled for the user. As changes are made to the local copy of User Profiles, the copy that resides on the server is updated—Windows 95 keeps the local and network image synchronized. System Policies should be stored in a directory that is accessible to all user logons and should be made read only for users to ensure that only network managers can modify the network-wide policies that the System Policies file may define.

System Management

Windows 95 systems have been designed to be managed well, both locally and remotely, using the Registry's remote capabilities. The Registry enables network managers to remotely manage the system software settings of Windows 95, including settings used by device drivers. For example, network managers can remotely change the network frame type in use on all the PCs under their oversight. Prior to

Windows 95, this task would, in many cases, be performed by directly editing the NET.CFG or PROTOCOL.INI files.

Plug and Play makes the hardware configuration of Windows 95 PCs much more manageable. It also addresses a paramount problem facing users and help-desk staff: that of proper hardware configuration. One of the more complex hardware/software configuration problems revolves around the use of portable-computer docking stations. Typically, portable-computer users have a "boot configuration" manager to help manage the different devices that need to be installed when the computer is docked or when it is remote. Creating these configurations is very time-consuming and must often be done for each system setup because of conflicts with other device drivers that may be installed. Plug and Play automates docking, as well as the use of PCMCIA cards, and helps with link management when moving from fast links to slower asynchronous links. The Windows 95 system detects events such as docking/undocking, PCMCIA card insertion/removal, and moving between fast/slow media and appropriately loads and unloads device drivers and configures them automatically. Windows 95 also notifies applications that the device is either available or unavailable.

The Windows 95 Tools

Windows 95 includes a variety of tools that allow users or network managers to configure the hardware and software on a Windows 95 PC. These include the following:

- **The Control Panel.** Most key system settings are accessible via the Control Panel, which has traditionally been the only interface available for directly modifying the configuration of hardware and software settings in Windows. The Control Panel in Windows 95, like its Windows 3.1 predecessor, is extensible and provides the best local mechanism for managing all system settings. In Windows 95, all network settings have been consolidated into a single Network tool, rather than being split between several discrete applications as in prior versions of Windows.

- **Context Menus and Property Sheets.** Context menus and property sheets list a number of actions that can be directly applied to system objects. They are displayed by right-clicking the object. For example, the Properties command on the context menu for a directory with sharing enabled allows users to invoke sharing of the directory. The Properties command on the context menu for a server tells whether the server is a NetWare server, a Windows NT server, or a Windows 95 system.

- **Plug and Play.** The current hardware configuration for the system is accessible via the Control Panel's System tool. All hardware device nodes in the hardware tree are shown, with current configuration settings. These settings are updated dynamically whenever a device's configuration changes or if the device is inserted or removed.

- **The Registry Editor.** For network managers or help-desk staff, the Registry Editor allows remote viewing and editing of the full Registry. Data contained in the Registry is represented in its hierarchical tree structure as pairs of keys and values.

- **The System Policy Editor.** System capabilities can be enabled or disabled using the System Policy Editor. For example, sharing can be disabled on a machine basis, or local Control Panel usage can be disabled for non-privileged users.

- **The DMI agent.** Remote desktop management, including hardware and software inventory and the ability to make remote changes to the system, is possible via the DMI agent for Windows 95.

Performance Monitoring

Windows 95 includes an enhanced performance monitoring utility that enables network managers and help-desk staff to more quickly troubleshoot performance problems caused by an invalid configuration or some other conflict. The System Monitor, shown in Figure 66, is the replacement for WinMeter in Windows for Workgroups. It provides more detailed information about the system's I/O performance, including file I/O and network I/O performance. Data is gathered on an FSD basis, which means information can be gathered from the FAT file system and any number of network redirectors that may be loaded. The interfaces to the System Monitor are open and are extensible by third parties.

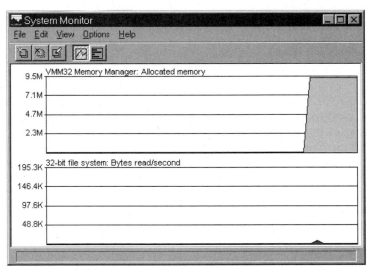

Figure 66. The System Monitor, which allows local and remote monitoring of system performance

For network managers, the key feature of System Monitor is its ability to monitor a remote system. This capability is built upon remote Registry access because performance data is registered with the system using dynamic keys contained within the Registry. For example, a network manager who is attempting to troubleshoot a "slow PC" can discover remotely that the NIC has an unusually high number of dropped frames and can then use the Registry Editor to see how the network card is configured.

Network Management

Windows 95 includes a number of features to facilitate the use of a variety of network management tools. Many of these tools require support in the client to enable their operation. In some cases a formal industry standard exists, and in others, a de facto standard has emerged. Either way, Windows 95 enables some of the key network management tools by building the necessary "agent" software into the client operating system.

Server-Based Backup

Windows 95 includes agents for the remote backup of the Windows 95 system by a server-based backup system. The following backup agents are included with Windows 95:

- Cheyenne ARCServe agent for backup to NetWare and Windows NT Server servers

- Arcada Backup agent for backup to NetWare and Windows NT Server servers

These agents make it possible to include Windows 95 systems in a scheduled, automatic remote backup scheme managed centrally via the server-based backup system. Their property sheets are shown in Figure 67 and Figure 68 on the following page.

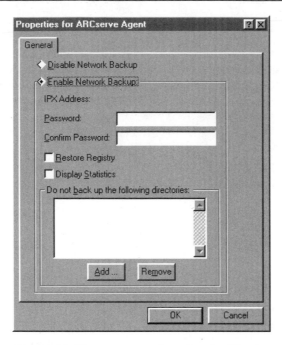

Figure 67. The property sheet for the Cheyenne ARCServe agent

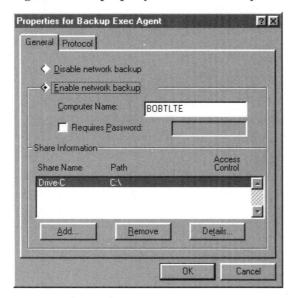

Figure 68. The property sheet for the Arcada Backup agent

Both backup agents include a number of enhancements for Windows 95. For example, both agents include the ability to backup and restore long filenames. (If the native tape format does not include a mechanism for storing long filenames, the agents provide special logic to facilitate saving and restoring the long filenames.) Both agents have also been enhanced to backup and restore the Registry.

Another enhancement for Windows 95 is the ability to secure operation of the backup agent by means of user-level security. By default, remote administration of the Windows 95 PC is enabled only for supervisor-privileged accounts, giving the ability to remotely back up Windows 95 systems only to network managers or help-desk staff. For example, only authorized personnel should be able to back up the hard disk of the CEO's and the corporate controller's PCs.

Network Management Tools

A category of tools is emerging onto the market that all claim to be network management tools. Many of these tools were actually designed to solve a specific problem but have been extended to become more general-purpose network management tools.

SNMP Support

Simple Network Management Protocol (SNMP) consoles are a good example of this trend. They are now being enhanced to monitor components of desktop systems as well as server applications such as database servers. Windows 95 includes an SNMP agent that supports the use of an SNMP console to manage Windows 95 PCs. The SNMP support in Windows 95 includes the following:

- An SNMP Agent
- An extensible MIB handler interface
- MIB-II support via TCP/IP

The SNMP agent provided with Windows 95 is extensible via its MIB handler interface, which enables third parties to include instrumentation of their software or hardware components and allows remote management via the SNMP console.

Because many corporations are beginning to migrate to TCP/IP as a standard protocol, the TCP/IP stack in Windows 95 has been instrumented for SNMP remote management. The MIB-II supports the Internet Engineering Task Force (IETF) Request for Comment (RFC) for the TCP/IP MIB definition. This support enables network managers to centrally monitor the performance of TCP/IP on the network from a central console.

DMI Support

Windows 95 also includes support for the Desktop Management Task Force (DMTF) by supplying a DMI Agent. (This support may become available after the release of Windows 95.)

The Windows 95 Tools

Windows 95 includes a number of built-in tools for network management, including NetWatcher (shown in Figure 69). NetWatcher allows local and remote management of users' connections to Windows 95 peer services. The tool shows all current connections to the Windows 95 system, who is connected, and which files and printers are in use. It allows disconnection of users and maintains a log of key system events, such as logon, logoff, system boot and shutdown, and failed attempts to connect.

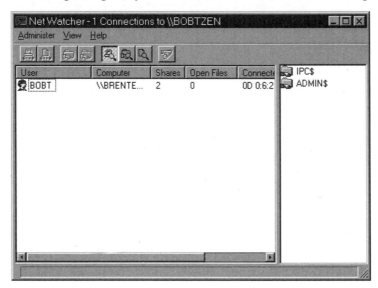

Figure 69. NetWatcher, which supports local and remote monitoring of connections to peer services

Additionally, Windows 95 includes the capability to access a special "administration share" of any capable Windows 95 PC. This share, which allows network managers to reconfigure the hard disks of remote PCs from their desktops, is accessed by displaying the property sheet for the remote PC from the Network Neighborhood. When this feature is activated, a window opens that appears to be a normal browsing window but is actually the remote PC's My Computer view. All files and other resources on the remote PC are then accessible.

CHAPTER 11

Printing

In Windows 95, several changes have been made to the way printing is handled to address requests from customers and independent software and hardware vendors. The improvements focus on the following three major areas:

- **Better performance.** Windows 95 has a new 32-bit printing architecture that supports preemptive multitasking and improves overall performance.

- **Easier.** Improvements in the UI in Windows 95 make printing easier, and Plug and Play support makes installing new printers easier.

- **Better integration of network printing.** Windows 95 has extended the local printing architecture to the network environment and ties together installation enhancements to shared network printers.

This chapter describes the printing architecture used in Windows 95 and discusses the areas where printing is improved over Windows 3.1.

Summary of Improvements over Windows 3.1

The primary improvements in printing for Windows 95 are the following:

- A new 32-bit print subsystem modeled after the subsystem in Windows NT, providing smooth background printing

- Increased printing performance through the use of enhanced metafile (EMF) spooling, which decreases the time needed to return control to the application

- Support for over 800 different printer models (versus over 300 for Windows 3.1) through the development of new printer mini-drivers

- Support for PostScript Level II printers

- Spooling of MS-DOS–based application print jobs along with those of Windows–based applications, with conflict resolution when MS-DOS and Windows–based applications try to print at the same time

- Image color matching support, which provides better WYSIWYG between color in images displayed on screen and color generated on an output device

- Deferred printing for mobile computer users, allowing users to issue the command to print while undocked and not connected to a printer, so that print jobs will be automatically started when the computer is docked into a docking station

- Simplified printer driver installation, configuration, ease of use, and ease of support through a new, consolidated user interface

- System support for new bidirectional printers and ports, providing improved I/O performance with fast parallel ports (ECP) and error status reporting

- Better integration of network printing support, including Point and Print support for the automatic installation of printer drivers from Windows 95, Windows NT Server, or Novell NetWare servers

- Plug and Play support for printers, simplifying installation and configuration

The 32-Bit Print Subsystem

Windows 95 features a 32-bit print subsystem that includes a multithreaded, preemptive spooler architecture and provides improved printing performance, smoother background printing, and quicker return to the application after a print job is initiated by a user in an application. The architecture of the print subsystem is compatible with the Windows NT 3.1 print subsystem.

The 32-Bit Preemptive Spooler

In Windows 3.1, print spooling functionality was handled by Print Manager and was supported by code in several different Windows components. In Windows 95, the print spooler is implemented as a series of 32-bit virtual device drivers and the spooler functionality is consolidated into a single architecture, with the following benefits:

- **Smooth background printing.** In Windows 3.1, Print Manager passed a fixed amount of information to the printer, whether or not the printer was ready to receive the information. If the printer wasn't ready, the system would be suspended until it was ready. Unlike Print Manager, the Windows 95 spooler passes data to the printer only when the printer is ready to receive it. This strategy helps reduce the "jerkiness" often experienced when printing documents with Windows 3.1 Print Manager.

- **Quick return to the application.** Because of the smooth background printing made possible by the new 32-bit print subsystem, Windows 95 spools enhanced metafiles (EMFs) rather than raw printer data when printing from Windows–based applications, resulting in a quicker return-to-application time. After it is spooled, the EMF is interpreted in the background by the printer driver, and output is then sent to the printer. For more details, see the following "Enhanced Metafile Spooling" section.

- **More power and flexibility.** The new architecture allows users to select printer attributes on a per-printer basis, instead of requiring global printing attributes as in Windows 3.1. For example, each printer can have a different separator page and the option of printing direct via a queue.

Enhanced Metafile Spooling

EMF spooling results in a quicker return-to-application time and hence quicker return of control to the user after a print job is initiated in a Windows–based application (Win16 or Win32).

Before discussing how EMFs fit into the printing architecture used by Windows 95, it is worth reviewing how print jobs are handled by Windows 3.1, because the improvements in Windows 95 result in much better printing performance than in Windows 3.1.

In Windows 3.1, all interpretation of print API calls were handled by the Windows printer driver *before* the information was spooled to Print Manager, as shown in Figure 70 on the following page. The interpretation of print information for printers was the most time-consuming operation in the print process. Users of PostScript printers were not impacted by this process because the printer driver sends high-level Page Description Language (PDL)–based information to the printer, rather than sending raw image data that must be interpreted by the printer itself. However, users of non-PostScript printers experienced a delay in returning to their applications after a print job was initiated, while the GDI print API calls were processed by the printer driver. After the output image file was created by the printer driver, the Print Manager spooler took over, and control was returned to the user's application. As a result, background printing under Windows 3.1 often seemed jerky.

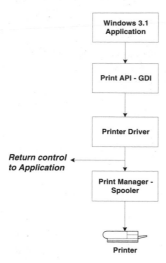

Figure 70. The spooler's relationship to printing in Windows 3.1

Windows 95 greatly improves the return-to-application time by spooling high-level command information generated by the GDI print API, collectively referred to as an enhanced metafile, rather than spooling raw printer data generated by the printer driver. For example, if a document contains a solid black rectangle, the EMF contains a command to draw a rectangle with the given dimensions that should be solidly filled with the color black. After the EMF is created, control is returned to the user, and the EMF file is interpreted in the background by the 32-bit print subsystem spooler and sent to the printer driver. This process, which is shown in Figure 71, results in control being returned to users in significantly less time because they don't have to wait for the print calls to be directly interpreted by the printer driver.

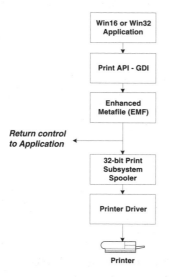

Figure 71. The spooler's relationship to printing in Windows 95

Try It!

Test the Quicker Return-to-Application Time

1. Under Windows 3.1, start Print Manager.

2. Turn off background printing if it is supported by your application—for example, Word for Windows version 6.0.

3. Print from your application, noting the time it takes for control to be returned to you.

4. Perform the same task under Windows 95, again noting the time it takes for control to be returned to you.

5. Print from an MS-DOS–based application under both Windows 3.1 and Windows 95, and again note the return-to-application time.

6. Compare the above.

Support for MS-DOS–Based Applications

Windows 95 improves on the support provided by Windows 3.1 for printing from an MS-DOS–based application in the Windows environment by allowing MS-DOS–based applications to spool print jobs to the 32-bit print subsystem spooler. With Windows 3.1, users printing from MS-DOS–based applications could not take advantage of the Windows–based spooling functionality offered by Print Manager, and they encountered device contention issues when trying to print from MS-DOS–based applications at the same time as printing from Windows–based applications.

Windows 95 addresses these printing problems by incorporating the functionality for an MS-DOS–based application to spool directly to the 32-bit print spooler. This support is integrated into a print spooler virtual device, which takes the output destined for a printer port and places it in the print spooler before sending the data to the printer. The print spooler is automatically installed and configured and its handling is transparent to users. It works with all existing MS-DOS–based applications and results in a quicker return-to-application time. Although MS-DOS–based applications do not benefit from EMF spooling, which is supported only for Windows–based applications, the print spooler mechanism means that users won't encounter device contention issues and will benefit from smoother background printing and improved printing performance.

Try It!

Spool from an MS-DOS–Based Application

1. In Windows 95, pause the print queue for your printer.

2. Print from an MS-DOS–based application. Notice that print jobs generated by MS-DOS–based applications show up in the print queue and can be manipulated just like print jobs from Windows–based applications.

Support for Deferred Printing

To benefit mobile computer users, the print subsystem in Windows 95 features support for deferred printing. This capability allows users not connected to a printer to generate print jobs that are stored on their local computers. Items not immediately printed are held in the print queue until the computer is connected to a printer. Using this feature, mobile users can create print jobs from Windows–based applications (Win16 or Win32) or MS-DOS–based applications while on the road and then print on a physical printer when they return to the office. This feature is also handy for users in the office who temporarily lose printer connections because of network or printer problems.

Image Color Matching Support

Using technology licensed from Kodak, Windows 95 provides Image Color Matching (ICM) support, enabling applications to offer greater consistency between the color of images displayed on the screen and the color of images generated by an output device. ICM support is included for display, printer, and scanner devices.

ICM provides consistent (predictable) color rendering from input through monitor preview to output. With ICM functionality, color information is portable across applications that manipulate the information; across users, providing consistent use of colors; and across platforms, allowing the information to be easily moved to different systems in which ICM has been implemented.

ICM support in Windows 95 provides the following benefits to application developers, which in turn result in benefits to users:

* Makes enabling color awareness in applications easy
* Allows for color
* Provides consistent color output across devices

Because Windows 3.1 did not provide ICM support as part of the operating system or in an external driver, this support was implemented in a proprietary manner by application developers, and the burden was on the developers to properly map the colors generated by a display device to the colors generated by a printer device. Windows 95 simplifies this process by including ICM support as part of the operating system, allowing application developers to integrate ICM functionality into their applications and thus take advantage of this new system service.

To provide support for device-independent color matching, colors used in applications are tied to international (CIE-based) colorimetric standards rather than specific hardware devices. The operating system does the appropriate color transformations to map the device-independent color representations to the colors supported by the physical device.

The key to ICM support is the use of a profile that represents the color properties of a monitor, printer, or scanner device. The profile format used by the ICM support in Windows 95 is the work of InterColor 3.0, an industry consortium made up of many industry hardware vendors—Kodak, Microsoft, Apple Computer, Sun, and Silicon Graphics, among others—and industry standard-setting bodies. The InterColor 3.0 efforts provide for a consistent cross-platform color standardization process that will result in industry-wide standards for defining the ICM properties of output and display devices.

Installing and Configuring a Printer

Unlike Windows 3 1, Windows 95 has no Print Manager and no Print icon in the Control Panel. Gone also is the confusion about which tool to use for managing print jobs, installing new printers, creating queues, and performing other tasks related to printing. Windows 95 consolidates the printer and printing functions into a single Printers folder, shown in Figure 72. The Printers folder provides easy ways of adding new printers, configuring existing printers, and managing print jobs.

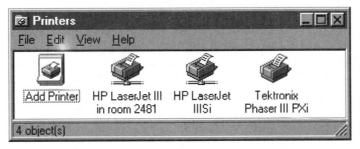

Figure 72. The Printers folder

Easy Printer Setup

Windows 95 makes it easy to install new printers by supporting the following installation mechanisms:

- **Plug and Play printer detection.** For Plug and Play printers, Windows 95 will automatically detect the printer at installation time or during the boot process. The Plug and Play detection code will prompt the user for the appropriate driver files if they are not resident in the Windows directory.

- **The Printer Installation Wizard.** Windows 95 provides a wizard that walks users through the printer installation process. Whether the printer is connected to the local PC or shared on another PC on the network, installing it is easier than ever before. Figure 73 shows the Printer Installation Wizard's first dialog box.

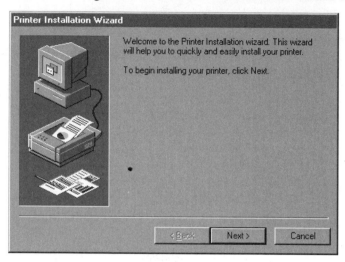

Figure 73. The Printer Installation Wizard, which walks users through the printer installation process

- **Point and Print printing.** The Point and Print feature enables users to quickly connect to and use a printer shared on another Windows 95 PC, a Windows NT Server, or a Novell NetWare server. When users connect to a shared printer, Windows 95 automatically copies and installs the correct driver for the shared printer from the remote Windows 95 PC, the Windows NT Server, or the Novell NetWare server. They can then simply begin printing.

- Point and Print printing is discussed in more detail in Chapter 9, "Networking."

Configuring a Printer

Configuring a printer in Windows 95 is much simpler than in Windows 3.1. All printer configuration is consolidated onto a single property sheet for the printer that can be accessed from the Printers folder. As shown in Figure 74, the property sheet contains all printer parameters, such as the printer port (or network path) that the printer is connected to, the paper options for the printer, the fonts built into the printer, and device options specific to the printer model.

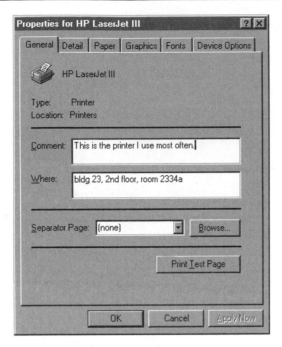

Figure 74. The property sheet for the Hewlett-Packard LaserJet III printer

To further simplify printer configuration, Windows 95 supports bidirectional communications between compatible printers—for example, HP LaserJet 4 models and PostScript printers that are connected to PCs via serial cables—and printer ports. With this functionality, Windows 95 can query the characteristics and configuration options directly from the printer and can automatically configure the printer driver to exactly match the configuration of the printer, including the amount of memory, the paper options, and the fonts installed in the printer.

Managing Print Jobs

Windows 95 provides better print job management capabilities than Print Manager does in Windows 3.1 and Windows for Workgroups. Improvements provided in Windows 95 include the following:

- **Direct integration with the UI in Windows 95.** The Printers folder serves as the centralized location for interacting with or configuring with printer devices. Opening a printer window and switching to Details view, as shown in Figure 75 on the following page, displays detailed information about the contents of active print jobs or jobs that are waiting in the queue, including the name of the document, the status of the document, the owner of the document, when the document was submitted to the print queue, the number of pages in the document (when printing, the status of the print job down to the page that is being printed is displayed), the size of the document, and the priority of the print job.

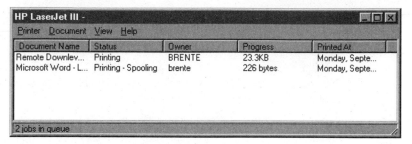

Figure 75. A Details view of a remote print queue's status

- **Local and remote management of print jobs.** With Windows for Workgroups, users had to physically walk over to a remote PC to cancel a printing operation on that PC's shared printer. With Windows 95, it is no longer necessary to walk over to the PC where the queue resides to terminate print jobs or resume the printer if an error occurs. Users can pause or cancel the printing of print jobs residing in a remote print queue on a Windows 95 PC. Users with administrator access to a Windows 95 PC that is sharing a printer can remotely manage and administer the print queue with the same UI and functionality available for a local printer.

Network Printing Improvements

Windows 95 provides better support than Windows 3.1 for printing in a networked environment. The enhancements include the following:

- **Network Point and Print functionality.** Users can print to a shared network printer connected to a computer running Windows 95, Windows NT Advanced Server, or Novell NetWare and have the appropriate printer driver automatically copied from the remote computer and configured on the local Windows 95 computer. Point and Print simplifies the printer installation process and ensures that the correct printer driver is installed for the remote printer.

- **Remote administration of print jobs.** Windows 95 provides full remote administration of print jobs for printers shared on computers running Windows 95. With the appropriate access privileges, operations such as holding a print job, canceling a print job, and resuming printing when the print queue is paused can be performed remotely.

More information about network printing enhancements in Windows 95 is provided in Chapter 9, "Networking."

Plug and Play Support

Installing and configuring printers in Windows 95 is much simpler than in Windows 3.1. As with other components of the Windows 95 system, setting up a new printer benefits from the Windows 95 Plug and Play capabilities. Using bidirectional parallel communications, Windows 95 detects that a Plug and Play–compatible printer is connected to the PC (see Figure 76) by means of a returned device ID value, as described in the IEEE 1284 Specification. Bidirectional parallel communications with the printer also enable Windows 95 to obtain information about other physical attributes of the device.

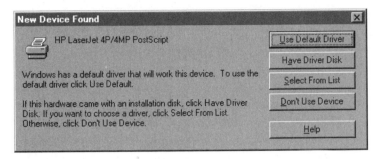

Figure 76. The New Device Found dialog box, showing detection of a Plug and Play printer

Windows 95 detects a Plug and Play printer in one of three ways: when Windows 95 is first installed on a PC, each time Windows 95 starts, or when a user explicitly requests that a detection be made. When Windows 95 is first installed on a PC and when Windows 95 starts, a Plug and Play printer connected to a bidirectional communications port attempts to identify itself by sending its detection code. If the connected printer is not presently configured in the Windows 95 system, the user is asked whether the printer should be installed. If the user says "Yes" and the appropriate printer driver is already present on the system, Windows 95 automatically installs and configures the driver for the printer. If the printer driver is not already present, Windows 95 prompts the user for the appropriate Setup And Installation disk for Windows 95. If the system doesn't recognize the printer, Windows 95 prompts the user to insert a disk containing the printer driver provided by the printer manufacturer.

Try It!

Test Plug and Play Support

1. Connect a Plug and Play printer to your computer before starting Windows 95. Supported printers include the Hewlett-Packard LaserJet 4 models (4L, 4Plus, 4P, 4MP, 4MPlus, and 4ML, 4si), the LexMark 4039 and 4039+, and the ValueWriter 600.

2. Start Windows 95. During the boot process, notice that the system automatically detects the Plug and Play printer and prompts you to install the appropriate printer driver.

CHAPTER 12

Communications

Windows 95 features a new 32-bit communications subsystem that provides higher throughput, better reliability, and greater device independence for communications operations than Windows 3.1. The new communications subsystem serves as the underlying architecture on which Windows 95 provides communications services that support telecommuting and dial-up network access, Microsoft At Work Fax services, access to online information services, computer-telephone integration, conferencing, and remote access to mail.

The communications subsystem addresses problems that users encountered with communications support in Windows 3.1 and provides a powerful, robust, and flexible communications architecture.

Summary of Improvements over Windows 3.1

Changes made to the Windows 3.1 kernel and communications architecture resulted in the following improvements and benefits to the Windows 95 user:

- Robust and reliable, high-baud-rate communications throughput

- Better multitasking of communications applications

- Simpler centralized setup and configuration

- Broader device support

- Better support for sharing communication devices, such as modems, among different communications applications

- Telephone network independence

The Communications Architecture

Around the time when Windows 3.0 was first developed, 2400-baud modems were the mainstream and 9600-baud modems were just becoming affordable. Windows was able to handle receiving data at these relatively slow rates without much difficulty. However, as mechanisms to transfer communications information at faster rates—for example, higher baud rates or the use of data compression—became more popular, the communications architecture of Windows needed to be examined closely.

When Windows 3.1 was released, 9600-baud modems were extremely popular, but because of communications barriers under Windows 3.1, the overall effectiveness of reliable high data throughput was limited, and the efficiencies of multitasking were eroded when running communications applications. These communications barriers included high interrupt latency and overhead that affected high speed communications, and a monolithic driver architecture that made it necessary for some third parties to replace the communications driver provided with Windows to allow their devices to run efficiently on the system.

Windows 95 greatly improves upon the Windows 3.1 architecture to support communications applications, support high-speed communications, and provide a modular communications architecture that allows third parties and communications device manufacturers to easily plug in new communications device drivers. This section describes the communications architecture used in Windows 95.

Communications Goals of Windows 95

The goals of communications support in Windows 95 are to deliver better performance than Windows 3.1, and to enhance ease-of-use through Plug and Play communications. The communications architecture of Windows 95 delivers the following performance benefits over Windows 3.1:

- **High-speed reliability.** Windows 95 supports reliable high-speed communications by keeping up with data coming in from the communications port, thereby incurring no lost characters because of interrupt latency. In addition, the use of a 32-bit protected mode file system and network architecture has less impact on the communications system because required mode transitions and interrupt latency are reduced.

- **Higher data throughput.** The 32-bit communications subsystem leverages the preemptive multitasking architecture of Windows 95 to provide better responsiveness to communications applications and support higher data throughput. Communications transfers in 32-bit applications are not as affected by other tasks running in the system as Win16–based applications under Windows 3.1.

- **Support for time-critical protocols.** The communications architecture provides support for time-critical protocols and allows for real-time serial device control.

- **Independence of underlying telephone networks.** Windows 95 allows application developers to build telephony applications that can run on a wide variety of telephone networks, including analog, proprietary digital PBXs, key systems, ISDN, and cellular.

The Plug and Play initiative provides ease-of-use enhancements throughout Windows 95, and communications support is no exception. Plug and Play support for communications delivers the following benefits:

- **Broad device support.** Windows 95 features a new communications driver architecture that makes it easier for third parties to extend the communications support provided as part of the operating system without sacrificing functionality or stability. In addition, the new communications architecture features APIs that support more robust communications devices beyond base RS-232 devices—for example, ISDN.

- **Easy-to-install and easy-to-use communications devices.** Windows 95 features centralized modem installation and configuration to simplify setup for users and simplify communications development efforts for application developers. Windows 95 leverages the use of a single universal modem driver (UniModem) to provide a consistent mechanism for communicating with modem devices. It also provides detection support for Plug and Play modems and supports existing hardware by including mechanisms for detecting legacy modems.

- **Device sharing among communications applications.** Through the use of the Telephony API (TAPI), Windows 95 provides consistent, device-independent mechanisms for controlling communications devices for operations such as dialing and answering incoming calls. Arbitration for the sharing of communications ports and devices is also handled through TAPI. For example, while dial-up networking in Windows 95 is waiting for an incoming call, a TAPI-aware fax communications application can send an outgoing fax without having to first terminate the already running communications application.

To further describe the improvements resulting from the new 32-bit communications subsystem in Windows 95, the rest of this section examines the components that comprise the communications support.

Kernel Improvements

When data comes into the system from a serial communications port, an interrupt tells the system that a piece of data has been received. If information was received at a high rate under Windows 3.1, the system sometimes could not keep up with the incoming data, resulting in errors or lost information at the port.

Whereas disk I/O and network I/O manipulate blocks of information at a time, serial communications I/O generates one interrupt on the system for *each* incoming character. The burden on the communications driver to keep up is quite high. To support high-speed throughput of information from a communications device, the system must be able to respond quickly to incoming data, but in Windows 3.1, real-mode drivers sometimes disabled system-wide interrupts for "long" periods of time (usually milliseconds), during which no incoming information could be received.

To address the issue of supporting higher, sustained communications throughput, the Windows 95 development team focused on areas in the Windows 3.1 kernel that resulted in periods of time when interrupts were disabled by the system. The Windows 3.1 kernel and other components were limited to reliable serial communications at rates of 9600 bps or slightly higher (dependent on CPU speed) because of high interrupt latency or other systems design limitations. In addition, when Windows 3.1 had to execute real-mode code, the use of real-mode file system and networking drivers blocked the system, thus preventing the system from being able to keep up with incoming data.

To improve performance and the rate at which the system can accept incoming data reliably, the code that can be used by only one process at a time (critical sections) was reduced and interrupt latency in the core system was also reduced. In addition, the use of new 32-bit protected-mode components for the implementation of the file system and network subsystem helped to improve the system responsiveness. Windows 95 is now truly limited in baud rate only by PC hardware characteristics, such as the processor speed and type of communications port.

Driver Architecture

The Windows 95 communications subsystem consists of a modular, 32-bit protected-mode architecture with new communications drivers. A new layer called VCOMM provides protected-mode services that allow Windows–based applications and device drivers to use ports and modems. To conserve system resources, communications device drivers are loaded into memory only when in use by applications. VCOMM uses the Windows 95 Plug and Play services to assist with configuration and installation of communications devices.

In Windows 3.1, a monolithic communications driver called COMM.DRV provided an API interface, through which Windows–based applications interacted with communications devices, and the code that serves as the communications port driver. The monolithic approach made it necessary to completely replace the Windows communications driver if new functionality was required by a hardware device. Figure 77 shows the relationship between the COMM.DRV driver and the hardware device in Windows 3.1.

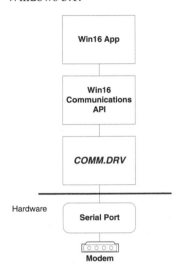

Figure 77. The communications architecture of Windows 3.1

Windows 95 provides a more flexible communications architecture than Windows 3.1, separating communications operations into three primary areas: Win32 communications APIs and TAPI, the universal modem driver, and communications port drivers. Figure 78 on the next page shows the relationship between the VCOMM communications driver and the port drivers to communicate with hardware devices. The flow path for a Win16–based application is also illustrated to show how compatibility is maintained for existing Windows–based applications. Compatibility is maintained for IHVs and ISVs that replace the Windows 3.1 COMM.DRV driver; however the vendor-specific communications driver communicates directly with the I/O port, rather than going through VCOMM.

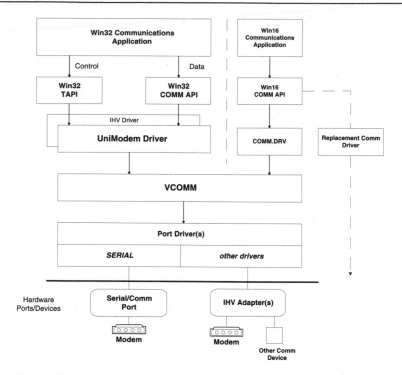

Figure 78. The communications architecture of Windows 95

The primary areas that make up this architecture are the following:

- **Win32 communications APIs and TAPI.** The Win32 communications APIs in Windows 95 provide an interface for using modems and communications devices in a device-independent fashion. Applications call the Win32 communications APIs to configure modems and perform data I/O through them. Through the Telephony API, applications can control modems or other telephony devices for operations such as dialing, answering, or hanging up a connection, in a standard way. TAPI-aware communications applications no longer need to provide their own modem support list because interaction with a modem is now centralized by Windows 95. The communications functionality provided with Windows 95 utilizes these services.

- **Universal modem driver.** Also new in Windows 95 is the universal modem driver, UniModem, which is a layer for providing services for data and fax modems and voice. Users no longer have to learn (and application developers no longer have to maintain) difficult modem AT commands to dial, answer, and configure modems. UniModem handles these tasks automatically, using mini-drivers written by modem hardware vendors. Application developers can use TAPI to perform modem control operations in a modem-independent manner.

- **Port drivers.** Port drivers are responsible for communicating with I/O ports, which are accessed through the VCOMM driver and provide a layered approach to device communications. For example, Windows 95 provides a port driver to communicate with serial communications and parallel ports, and third parties and IHVs can provide port drivers to communicate with their own hardware adapters, such as multiport communications adapters. With the port driver model in Windows 95, third parties no longer have to replace the communications subsystem as they did in Windows 3.1.

The Telephony API (TAPI)

The Windows Telephony API is part of the Microsoft Windows Open Services Architecture (WOSA), which provides a single set of open-ended interfaces to enterprise computing services. WOSA encompasses a number of APIs, providing application and corporate developers with an open set of interfaces to which applications can be written and accessed. WOSA also includes services for data access, messaging, software licensing, connectivity, and financial services.

Like other WOSA services, the Windows Telephony API consists of two interfaces: the applications programming interface (API) that developers write to, and the service provider interface (SPI) that is used to establish the connection to the specific telephone network. This model is similar to the one whereby printer manufacturers provide printer drivers for Windows–based applications. Figure 79 shows the relationship between the "front-end" Windows Telephony API and the "back-end" Windows Telephony SPI.

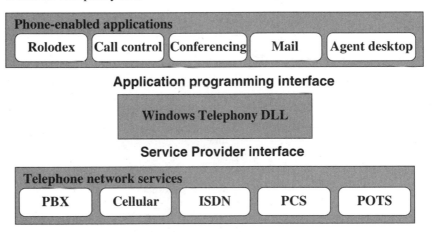

Figure 79. The seamless integration of applications and telephone networks by means of the Windows Telephony API and the Windows Telephony SPI

The Windows Telephony API provides a standard way for communications applications to control telephony functions for data, fax, and voice calls. The API manages all signaling between a PC and a telephone network, including such basic functions as establishing, answering, and terminating a call. It also includes supplementary functions, such as hold, transfer, conference, and call park, found in PBXs, ISDN, and other phone systems. In addition, the API provides access to features that are specific to certain service providers, with built-in extensibility to accommodate future telephony features and networks as they become available.

The Telephony API supports four models for integrating Windows 95 PCs with telephone networks, as illustrated in Figure 80. Applications using the Telephony API can work in any of these four connection models, whether they involve a physical connection between a PC and phone on the desktop, such as the phone or PC-centric models, or a logical connection in either of the client-server models.

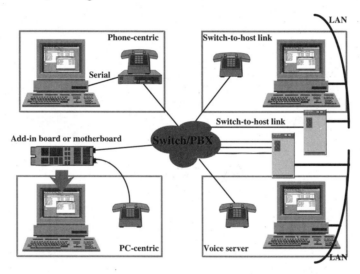

Figure 80. Four models for integrating Windows 95 PCs with telephones

Through the use of the TAPI services, applications that support communications services have a device-independent means for interacting with telecommunications networks. TAPI also provides a common access mechanism for requesting the use of communications ports and devices, thus providing a means for multiple communications applications to share a single modem—data, fax or voice—in the computer.

Windows 95 includes TAPI support in the base operating system, allowing application developers to leverage this functionality in their Windows 95–aware applications. In addition, all communications components included as part of Windows 95 are TAPI clients.

Sharing Communications Devices

Through the TAPI interface, communications applications can ask for access to the modem or telephone device, allowing the communications subsystem in Windows 95 to arbitrate device contention and allow applications to share the communications device in a cooperative manner.

Win32–based applications can utilize TAPI functionality to allow some applications to make outgoing calls while others are waiting for inbound calls. For example, while a dial-up network service that is configured for auto-answer mode is for an incoming call, a Win32–based communications application can call the TAPI services to request the use of the modem to perform an outgoing call. Only one call can be performed at a time, but users no longer have to terminate other applications that are using a communications port in order to run a different application. The TAPI services arbitrate requests to share communications ports and devices.

Try It!

Test the Power of the Telephony API

1.   In Windows 95, install and configure a modem for use on your system.

2.   Run TAPI-enabled applications, such as Phone Dialer, HyperTerminal, Dial-Up Networking, and Microsoft At Work Fax software, and note that after the modem is configured you don't have to change modem settings in any of these applications.

Centralized Modem Setup and Configuration

Support for installing and configuring a modem under Windows 95 is greatly simplified over Windows 3.1. Configuring each individual communications application for the correct serial port, modem type, and other related modem configuration parameters is no longer necessary. Windows 95 provides central configuration of communications devices through a tool in the Control Panel. Win32–based applications that take advantage of the TAPI services implemented in Windows 95 can completely leverage the user's configuration of their communications hardware, making subsequent configuration of communications applications easy.

Windows 95 brings the following benefits to modem configuration:

*   Easy modem configuration of new communications applications for use by entire system
*   Centralized communications port status and configuration
*   Supported by TAPI and Win32 communications APIs
*   Support for 100+ modems

Modem Configuration in Windows 3.1

With Windows 3.1, when users added a new communications application to their computer, they first had to configure the application to communicate with their modem by specifying the COM port to use and the type of modem, in addition to other communication parameters. Communications and modem configuration was either handled by the application developer and specified as a series of default modem AT commands, or users had to read through the modem manual and type in the appropriate command strings. For example, Figure 81 shows the Modem Commands dialog box in Terminal. Many Windows 3.1–based communications applications support only a limited set of modems because, given the number of modems available on the market, the burden on the application developer of providing global support is too great.

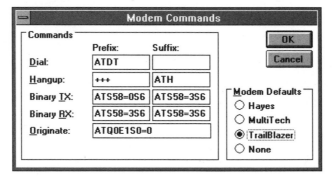

Figure 81. Configuring a modem in Windows 3.1 Terminal

Modem Configuration in Windows 95

As with support for printers, the support for modems in Windows 95 is centralized. When users first install Windows 95, they are prompted to detect or identify the modem device that they have connected to or installed in their computer. When a modem has been selected and configured, any communications application that supports TAPI services can interact with the modem in a device-independent way. Users no longer need to know or understand AT command sequences to customize their communications application.

Configuring a modem under Windows 95 is as easy as performing three simple steps: identifying the new modem device, configuring the modem device, and configuring the Telephony services.

Identifying a New Modem Device

If a modem is not selected when Windows 95 is first installed, The Modem Wizard can be used to identify a new modem, by using the Modems tool in the Control Panel. When the Modem Wizard dialog box is displayed, as shown in Figure 82, the user can have the Wizard detect the modem connected to the PC or can manually select a modem from the list of known manufacturers and modem models. The detect option uses Plug and Play to configure the correct device. If the Wizard cannot detect the device, the user can still manually select the correct modem.

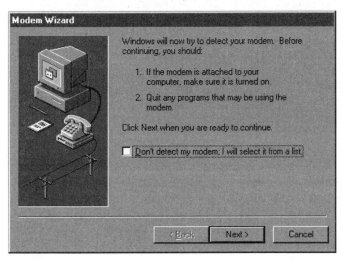

Figure 82. The Modem Wizard, which can detect and install a modem

Configuring a Modem Device

After the correct modem has been selected, users can optionally change configuration parameters, such as the volume for the modem speaker, the time to wait for the remote computer to answer a call, and the maximum baud rate to use, on a property sheet like the one shown in Figure 83 on the next page. (The maximum baud rate is limited by the speed of the PC's CPU and the speed supported by the communications port.)

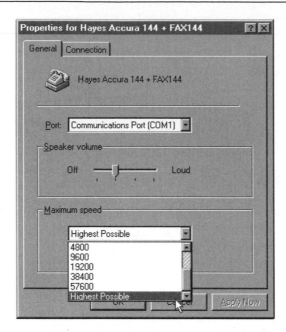

Figure 83. A Modem property sheet

Configuring Telephony Services

In addition to configuring the modem device, users configure telephony services to identify the various dialing parameters associated with the different locations where the PC will be used. For each location, information is stored for use by TAPI-aware applications, including information needed to dial a local call and a long distance call, the location's area code (for use in determining whether the call is inside or outside the calling area code), and calling card information. For a desktop PC, the default location would commonly be used—the default name could be changed to *in the office*—whereas for a portable computer, a mobile user might add several different locations to accommodate those where the computer is commonly used. For example, a mobile user might use the computer in the office, on the road, or in a remote city. Figure 84 shows three location configurations that are selectable depending on the location where the computer is being used.

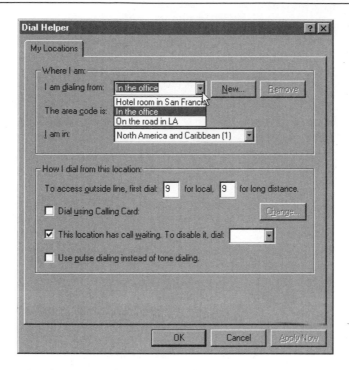

Figure 84. A Dial Helper property sheet for configuring location information

Device/Hardware Support

Windows 95 provides improved communications device and hardware support over Windows 3.1. A few areas of improvement are discussed below.

Support for 16550A UART FIFO

Windows 95 provides greater robustness and performance at high baud rates for MS-DOS–based and Windows–based communications applications using local serial ports with 16550A-compatible UARTs. The 16550A UART contains a 16-byte FIFO buffer to prevent character overflow resulting from interrupt latency, and help to reduce overall interrupt overhead. Because the Windows 3.1 communications driver did not fully support the use of the 16550A UART, some third-party communications vendors had to replace the driver. Improvements in Windows 95 communications should alleviate this problem.

Support for More Ports

Windows 3.1 limited the number of logical names that could be used to address serial communications ports to nine and the number that could be used to address parallel ports to four. This limit inhibited the use of multiport serial devices in Windows 3.1. The communications APIs in Windows 95 have been enhanced to support the same number of logical ports as MS-DOS: 128 serial ports and 128 parallel ports. Obviously, the number of usable ports is still a function of the number of physical ports available to the system.

Support for Future Parallel Port Modems

Windows 95 supports Enhanced Capabilities Ports (ECP) to facilitate higher speed communications than is possible over a serial device. This support provides for the use of future parallel port modems.

Plug and Play Support

Plug and Play support for communications devices in Windows 95 facilitates the detection of connected modem devices and assignment of system resources—for example, IRQs and I/O addresses for communications ports—which simplifies configuration and setup. In addition to Plug and Play detection, Windows 95 provides for manual detection of non–Plug and Play communications devices, such as modems. Because no standard for automatically obtaining device information using the AT modem command strings presently exists, detection of legacy modems is handled manually by querying the modem device and checking the information returned against a database of known modem information. As part of a Telecommunications Industry Association (TIA) proposed standard called IS-131, Microsoft is working with other leading industry manufacturers to standardize the modem command set. When this proposal is adopted, Windows 95 will support the standardized command set, which will aid detection of legacy modems.

Modems

External modems require new firmware to return the required Plug and Play ID information, whereas internal modems utilize the ISA Plug and Play specification. PCMCIA communications devices are supported as part of the Plug and Play services for the PCMCIA specification. Some modem manufacturers will improve their communications product offerings by revising their existing modem lines, while others will produce a new line of Plug and Play modems.

Detection of Plug and Play serial devices, such as modems, is handled when Windows 95 is initially installed, during the boot process, or when a new modem device is connected to the system. As with other Plug and Play devices, the user is notified that the new device has been detected and is asked to confirm the installation and configuration of the device.

Support for legacy modems is provided by using device-specific information to provide a manual detection mechanism, or by displaying a list of supported modems from which a user can choose the appropriate one. After the modem has been identified for the system, it can be used by TAPI-enabled communications applications, including dial-up networking, Microsoft At Work Fax services, and the new HyperTerminal communications application.

HyperTerminal

Windows 95 includes a new 32-bit communications application called HyperTerminal that has all the qualities of a good Windows 95 communications application. HyperTerminal offers the same base communication capabilities as the Terminal program included with Windows 3.1, but integrates well with the UI in Windows 95 and demonstrates how the Win32 communications APIs and TAPI services support more flexible communications applications than Windows 3.1–based applications.

Good communications applications utilize the Windows 95 services and capabilities to offer a more robust and powerful product, as follows:

- They are Win32–based applications that use the Win32 communications APIs.

- Their internal architecture uses multiple threads of execution to provide good responsiveness to the user and great error-free high-speed communications. Multiple threads allow full preemptive multitasking of communications tasks and support concurrent interaction with the user, downloading of remote data, and display of communications status.

- They take advantage of TAPI services for making remote connections and controlling the modem device.

Try It!

Run Communications Applications in the Background

1. Start Windows 3.1.

2. Run an MS-DOS–based communications application in the background with other foreground activities.

3. Run a Win16–based communications application and perform other CPU or disk-intensive tasks, such as copying files, accessing a network, or formatting a floppy disk.

4. Now start Windows 95 and repeat steps 2 and 3.

5. Run the 32-bit HyperTerminal communications application and perform other CPU or disk-intensive tasks, such as copying files, accessing a network, or formatting a floppy disk.

The Phone Dialer

The Phone Dialer application in Windows 95 provides basic support for making telephone calls. As shown in Figure 85, it includes a telephone dial pad, user programmable speed dials, and a call log.

Figure 85. The Phone Dialer

Increasingly, new communications hardware will support voice communications in addition to data and fax. The next generation of modems will support the AT+V standard (TIA IS-101), which adds voice support to the standard AT command set, effectively turning the modem into a telephone designed to be a PC peripheral. Other devices, such as those built on digital signal processors (DSPs), will also include voice telephony support. Windows 95 communications applications will bring control of the telephone to the PC, enabling programmable "smart" answering machines, dynamic call filtering and routing, dialing from any PC application or directory, drag-and-drop setup of conference calls, and other types of computer-telephone integration.

C H A P T E R   1 3

Mobile Computing Services

As computing moves beyond its traditional desktop environment, Microsoft is committed to leading the market by delivering system services and end-user functionality that dramatically improve the ease-of-use and power of mobile computing.

The Windows 95 Vision of Mobile Computing

The goal for mobility in Windows 95 is to enable users—wherever they are and whatever computing they want to do—to do it easily. The strategy for achieving this goal is based on the following tenets:

- **Mobile computing encompasses anyone who moves computing capabilities away from the desktop PC.** The strategy includes everyone, from people who move from meeting to meeting in an office building, to those who shuttle between their homes and offices, to business travelers, to those who have no office at all and move from customer site to customer site.

- **The tasks people want to perform away from their desks are fundamentally similar to those that they perform on their desktop.** On desktop PCs, users want to draft a memo, review a budget spreadsheet, query a database, browse e-mail, peruse a presentation on the network, send a fax, or look at their schedule for the day. Away from their offices and their desktop PCs, users want to continue performing these same tasks.

- **The "mobile" computer environment is fundamentally different from the desktop environment.** When users move away from their desktop PCs, their computing environment changes dramatically. Their hardware environment is dynamic, as they plug in and unplug different components to deal with the task at hand. Portable PC users may be operating in a power-constrained environment with video displays often half the size of their desktop displays. They can't easily access a file on a server or receive e-mail. As a result, the mobile computing environment can be constrictive to users.

The challenges that mobile computer users face stem from the following three fundamental problems:

- **Staying connected.** At their desks, users have a wide array of communications capabilities to keep them connected to other people, both inside and outside their organizations. They have access to the LAN and all its services, such as e-mail, file sharing, and print sharing. A phone, a fax machine, and perhaps a modem are close at hand. When they leave their desks, these users become communications islands. They are cut off from their network and all its services. Phones, faxes, and modems are not readily available. Being mobile entails a constant struggle to stay in touch. The ideal for most mobile users is to be as productive while mobile as they would be at a desk. To achieve this ideal, users must have easy access to powerful communications tools, regardless of location. Channels of communication must exist between their portable and desktop PCs, between themselves and the rest of their workgroup, and between themselves and the broader community of PC, fax, and other equipment users.

- **Moving to and from the desk.** Desktop PCs operate in a fairly constant hardware environment. Mobile computers do not. For example, portable computer owners usually change the video resolution, pointing device, and network state every time they undock or otherwise change location. Changing locations means tweaking configuration files, contending with error messages, and restarting the computer a lot. Being mobile involves a constant struggle to get the hardware to adapt to the new conditions in which the user is computing.

- **Dealing with the mobile environment.** Mobile users face problems and challenges that simply do not exist for desktop computer users. Examples include keeping multiple versions of files in synch—for example, the copy of the proposal on a laptop and the copy on the file server—or transferring files from the desktop to the portable, including over the phone lines, or working with limited disk storage. In addition, many activities that are simple on the desktop—for example, sending a fax, using electronic mail, or printing a document—become needlessly complex in the mobile environment. Although solutions to some of these problems exist today, these solutions are often provided as utilities that are difficult to use and are not well-integrated into the overall computing environment.

The development investments for mobile computing in Windows 95 have focused on delivering solutions that make it easier and more powerful to stay connected, adapt to changing hardware configurations, and deal with the mobile computing environment. The following table shows features that address the needs of mobile users.

How Does Windows 95 Improve Mobile Computing?			
	Staying Connected	**Moving to and from the Desk**	**Dealing with the Mobile Environment**
Easier	Dial-Up Networking Wizard Implicit connections Password management	Hot-docking Automatic device detection and setup PCMCIA support Hardware suspend UI Battery monitor	File synchronization: Briefcase UI, automatic reconciliation Deferred printing File viewers At Work Fax
More powerful	PPP, SLIP protocols Support for faster baud rates Dynamic networking Modular, extensible network architecture More network APIs	Power management messages and APIs baked into operating system Dynamic video resolution Dynamic networking	Direct cable connection OLE reconciliation engine Remote Mail Integrated compression
Compatible	UniModem drivers Built-in support for Windows, NetWare, and Internet hosts	Supports PCMCIA standards APM 1.1 specification	

The following sections detail how Windows 95 provides improved communication, hardware-adaptability, and productivity features for the mobile user.

Staying Connected

To establish the connections needed for mobile computing, Windows 95 provides powerful, easy-to-use, end-user communications capabilities and an open, extensible set of services for applications.

Dial-Up Networking

In the office, well over 50 percent of PC users have become accustomed to full workgroup computing capabilities—printing to a network printer, sending and receiving e-mail, and accessing shared files. However, when users leave the office, they cannot take all the shared resources from their workgroup environment with them.

The dial-up networking features in Windows 95 give users complete workgroup computing capabilities while mobile. Dial-up networking is smoothly integrated into the Windows 95 shell. Whether users are running a client-server application, accessing a customer database, downloading and/or browsing e-mail, or accessing shared files, network access while mobile looks and works exactly like network access in the office, and establishing a remote connection works the same as establishing a connection in the office. Users simply double-click the desired network object. Similarly, if users double-click Mail, a remote connection is automatically established.

The Dial-Up Networking client software component, like the rest of networking in Windows 95, provides an open architecture and connects to a broad set of networks, including Windows NT, NetWare Connect, and the Internet. Support is included for TCP/IP, IPX, and NetBEUI network protocols, using industry standard point-to-point protocol (PPP) over the wire, as shown in Figure 86. Because remote access is part of the dynamic 32-bit protected-mode network architecture of Windows 95, users don't have to reconfigure or reboot their computers to continue working after establishing or ending a connection.

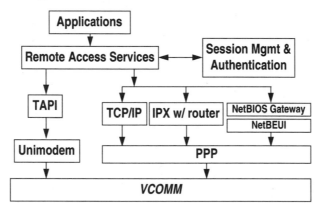

Figure 86. The Windows 95 remote access functionality, which supports TCP/IP, IPX, and NetBEUI over PPP

As Figure 87 shows, a Windows 95 desktop PC can be used as a convenient access point to a small LAN or simply to the desktop PC itself. (Windows NT Server 3.5 supplements the remote network access functionality in Windows 95 to provide a large network solution that allows for as many as 256 simultaneous dial-in sessions.) When used as a host computer—that is, the computer the user dials into—a Windows 95 PC provides an easy-to-use, single-port host, capable of multiprotocol routing for IPX and NetBIOS with pass-through user-level security. The Windows 95 security scheme employs the Windows NT or NetWare authentication mechanism and user database to validate the user. Share-level security is also available. Using the desktop management capabilities in Windows 95, an administrator can disable dial-up access so users cannot dial into a particular desktop PC or cannot remotely access the entire network. (For more details about the desktop management infrastructure in Windows 95, see

Chapter 9, "Networking.") If the user dials into a host system, such as Windows NT, Shiva Netmodem/ LanRover, or NetWare Connect, Windows 95 offers full connectivity.

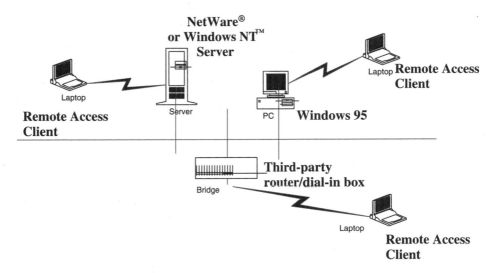

Figure 87. The flexible remote connectivity options and broad network access provided by Windows 95

Windows 95 provides a modular, open architecture that enables applications to establish a "pipeline" to the remote network. The Remote Access API, a component of the Win32 API, provides ISVs with services to initiate and resume a remote connection, as well as to gather information about the type and status of the connection. These APIs enable applications to adjust their behavior depending on the transmission speed and other characteristics of the network connection.

Another key component of the Windows 95 architecture is the Remote Access subsystem. This open subsystem is network-independent and device-independent to enable universal connectivity. For example, Windows 95 supports ISDN boards, PBX modems, and so on. This capability is accomplished through service providers—software components that manage physical connections and network traffic over the remote media.

The Remote Access subsystem includes a modular authentication provider that can be supplemented or replaced to provide custom security services. For example, if a company wants to provide its own custom services, that company can replace the authentication DLL in Windows 95 with its own to take advantage of company-specific security features.

Figure 88 on the following page highlights the various components of the Remote Access subsystem that can be replaced by third-party service providers. The shadowed items can be replaced to add functionality not provided by Windows 95.

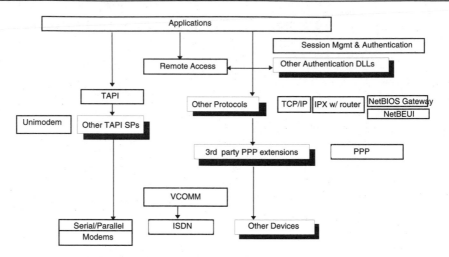

Figure 88. The Windows 95 Remote Access architecture, which allows direct integration by third-party service providers

Telephony API

To communicate in a mobile environment, users and applications must dial phones or modems. Whether the device is a phone on a PBX system, an ISDN board, or a modem, applications can use the Telephony API (TAPI) in Windows 95 to dial. TAPI provides services that allow applications to share a line so that more than one application can wait for an incoming call while another dials out. TAPI itself is extensible, so third-party developers can write TAPI service providers to extend dial support to new devices. One such TAPI service provider is UniModem, which is discussed in detail in the following section.

TAPI also provides the Dial Helper to guide users through the process of defining a correct phone number, given their location and telephone system. The Dial Helper gives users the opportunity to define phone numbers in a location-independent fashion. Users enter an area code and phone number, and the Dial Helper applies location-specific parameters to the number, such as a prefix to get an outside line. When users dial this same number from a different location, they simply switch their location, and Dial Helper automatically adjusts the prefixes, area codes, and other parameters.

UniModem

Windows 95 provides an easy, central, extensible mechanism for installing and configuring modems. (This mechanism is similar to the Window 95 infrastructure for printers.) Windows 95 automatically detects the modem and provides a default configuration for it. After the modem is installed, it is available to all applications, which no longer need to store modem commands or data about the capabilities of different modems. Windows 95 ships with support for the top 200 modems worldwide. Adding new modems is as simple as supplying the appropriate installation data (.INF) file. Microsoft will certify the .INF files for each new modem and provide a logo identifying it as Windows-compatible.

Both TAPI and UniModem use the extensible 32-bit communications architecture in Windows 95. For more information, see Chapter 12, "Communications."

Dynamic Networking

Historically, network users with portable computers have dealt with CONFIG.SYS files and a regular stream of error messages as they connected and disconnected from the network.

To adapt to changes in link speed and configuration, the network architecture in Windows 95 is completely dynamic, regardless of whether users are using the NetWare–compatible components or the Microsoft networking components. All the underlying drivers, transports, and redirectors are robust, 32-bit, dynamically loadable, protected-mode virtual devices that support Plug and Play. This architecture enables Windows 95 to load and unload components of the network stack as demanded by hardware events. For example, when the user docks a portable PC or inserts a PCMCIA network card, the appropriate network components are loaded and connections are established without user interaction. Even assigning a TCP/IP address is now dynamic, using the Dynamic Host Configuration Protocol (DHCP) servers to allocate addresses on demand.

Users can forget about the intricacies of network hardware and configurations. Virtually every aspect of networking, including dynamic configuration, is handled transparently by Windows 95

Password Management

Users constantly strive to protect the data on their portable computers from prying eyes and hands. This chore is not easy. Password protection at boot-up, after a suspend (reduced power) state, and at network logon means users must often contend with inconsistent user interfaces and multiple passwords.

The Security icon in the Windows 95 Control Panel provides a central, extensible mechanism for users to easily manage the security of their computers. The Master Password gives users the opportunity to unify all their different passwords under a single password.

The interface for the Control Panel's Security tool is open and extensible. As a result, ISVs and portable PC manufacturers can add their own security property sheets and hook their password services to the Master Password.

Moving to and from the Desk

To achieve easy, seamless mobility, any changes in hardware must be transparent to users. The portable computer should correctly reconfigure itself to match the current environment, with no special user intervention. Microsoft's Plug and Play architecture, defined in partnership with other industry leaders such as Intel and Compaq, provides an infrastructure to effectively tackle these problems.

Hot-Docking Support

Many portable PC users have had to compromise storage, extensibility, and display size and resolution in favor of mobility. Docking stations (or simpler port replicators) provide users with both the mobility of the portable PC and the storage, extensibility, and versatile display capabilities of a desktop PC. However, users with docking stations spend a lot of time reconfiguring and rebooting their machines when they take them in and out of their docking stations.

Microsoft forged partnerships with leading portable vendors like Toshiba and Compaq, and BIOS vendors like Phoenix Technologies to achieve a level of integration between hardware and software never achieved before. On the hardware side, docking stations have enabled docking and undocking operations without powering off the computer. On the software side, Windows 95 detects the impending changes in configuration and anticipates the resulting changes in hardware, manages any conflicts (such as open files on an external hard drive or network), and loads the hardware drivers appropriate to the new configuration.

Instead of rebooting and fooling with configuration files, users now simply click the UI's Start button and choose Eject PC from the Start menu. Windows 95 checks for any potential problems and then undocks, without users having to power down. After undocking, the system automatically reconfigures itself for the different hardware—for example, changing the video resolution to match the resolution of the built-in display—and continues running.

New Message Support

The Windows Plug and Play initiative provides a new set of Windows messages that alert applications and device drivers to changes in the hardware so that they can react intelligently. These messages include the following:

- **Docking.**
  - About to change configuration (for example, when the user is about to undock)
  - Device about to be removed
  - Configuration changed (for example, when the user just undocked)
  - Device about to be added

- **Power management.**

  - System about to suspend
  - System suspended
  - System resumed

- **PCMCIA.**

  - Device inserted
  - Device removed

- **Miscellaneous.**

  - New device inserted (for a device that needs to be set up)
  - Serial mouse inserted
  - Parallel cable inserted

These messages enable applications and system services to better support portable PC users. Windows 95 itself takes full advantage of these messages. For example, the applications shipped with Windows 95 use the *Configuration changed* message in the following ways:

- The Briefcase uses it to try to start updating.
- The print spooler uses it to print all deferred print jobs.
- Mail uses it to try to reestablish a network connection.

The Registry

The Registry provides a centralized, dynamic datastore for all Windows settings. The Registry defines a current-configuration branch to enable ISVs to better serve the needs of mobile users. This branch stores information on a per-configuration basis. For example, the Control Panel's Desktop tool stores per-configuration information about video resolution changes and Print Manager stores per-configuration information about the default printer.

Configurations are created when Windows 95 queries the BIOS for a dock serial ID, asks the user for a name for the configuration, and then stores information about hardware and software associated with this configuration. Applications access and store information for each of the different hardware configurations used by mobile users. This Registry support enables applications to gracefully adapt to different hardware configurations.

PCMCIA Support

The emergence of PCMCIA cards has been one of the most exciting advances in the portable computer market. However, users were never sure whether a particular card was compatible with their portable PC, they had to struggle through installation and configuration of card drivers and socket services, and card insertion and removal were anything but dynamic.

Through the Plug and Play architecture, Windows 95 delivers power, compatibility, ease of installation, and dynamic card insertion and removal to PCMCIA users. PCMCIA drivers in Windows 95 are robust, 32-bit, dynamically loadable virtual device drivers with zero conventional memory footprint. Windows 95 ships with an updated version of card and socket services. Microsoft's compatibility testing/logo program ensures compatibility with these standards.

Installation of a PCMCIA device is as simple as inserting the card, and insertion and removal of cards happens dynamically. For example, when a user plugs in a PCMCIA network card, the portable computer detects the network card, loads the network drivers, and establishes a network connection. Then the shell updates its user interface to reflect that the mapped network drives are now active. Prior to Windows 95, users would have needed to shut down their systems and reboot in order to begin using the device.

Power Management

One of the curses of portable computer users' existence is battery life. Windows 95 supports Advanced Power Management (APM) 1.1, which represents a major step forward from APM 1.0.

From an end-user perspective, APM 1.1 offers three major benefits:

- The Windows 95 shell includes a battery meter that provides users with an accurate representation of the battery life they have remaining.

- Users can put their systems in Suspend mode directly from the Start menu, as opposed to going to a hardware control.

- Users have the option of automatically powering their PCs off when they shut down Windows, instead of having to shut down Windows and then use the hardware power switch to shut off the PC.

From a software vendor's perspective, Plug and Play APM messages allow applications to react to changes in the power state and battery life. For example, a mail program or a utility that does background disk compression could disable this feature when running on limited battery power.

Flexible Video Resolution Support

"Poor displays" have been cited as the number one limitation of portable computers. To overcome that limitation, portable computer vendors are putting high-end video controllers into portable PC systems, and users are plugging external monitors into their portable PCs when they are at their desks.

Windows 95 stores video resolution on a per-configuration basis and supports dynamic resolution changes. As a result, when users have monitors attached to their portable PCs, they can set the video to a higher resolution—for example, 1024x768. When they undock (or detach the monitor), the video resolution changes to 640x480. Whenever they return to their connected or docked configuration, the resolution automatically returns to 1024x768.

Pointing Devices

Portable PC users often describe difficulties in switching between the integrated pointing device on their portable computers—for example, a trackball or clip-on mouse—to a desktop pointing device. Windows 95 addresses these difficulties in two ways:

- When users change configurations, Windows 95 automatically detects which pointing device is available and enables it.

- When users connect a Plug and Play serial mouse, the system detects the new mouse and dynamically reconfigures itself to enable its use. No manual configuration changes are necessary.

Dealing with the Mobile Environment

Windows 95 includes a variety of features specifically designed and optimized to simplify the lives of mobile computer users. Rather than learning new and different ways to handle the challenges of mobile computing, users can concentrate on the task at hand and delegate the intricacies of the mobile environment to the operating system.

The Briefcase

Portable PC users who also have desktop PCs (or who connect to a network) need to keep the most up-to-date files on the computer they are currently using. Users most often stay up to date by comparing the dates stamped on files and manually copying files from one machine to another—a tedious, unintuitive, and error-prone process.

The Windows 95 Briefcase minimizes the headaches of staying up to date by keeping track of the relationships between different versions of a file on different computers. As shown in Figure 89 on the following page, the user interface for this feature employs a simple metaphor that users are already comfortable with: a briefcase.

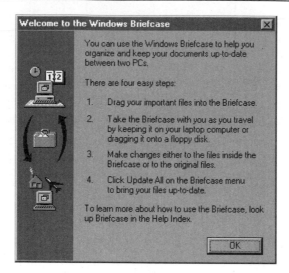

Figure 89. The initial Briefcase screen, outlining the Briefcase process

After installing the Briefcase software on their portable PCs, users can specify which files and directories they want to keep up to date, by dragging and dropping those objects into the Briefcase. When users reconnect their portable PCs to a network or their desktop PCs, the Briefcase automatically updates unmodified files on the host with the recently modified files from the portable computer. Figure 90 shows the contents of a typical Briefcase.

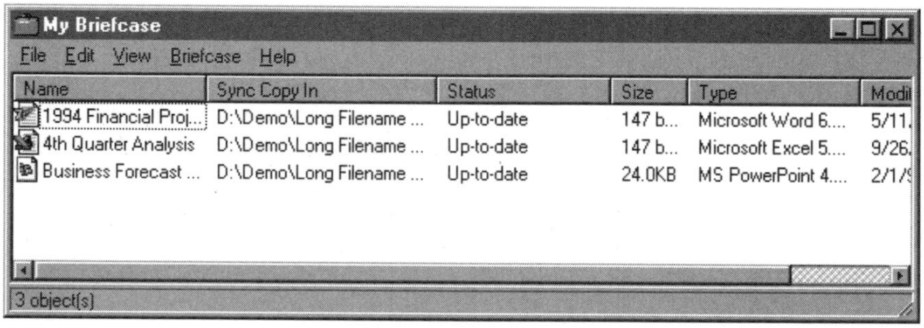

Name	Sync Copy In	Status	Size	Type	Modi
1994 Financial Proj...	D:\Demo\Long Filename ...	Up-to-date	147 b...	Microsoft Word 6....	5/11.
4th Quarter Analysis	D:\Demo\Long Filename ...	Up-to-date	147 b...	Microsoft Excel 5....	9/26.
Business Forecast ...	D:\Demo\Long Filename ...	Up-to-date	24.0KB	MS PowerPoint 4....	2/1/9

3 object(s)

Figure 90. Sample Briefcase contents, showing document status

Windows 95 provides a set of OLE 2.0 interfaces that allow applications to define "reconciliation handlers." When both the file in the Briefcase and the corresponding original document have changed, Windows 95 calls the appropriate reconciliation handler to merge the two files. (The Windows 95 reconciliation APIs will also serve as the foundation for Cairo's reconciliation APIs. As a result, ISVs writing to the reconciliation APIs in Windows 95 can leverage that investment as they write Cairo applications in the future.)

Microsoft At Work Fax

Fax is one of the most common tools mobile users employ to send messages and documents. Rich fax services are seamlessly integrated into the Microsoft Exchange e-mail client provided with Windows 95. Users of Windows 95 send a fax message the same way they send any other electronic message.

Microsoft At Work Fax services extend the capabilities of today's "paper-based" fax machines. For example, users can address a fax message in the Microsoft Exchange client and attach a binary file, such as a word processing document. Depending on the capabilities of the recipient's PC or fax machine, the message could appear as a message in their inbox with an attachment or, in the case of Class 3 fax machines, the attached document could be rendered and printed with a cover sheet. Microsoft At Work Fax provides security to ensure the correct recipient via an RC4 encrypted password or public key and private key encryption.

If users want to send faxes when they are not connected to a phone line or network, they can spool them to their outbox. When they reconnect, the faxes are automatically sent

Microsoft At Work Fax uses the open, extensible architecture of MAPI, plugging in as a transport provider and then leveraging the user interface provided by the Windows 95 client. Users do not need to learn how to operate a separate fax software package. For more information, see Chapter 14, "Microsoft Exchange: E-Mail, Faxes, and More."

"Local" Connections

Roughly 70 percent of portable PC users also use a desktop PC. As a result, they constantly need to transfer files and other data between the two machines. A simple way to effect these transfers is via a direct parallel or serial cable connection. Windows 95 makes this process significantly easier than it was under Windows 3.1. Like remote access, establishing a local connection is seamlessly integrated into the shell and provides full participation for the client on a variety of networks. The services provided by a direct cable connection are much the same as those provided via a dial-up connection, only faster!

Wireless technologies, such as infrared (IR), provide another form of local connection. Using the extensible device driver architecture in Windows 95, Microsoft is working closely with creators of wireless devices to develop and ship Windows drivers for these new technologies.

Document Viewers

Like other PC users, portable PC users often exchange documents with customers or other people in a different work environment. Because of limited disk space or lack of network access, however, mobile users often don't have the applications needed to view the files they receive.

An extensible, replaceable File Viewer technology has been seamlessly integrated into the Windows 95 UI. Users simply select a file and choose Quick View. Windows 95 directly supports more than 30 file types and publishes interfaces to allow applications to add support for additional formats (and even to add their own viewer). For more information, see Chapter 4, "The Windows 95 User Interface."

Deferred Printing

Users generate print jobs regardless of where they are. Windows 95 supports "deferred" print jobs, enabling users to generate print jobs even if a printer is not currently available. The print jobs are stored by the system until a printer becomes available, at which time Windows 95 detects the connection and automatically spools the print jobs as a background process.

Windows 95 also gives users the ability to print to a generic printer. If they aren't sure which printer they will be connected to, they can queue the print jobs and specify the printer only when a physical device is available. This functionality enables users to easily use printers available at customer sites, in copy centers, and so on.

Finally, to better support the mobile user, Windows 95 stores the default printers on a per-configuration basis. If users have a different printer at home than they do the office, Windows 95 changes the default printer when it detects the computer's change in location—for example, from docked status to undocked status.

Remote Mail

Historically, when users left the office, they left behind robust e-mail capabilities. Microsoft, Lotus, and other e-mail vendors are changing this scenario. Windows 95 delivers the next generation of remote mail so that users can simply connect a phone line to their modem and start using mail. The remote connection is established automatically using Remote Access services.

Windows 95 has also optimized Mail to gracefully handle remote network connections and slow network links. Performance over the wire has been enhanced, and users can browse message headers and download specific messages, getting an estimated time to download and status of the download process.

The Messaging API

More than any other class of users, mobile users need access to multiple messaging providers and the ability to seamlessly move between these providers. While desktop users receive most of their electronic mail through a corporate or network-based electronic mail system, mobile users frequently connect to several different messaging providers—for example, both CompuServe and their corporate network.

The Windows 95 Messaging API (MAPI) makes the communications abilities of mobile users significantly more powerful. MAPI is an open, extensible messaging infrastructure standard that ensures complete independence of Windows applications and client software from underlying messaging systems, while enabling vendors to supply a wide array of providers. To the end-user, each messaging provider looks more or less the same. MAPI provides the support to dynamically switch between providers and associate multiple providers and preferences with a "profile."

CHAPTER 14

Microsoft Exchange: E-Mail, Faxes, and More

Personal computers today are being used for an increasingly wide range of tasks, beyond simply creating and editing documents. Electronic mail has become a primary communication vehicle, not only within many companies, but also among individuals, families, and the public at large. Additionally, usage of online information services has dramatically increased, due in large part to e-mail. Witness the astounding 15 percent *per month* growth rate seen by the Internet, in addition to the rapid growth in online commercial services, such as CompuServe and others.

The growing use of messaging and communication services has resulted in a plethora of software tools. A very real problem users face today is that each of these different information sources and services comes with its own unique software and user interface. Users often have software for an e-mail client such as Microsoft Mail, a groupware client such as Lotus Notes, an online services client such as CompuServe Information Manager, and perhaps some electronic fax software that came with their modem—all in addition to the basic File Manager they use for accessing and manipulating documents.

Windows 95 addresses this growing complexity by including an integrated messaging and workgroup communications system that provides universal e-mail, fax, and information-sharing solutions. These different services are all presented in Windows 95 with a single user interface called Microsoft Exchange. Microsoft Exchange includes the following features:

- The ability to send and receive rich-text e-mail messages over virtually any e-mail system, including public networks such as the Internet.

- The ability to send faxes directly from the desktop and receive incoming faxes directly in Microsoft Exchange's universal inbox.

- A complete, built-in e-mail system to quickly get workgroups up and running, including the Microsoft Mail Post Office. The system can be easily upgraded to a full Microsoft Mail Server or Microsoft Exchange Server to connect multiple workgroups or the entire enterprise.

- The ability to move messages and documents between the file system and mail folders, and to organize documents using sophisticated custom views with searching and filtering capabilities.

- Support for taking full advantage of MAPI-enabled applications, ranging from desktop productivity to workflow and document management.

This chapter introduces the Microsoft Exchange client and other components of the Windows Messaging subsystem, including Microsoft At Work Fax software, MAPI, and the Microsoft Mail Post Office.

The Windows Messaging Subsystem

Microsoft Exchange is built upon the open Messaging API (MAPI) 1.0 architecture, so it can work with many different e-mail systems and information services simultaneously and provide a universal inbox for communication between individuals and workgroups. Because e-mail and other messaging-enabled applications are becoming so ubiquitous, Windows 95 includes a set of operating system–level components that provide built-in messaging services to any application that wishes to take advantage of them.

Windows 95 ships with a number of components that together make up the Windows Messaging subsystem. (The term *Windows Messaging subsystem* is sometimes used synonymously with MAPI 1.0, because Windows 95 represents the first complete implementation of the "extended" MAPI architecture.) These components include the following:

- **The Microsoft Exchange client.** The built-in universal inbox in Windows 95, which is used to send, receive, and organize e-mail, faxes, and other information, includes an OLE-compatible rich-text editor used for composing and reading messages, as well as powerful custom views, searching, and filtering. Through the use of MAPI drivers (described later), the Microsoft Exchange client can work directly with most public or private e-mail systems.

- **The Personal Address Book**. The Personal Address Book contains not only e-mail addresses, but names, phone/fax numbers, mailing addresses, and other personal contact information. Through the open MAPI interfaces, the Personal Address Book is accessible from a wide variety of applications, and through the use of MAPI drivers, it is also the user interface for corporate e-mail and information services directories. The Personal Address Book can store addresses for multiple e-mail systems at the same time.

- **The Personal Information Store**. This sophisticated local "database" file allows users to store e-mail messages, faxes, forms, documents, and other information in a common place. The Personal Information Store functions as the user's mailbox and includes a universal inbox and outbox, as well as any other mail or document folders the user wishes to create. It supports long filenames, plus sorting and filtering on various fields of the stored objects. Custom views can be created and saved in the Personal Information Store.

- **The Messaging Application Programming Interface (MAPI) 1.0.** These core system components seamlessly connect the Microsoft Exchange client and other mail-enabled and workgroup applications to various information services. MAPI also defines a Service Provider Interface (SPI) that allows MAPI drivers to be written for nearly any messaging or workgroup service.

- **The Microsoft Mail drivers.** This set of MAPI drivers allows the Microsoft Exchange client to be used with a Microsoft Mail Post Office—either the "workgroup edition" that's provided with Windows 95 or the "full" server edition that's available separately.

- **The Microsoft At Work Fax drivers.** These MAPI drivers allow the Microsoft Exchange client to send and receive electronic faxes in the same way as any other piece of e-mail.

- **The Microsoft Internet Mail drivers.** This set of MAPI drivers lets the Microsoft Exchange client send and receive mail directly on the Internet using the built-in TCP/IP and PPP communications protocols provided with Windows 95.

- **Optional third-party MAPI drivers.** Drivers for other messaging systems are available separately from a large number of vendors. Examples of vendors working on MAPI drivers that integrate into the Microsoft Exchange client include the following:

  - America Online

  - Apple

  - AT&T

  - Banyan

  - CompuServe

  - DEC

  - Hewlett-Packard

  - Novell

  - Octel

  - RAM Mobile Data

  - Skytel

An Open Architecture for Open Connectivity

The Microsoft Exchange client is designed to work with virtually any messaging or workgroup system, whether it is LAN-based, host-based, or an online service. Transparent access to these various messaging systems is available to *any* application, not just Microsoft Exchange. The key to this open architecture is MAPI, which is illustrated in Figure 91.

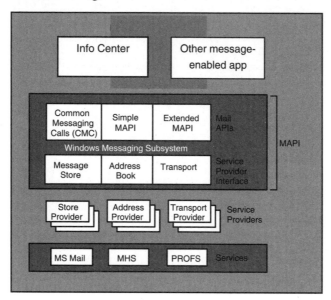

Figure 91. The open MAPI architecture

MAPI defines both an Applications Programming Interface (API) and a Service Provider Interface (SPI). The API is used by end-user applications, including Microsoft Exchange, whereas the SPI is used to write drivers (sometimes called *providers*). As Figure 91 shows, MAPI defines three different types of drivers:

- Transport drivers provide the ability to send and receive e-mail on any messaging system.

- Address Book drivers allow seamless access to any directory service, mailing list, or other name database.

- Store drivers let MAPI applications read and write to local or server-based message stores, mailboxes, and workgroup databases.

As Figure 92 shows, Windows 95 users can install any combination of drivers so that their Microsoft Exchange client can be used for multiple e-mail or workgroup systems at the same time.

Figure 92. Configuring the Microsoft Exchange client for use with multiple services

Microsoft Exchange

As already mentioned, Windows 95 has a built-in advanced e-mail and workgroup client called Microsoft Exchange. Far more than a "basic" bundled e-mail client, Microsoft Exchange actually provides more features than almost all existing e-mail clients on the market, including the current version of Microsoft Mail.

Summary of Improvements over Current Microsoft Mail

Microsoft Mail is currently available as part of Windows for Workgroups and Windows NT, as well as separately for Windows 3.1 users. The Microsoft Exchange client goes beyond the current Microsoft Mail by providing the following features:

- Rich-text e-mail, including full use of fonts, colors, bullets, and so on, that supports drag-and-drop text editing and Find/Replace

- Full OLE support, including Visual Editing and cross-application drag and drop

- Built-in Remote Mail—no separate "remote" product is required—that uses TAPI and Remote Network Access to support all common modems and network protocols

- Full integration with the Windows 95 file system so that messages can simply be dragged to hard drive directories or files can be dragged into mail folders

- A customizable Toolbar with Tooltips and right-click "shortcut" menus for commonly used tasks

- A Blind Carbon Copy (BCC:) feature

- Intelligent message replies that are automatically indented and rendered with a personal font/color, for better tracking of who made which comments

- The ability to connect to multiple mailbox files simultaneously

- Custom views of any folder, with user-defined columns and sorting/filtering/categorization

- Integration with the Windows 95 Registry so that use can be made of Master Password logon

Working with Microsoft Exchange

Note: Microsoft Exchange and the other Windows Messaging subsystem components are optionally installed by selecting Custom setup and then selecting the components during the installation of Windows 95. After installation of Windows 95, Microsoft Exchange can be installed by opening the Control Panel, running Add/Remove Programs, clicking the Maintain tab, and selecting Microsoft Exchange.

Microsoft Exchange can be started in several ways. The simplest is to double-click the Microsoft Exchange icon and start viewing e-mail and messages from the inbox, as shown in Figure 93.

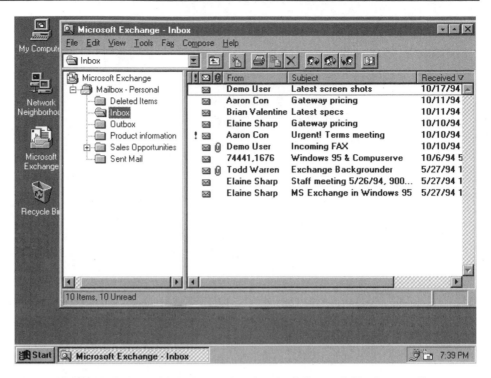

Figure 93. The Windows 95 desktop, showing the Microsoft Exchange client

To start Microsoft Exchange and read new e-mail, by far the easiest way is to choose Open Inbox from the Start button's Programs menu, as shown in Figure 94.

Figure 94. The Open Inbox item on the Start button's Programs menu

No matter what application is active in Windows 95, new e-mail is announced by a notification at the right end of the Taskbar, as shown in Figure 95. Other notifications indicate whether the system is currently sending or receiving mail, in addition to standard system notifications, such as print status and the time, as well as the battery power indicator.

Figure 95. A new mail notification on the Taskbar

Rich-Text Mail Messages

When designing Microsoft Exchange, Microsoft conducted extensive activity-based planning research into how people actually use e-mail during their work day. One of the strongest findings was that people use e-mail six to eight times more often than their word processor for tasks such as sending memos to people. Customers expressed a strong desire to be able to combine the power and immediacy of e-mail with the expressive capabilities of their word processor, but most e-mail packages on the market limit messages to a single font. To accommodate this desire, the Microsoft Exchange client includes a complete rich-text editor that is fully compatible with OLE. Figure 96 shows a message composed in Microsoft Exchange.

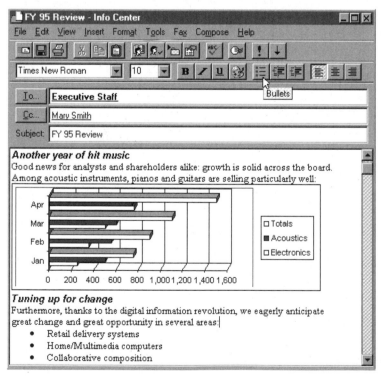

Figure 96. A rich-text e-mail message with an embedded OLE object

Because the Microsoft Exchange client works as a universal e-mail client, it has been designed to correctly transmit rich text and formatting over any mail system, even those that were not originally designed to handle rich text, such as the Internet. The rich-text information is automatically packaged as a separate compressed file attachment and is decompressed on the receiving end by another Windows 95 client. If the message is sent to someone who doesn't use Windows 95—for example, over the Internet—the "plain text" equivalent of the message is received, and any embedded objects are sent as binary attachments.

Messages received in the inbox can be saved for future reference by dragging the messages into any of the other folders (message stores) in the mailbox. Users can also drag a message to any directory on their local or network hard drives. In the latter case, the message becomes an .MSG file but maintains all of the messaging-specific fields, such as Sender, Recipient, and so on. At any time in the future, the user can still double-click the .MSG file to open it and then forward it to other e-mail users.

The Personal Address Book

A universal e-mail client needs to work with a universal address book—one that can seamlessly handle e-mail addresses of different types. Windows 95 includes a Personal Address Book that is implemented as a MAPI service. As a result, in addition to the local address book that the user maintains, Microsoft Exchange has transparent access to the address books and directory services of any other e-mail system that supports MAPI. For example, the same Personal Address Book could show a Microsoft Mail global address list or a corporate X.500 directory service.

For each new set of MAPI drivers installed, the Personal Address Book adds a new "template" to help the user in composing addresses of different types—for example, Internet e-mail addresses are typed on a predefined Internet template. After names have been entered, the user simply addresses e-mail to those people using their names, without having to remember complex addressing conventions.

As shown in Figure 97 on the following page, the Personal Address Book also allows users to keep vital personal information about people, such as their telephone numbers, postal addresses, and office locations. Any phone number in the address book can be auto-dialed using the built-in Windows 95 TAPI services.

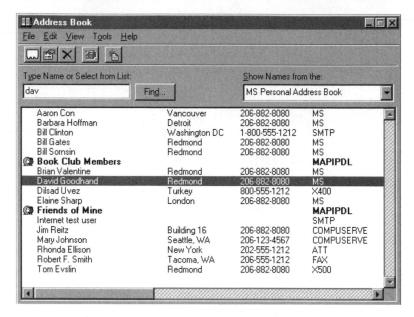

Figure 97. The Personal Address Book, showing entries for people on different e-mail systems

The Information Stores

Messages are typically stored in the user's Personal Information Store. Although the Personal Information Store is a single file, users see this file as sets of folders containing messages or documents. Normally, users have a single information store containing an inbox, an outbox, and perhaps other mail folders. However, Microsoft Exchange allows users to create as many "stores" as they like—for example, one store for current e-mail and another for backup or archive purposes. The built-in Personal Information Store is only one kind of information store. Any e-mail or workgroup system can expose its mailboxes or databases to users as information stores by creating an appropriate MAPI driver.

Information stores can be physically stored in local files, or they can represent a database on a network server. For example, when the Microsoft Exchange client is connected to a Microsoft Exchange Server, users see sets of folders (information stores) that represent replicated databases or "groupware" applications on the server in addition to their standard mailbox folders.

In addition to storing mail messages, users can store files or documents in information stores by dragging the files or documents into these folders. (Additionally, any MAPI-compatible forms software can store its form data and form definitions in an information store.) Users might want to store these items in an information store, rather than in the regular file system, for the following reasons:

- **MAPI properties.** MAPI associates additional fields with items in information stores, such as Sender, Subject, Received Time, Size, Importance, and Sensitivity. These "properties" can be used for searching, filtering, and sorting.

- **OLE document properties.** Documents that are stored as OLE compound documents have many additional built-in properties, such as Title, Author, Keywords, Comments, Last Edited Time, and Number of Pages. When a document is placed in an information store, these built-in properties can be made available to the user through custom views.

- **Rich custom views.** Unlike the regular file system, which displays only a few standard views based on filename, date, size, and so on, information stores allow users to create rich custom views of information by defining the following:

  - Which columns to show, including any of the MAPI or OLE document properties just described

  - How to sort and filter the items to show only those of interest

  - Custom grouping, which allows for multilevel categorized (or "outline") views of the information

Figure 98 shows a custom view of a folder created in an information store to display the OLE properties of the folder's documents. This particular view uses the grouping feature to categorize the information by author.

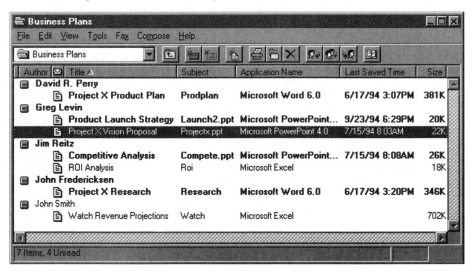

Figure 98. A custom view of a folder, showing OLE document properties

Users can create as many custom views of individual folders as they like, or they can create views that are shared among all folders. Custom views are useful in the universal inbox as well as in other folders. Two possible views are the following:

- View the inbox by Subject to create a "conversation thread" view, in which all the messages and responses on a particular topic are, categorized together.

- View the inbox by From to quickly locate and track all e-mail from a particular person.

Remote Mail

Windows 95 includes MAPI drivers for the Microsoft Mail e-mail system, so the Microsoft Exchange client can send and receive mail as a member of a Mail network—either a full, enterprise-wide mail system or a local workgroup mail system that uses the Windows 95 built-in Microsoft Mail Post Office. Microsoft Exchange users can fully interoperate with existing Microsoft Mail users on other platforms, although rich-text messages are converted to plain-text messages when sent to an existing Mail client.

To use mail on the road or from home, existing users of Mail typically purchase a separate product called Microsoft Mail Remote for Windows and dial into a special Mail remote gateway. They can then preview their waiting mail messages, decide which ones they really want to receive, and then download only the selected messages. They can compose new messages off line and have the messages sent automatically the next time they connect.

In keeping with the Windows 95 focus on facilitating mobile and remote computing, the Microsoft Exchange client is designed to provide the benefits of remote mail without requiring any additional client software or a special gateway to dial into. Mobile or remote users can easily send and receive e-mail using the following features:

- **Remote preview**. Using the built-in Mail drivers, Microsoft Exchange users can dial into their network and preview the headers of their new messages—that is, they can see who sent the new mail, what the subject is, how large the message is, and the estimated time it will take to download the message.

- **Selective download**. After the headers are retrieved, users can mark which messages they want to download and which messages should be deleted without downloading. Users can either download the selected messages immediately after retrieving the headers, or they can make another call later to download them.

- **Remote network access.** Rather than using a specialized e-mail gateway for remote mail, Microsoft Exchange relies on the standard Dial-Up Networking that is built into Windows 95. Users can dial into another computer running Windows 95, Windows NT Server, or a third-party remote access server such as

Shiva LanRover. Remote e-mail then becomes protocol-independent, because RNA supports standard network protocols such as TCP/IP, IPX, and NetBEUI.

- **Offline use.** Microsoft Exchange users can compose messages while off line and have the messages queued up in the outbox until the next time they connect to the appropriate mail service. For example, a user can download new mail at an airport, read the messages and compose replies while on an airplane, dial in from a hotel, and then send the responses automatically.

- **Scheduled connections.** Users can dial in as needed to retrieve mail remotely, or they can set up scheduled connections to dial in at a specific time or on a regular basis—for example, if the computer is permanently remote.

- **Telephony API.** Microsoft Exchange uses the Windows 95 TAPI facilities to dial in and retrieve mail remotely, allowing for effective sharing of modem resources between applications. For example, if users set their modems to listen for incoming faxes while still making a call to get e-mail, TAPI handles the resource management between the relevant applications. Microsoft Exchange also uses the TAPI Dial Helper feature to easily handle multiple locations, hotel dialing prefixes, and credit card calls.

The Microsoft Mail Post Office

Windows 95 includes the workgroup edition of the Microsoft Mail Post Office, providing everything that is needed to set up and manage a complete e-mail system for a workgroup. Typically, one workgroup member, who is designated as the Mail Administrator, creates a Post Office by using the Workgroup PO applet in the Windows 95 Control Panel. The Post Office is simply a shared directory on the administrator's computer where e-mail is stored. A Wizard steps the administrator through the process of creating the Post Office, and is also used to add new users, delete users, and manage shared folders. After the administrator shares the Post Office directory, users can start Microsoft Exchange, enter the shared directory name, and connect to the Post Office in order to send or retrieve mail.

The Microsoft Mail Post Office included in Windows 95 is a workgroup edition, meaning that it is limited to exchanging mail with users of a single Post Office. A single Post Office can potentially support dozens of users, depending on the server performance of the Post Office computer. However, a large group may need to be split up into separate workgroups, each accessing their own Post Office. In that case, a full Microsoft Mail Server will be needed. The full edition of the Microsoft Mail Post Office allows mail to be routed between multiple Post Offices, as well as to other e-mail gateways.

The Microsoft Mail Post Office that comes with Windows 95 can easily be upgraded to a Microsoft Exchange Server, a client/server messaging system that provides not only e-mail services, but also personal/group scheduling, information sharing applications ("groupware"), and forms and application design tools.

The Microsoft Internet Mail Drivers

Windows 95 includes a set of MAPI drivers that allows the Microsoft Exchange client to send and receive mail directly on the Internet. Because Windows 95 already includes great support for TCP/IP—including remote TCP/IP over PPP dial-up lines—everything needed to connect to the Internet and start sending and receiving mail is "in the box." Users can make a LAN connection if their company has direct access to the Internet, or they can obtain access through one of many Internet service providers. MAPI enables configuration of the Microsoft Exchange client to simultaneously support Internet mail along with other e-mail systems, such as the built-in Microsoft Mail.

The following benefits are provided by the Microsoft Internet Mail drivers:

- Supports Internet e-mail standards, including SMTP and POP

- Leverages the great built-in TCP/IP support of Windows 95—a true Windows Sockets application

- Runs either via direct LAN connection or using Dial-Up Networking and PPP

- Supports the Multipurpose Internet Mail Extensions (MIME) to allow interchange of video, images, voice, text, and graphics with other Internet users in e-mail messages. (The MIME Associations Option allows association of multimedia elements with programs on PCs so that they can be directly "launched" from the programs.)

- Supports remote preview, including the Microsoft Exchange header and selective-download options, to make the most of users' connect time on the Internet (see the earlier section titled "Remote Mail")

- Automatically uses standard encoding (UUENCODE) to send and receive binary attachments to and from other Internet or UNIX mail users

- Provides great international support, including support for character sets of all countries that have rapidly growing Internet usage

- Can send rich-text e-mail over the Internet to Windows 95 users (other users receive plain-text messages)

- Provides complete integration with all other Microsoft Exchange client features, including custom views, filtering, searching, and so on

- As shown in Figure 99, provides simple, graphical configuration and management tools, including detailed troubleshooting and logging facilities

Figure 99. Graphically configuring the Microsoft Internet Mail driver

Microsoft At Work Fax

Windows 95, in conjunction with Microsoft Exchange, provides PC users with the ability to send and receive faxes directly from their desktops. This capability, called Microsoft At Work Fax, sets the standard for desktop faxing as an easy-to-use messaging facility that is well-integrated with Windows.

Microsoft At Work Fax provides the following key features:

- High-resolution printed documents are faxed from within Windows–based applications using a fax printer driver.

- Microsoft At Work Binary File Transfer (BFT) capability sends original documents to users of Windows 95, Windows for Workgroups 3.11, and other Microsoft At Work–enabled platforms as e-mail attachments via fax.

- The use of encryption and digital signatures makes the exchange of confidential documents secure.

- High-speed communications with popular Class 1 fax modems and the millions of traditional Group 3 fax machines worldwide is supported.

- Networked Windows 95 users can send and receive faxes through a shared fax modem on one of the Windows 95 workstations on the network.

- A fax viewer allows users to browse multipage faxes using either "thumbnails" or full-page view mode.

- A cover page designer enables users to easily create new fax cover pages that incorporate graphics and text, or to customize one of the predefined cover pages included with Microsoft At Work Fax.

- Users can easily connect to fax-on-demand systems, using a built-in "poll-retrieve" feature that allows them to download faxes directly to their desktops.

Microsoft At Work Fax is integrated into Windows 95 as a MAPI transport service provider, leveraging Microsoft Exchange's universal inbox, rich-text message creation, and browsing capabilities to deliver ease of use and consistency to the management of fax messages. The fax provider coexists with other information or messaging services that users may have installed, and leverages Microsoft Exchange's common address book and inbox.

Windows 95 users can take advantage of Microsoft At Work Fax innovations that provide the secure exchange of editable documents. Users can send faxes from within mail-enabled Windows–based applications, such as Microsoft Word and Microsoft Excel, by using the File/Send command. Additionally, a fax printer driver lets users "print" documents to their local fax modems, either via the File/Print command or by dragging the documents to the Fax icon.

Microsoft At Work Fax leverages the power of the Windows 95 operating system through the Win32 API. As a 32-bit application, Microsoft At Work Fax integrates seamlessly with other Windows 95 applications through its support for MAPI, TAPI, and OLE. In addition to tight integration with Windows 95, Microsoft At Work Fax incorporates Microsoft At Work technologies that support Binary File Transfer (BFT), security, and high-quality document rendering. These technologies put powerful desktop fax messaging at the fingertips of Windows 95 users.

When faxes are sent to other users of Windows 95 (or Windows for Workgroups 3.11 and other Microsoft At Work Fax devices), the Microsoft At Work Binary File Transfer capability can be used to send the original file over the fax connection. For example, a user can attach a Microsoft Word document to an e-mail message and address the message to a customer's fax number. If the customer receives the fax via Microsoft At Work Fax, the Word document is attached to an incoming e-mail message. By clicking on the Word icon, the customer can open the original document. However, if the customer receives the fax via a traditional Group 3 fax machine, Microsoft At Work Fax automatically renders the Word document as an appropriate Group 3 fax image. The highest speed and image compression that is supported by the customer's fax machine is used when transmitting the fax.

Working with Microsoft At Work Fax

Microsoft At Work Fax has been designed to allow Windows 95 users to exchange printed documents and binary files easily and with a minimum of setup. Because fax capabilities are provided as a core system service, they are always available from within Windows 95–based applications or via Microsoft Exchange. Faxes can be transmitted using Microsoft Exchange's e-mail client or by printing documents to a fax printer. Faxes that have been received from other sources are always delivered via the Microsoft Exchange client.

Users can identify a fax recipient by selecting a fax address from an address book—for example, the Personal Address Book—or by directly entering an address, such as *[fax:555-1212]*. The MAPI service provider architecture allows users to mix different types of recipients in the same message. For example, users can send a message simultaneously to Microsoft Mail, CompuServe, Internet, and fax users as long as the Microsoft Exchange client contains profiles for these destinations.

Attaching a document to a Microsoft Exchange e-mail message is the easiest way to fax original or editable documents from Windows 95. The Send command on the File menu within any MAPI-enabled application   for example, Microsoft Word or Microsoft Excel—displays Microsoft Exchange's Send dialog box, in which fax users can address the intended recipient. The attached faxed document appears as an icon within the body of the message.

An easy way to fax a document to Group 3 fax machines is to send the document either by using the Print command on the File menu or by dragging and dropping the document to the fax icon. Microsoft At Work Fax then activates a dialog box asking for the recipient's address and transmits the rendered fax.

Rich Messaging Capabilities

Microsoft At Work Fax supports the rich-text capabilities of the Microsoft Exchange client and the advanced capabilities provided by Microsoft At Work Binary File Transfer (BFT) and Rendering technologies. The Microsoft At Work capabilities are effective when a Windows 95 fax user connects to a user of a Windows 95–enabled, a Windows for Workgroups 3.11–enabled, or a Microsoft At Work–enabled device. Microsoft At Work Fax exchanges information with the receiving device about their respective capabilities to determine whether the receiving device is a Microsoft At Work–enabled device or a Group 3 fax machine. It can then proceed as follows:

- If the receiving fax device supports Microsoft At Work Fax, an editable document attached to an e-mail message is transferred in its native format. In this case, fax works exactly like electronic mail between the originator and recipient. This fax capability supports the universal inbox provided by Microsoft Exchange.

- If the receiving fax device is a traditional Group 3 fax machine, Microsoft At Work Fax converts the document to the most compact fax supported by the machine—that is, MH, MR, or MMR format—and transmits the image at the highest speed supported by the mutual connection (up to 14.4 KB per second).

- If the receiving fax device is Windows 95 or Windows for Workgroups 3.11, and the originating computer sent a printed document, the file is transmitted between the two computers using a special Microsoft At Work rendered (printed) document format. The exchange of printed documents between Microsoft At Work devices is always faster than between Group 3 fax machines because the Microsoft At Work rendered image format achieves greater compression ratios than Group 3 MMR.

Figure 100 shows the property sheet displayed when Microsoft Exchange's Fax command is chosen:

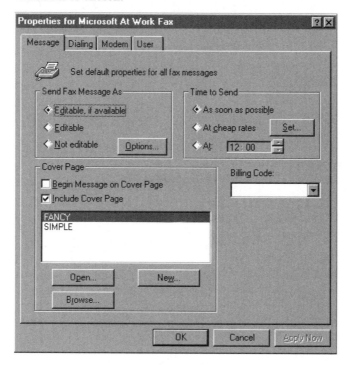

Figure 100. The Microsoft At Work Fax Message property sheet

Workgroup Fax Features for MIS Organizations

Microsoft At Work Fax supports Windows 95 users on local area networks by providing a shared modem fax capability.

If a local fax modem is installed in one Windows 95 workstation, all other Windows 95 users who are on the same physical network can send and receive faxes through the shared modem. The Windows 95 workstation to which the modem is connected is called the "fax server." Other Windows 95 users who are connected via the shared modem can have their incoming faxes routed directly to their desktops. Otherwise, an administrator can use Microsoft Exchange to manually route faxes from the fax server to the final recipients.

In a similar way, Windows users can connect to Microsoft At Work–enabled fax servers and fax machines over a network connection. Microsoft and a variety of hardware and software vendors are in partnership to develop fax products and services that incorporate Microsoft At Work technologies. These products and services will all be compatible with and leverage the capabilities of Microsoft At Work Fax in Windows 95.

Easy Access to Fax Information Services

Microsoft At Work Fax provides the capability to retrieve documents, software, binary files, and fax images from fax-on-demand systems and fax machines that support the Group 3 poll-retrieve capability. The ability to easily download information directly into a Windows 95 workstation via fax helps increase the popularity of fax on demand as a way for companies and information services to cost-effectively distribute information.

For example, the distribution of information could include the automatic distribution of software updates. A Windows 95 workstation with Microsoft At Work Fax could make a connection to a fax-on-demand server and request the name of a binary file via its poll-retrieve capability. The server would respond to the request by downloading the binary file to the Windows 95 workstation. This exchange could be accomplished using a single fax call to the fax-on-demand system. Figure 101 illustrates how a Windows 95 user can request that a binary file be downloaded from a fax information service that supports poll retrieve.

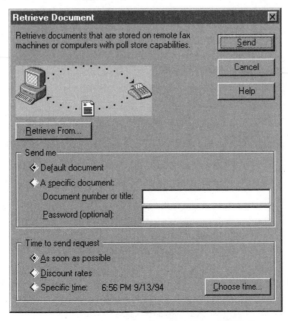

Figure 101. Retrieving a document from a fax information service that supports poll retrieve

The Fax Viewer and Fax Cover Page Designer

Windows 95 includes a Fax Viewer for viewing incoming faxes and a Fax Cover Page Designer for creating customized cover pages for faxes sent to other users. These tools are provided in Windows 95 as accessories.

When a Windows 95 user receives a fax image (as opposed to an editable document), the Fax Viewer is automatically activated when the fax message is opened in Microsoft Exchange. The viewer allows the user to scale, rotate, print, and visually enhance "fuzzy" faxes. For multiple-page faxes, the viewer provides a thumbnail view of the fax that makes it easy to quickly scan the contents of the fax. Figure 102 illustrates this capability.

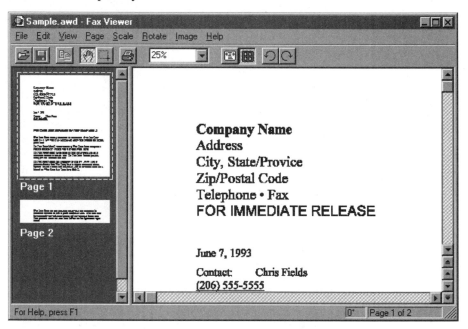

Figure 102. The Fax Viewer in "thumbnails" view

The Microsoft At Work Fax Cover Page Designer allows users to create customized fax cover pages or to modify one of the predefined cover pages included with Windows 95. The Fax Cover Page Designer is an OLE application that makes it easy for the casual user to create attention-grabbing cover pages.

Secure Faxing with Encryption and Digital Signatures

Microsoft At Work Fax protects valuable and confidential documents through encryption and digital signature capabilities. The sender of a document or traditional fax can encrypt the fax using either a simple password or sophisticated RSA public/private key security. The fax software includes the capability to exchange public keys with other users, and users can store and maintain the public keys they receive from other users in their Personal Address Book.

When an encrypted fax is transmitted to a recipient, it cannot be read unless the recipient knows either the password that was used to encrypt the file or the originator's public key, depending on the security mechanism used.

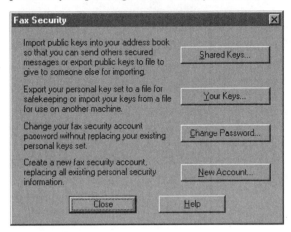

Figure 103. The Fax Security dialog box, showing encryption and digital signature support

Faxed documents can be "signed" with a digital signature to ensure that the fax data is not modified during transmission. A sender uses a private key to sign the fax, and anyone with that sender's public key can read it, but with the knowledge that only the owner of that specific private key could have sent the fax.

The ability to protect confidential documents in a fax environment is an extremely important feature that puts Microsoft At Work Fax ahead of other desktop fax applications.

Compatibility with Fax Modems and Fax Machines

Microsoft delivered the first Microsoft At Work Fax capability with Windows for Workgroups 3.11. This large installed base, along with the installed base of millions of Group 3 fax machines, has made compatibility a priority for fax in Windows 95.

To ensure fax connectivity with the widest possible variety of fax applications, fax machines, and fax modems, Microsoft At Work Fax in Windows 95 supports the following:

- The ITU (International Telecommunications Union, formerly the CCITT) T.30 standard for Group 3 fax. Microsoft At Work capabilities such as BFT are implemented as T.30 nonstandard facilities (NSF), thereby maintaining compatibility with the installed base of Group 3 fax machines.

- The ITU V.17, V.29, and V.27ter standards for high-speed fax communications (up to 14.4 KB per second).

- Class 1 and Class 2 fax modems. A Class 1 modem, or a Class 2 modem that supports NSF and ECM, is required for Microsoft At Work BFT and Security. Fax printing to traditional Group 3 fax devices is available on both Class 1 and Class 2 modems. Microsoft is working directly with fax modem manufacturers to ensure excellent compatibility.

- MH, MR, and MMR compression for Group 3 fax communication.

Coexistence with Windows–Based Telecommunications Applications

The ability of the Microsoft Exchange client to support multiple simultaneous MAPI service providers in Windows 95 means that users will want to have available connections to the Internet, CompuServe, and fax. Well-behaved telecommunications applications that support the Windows Telephony API (TAPI) can coexist and share a local modem in a Windows 95 computer.

The implication of TAPI support for fax is that fax can be listening to the phone line in auto-answer mode while other telecommunications applications and Microsoft Exchange providers dial out to information sources over the phone network. TAPI provides the call arbitration to ensure that physical modem resources are allocated to the appropriate telephony applications when they are needed.

Fax also leverages TAPI concepts such as locations and the Dial Helper dialog box to ensure that fax calls are made consistently, whether the fax user is connected to the network, is at home, or is on the road.

Integration of Fax and Applications

The fax capability in Windows for Workgroups 3.11 has evolved into Microsoft At Work Fax, which creates a powerful and extensible integration platform for fax-enabled applications. The extensibility, through MAPI, of Microsoft At Work Fax and Microsoft Exchange makes it easier for third-party software developers to deliver new fax-enabled applications and enhanced fax services.

Because fax is implemented in Windows 95 as a MAPI transport service provider, users can fax information to other users from any MAPI-enabled application by using the File menu's Send command. In addition, fax features such as poll retrieve have been added to ensure that Microsoft At Work Fax is an excellent client for enhanced fax services.

CHAPTER 15

The Microsoft Network

Microsoft has a vision of creating a world of "Information at Your Fingertips." Online services play a significant role in this vision because they offer "any time" access to the rapidly expanding world of electronic information and communication. Microsoft's goal is to bring these online benefits to mainstream PC users, and to achieve this goal, Microsoft has created a new online service called The Microsoft Network (MSN). Worldwide access to MSN is included as a feature of Microsoft Windows 95.

The Microsoft Network offers all Windows 95 customers affordable and easy-to-use access to a wide range of online information and services, including the following:

- **Electronic mail.** For sending messages to and receiving them from other MSN members or anyone with an electronic mailbox on the Internet.

- **Bulletin boards.** For in-depth discussions of a variety of topics, such as hardware or software support from computer companies.

- **Chat rooms.** For online conversations and special events with celebrities or business personalities.

- **File libraries.** For easy access to images, add-ins, utilities, and programs that can be copied to the user's PC.

- **The Internet.** For e-mail and "newsgroup" bulletin boards.

In particular, Microsoft customers will find MSN the single best place to go to get information about and support for Microsoft products.

Easy to Get Started

Access to The Microsoft Network is a feature of Windows 95. Users don't need to install any software, and the modem detection support in Windows 95 automatically sets up the modem correctly. To get started, all users of Windows 95 have to do is run the Windows 95 online registration and accept the MSN trial offer.

Easy to Use and Understand

The Microsoft Network is tightly integrated into Windows 95, in terms of both functionality and look and feel. Because of the consistent interface, Windows 95 users immediately feel comfortable moving around in an environment that is as familiar as their local system, with no new commands or concepts to learn. In fact, MSN's integration is so complete that experienced users can also use the more powerful Windows Explorer navigation tool to move around.

Highlights

The Microsoft Network incorporates features such as shortcuts, multitasking, and advanced e-mail services, all presented in an engaging, highly graphical format. Windows 95 users worldwide can access MSN by means of a local phone call.

Shortcuts

Shortcuts—OLE links to services on The Microsoft Network—provide a way to jump immediately to specific areas within MSN. When MSN members double-click a shortcut, they jump directly to the appropriate area on MSN. If they are not logged onto MSN, the shortcut starts MSN and prompts them to log on before executing the shortcut. Members can create shortcuts to anything on MSN: any folder, forum, or bulletin board or even a particular file in a file library.

The most-used shortcuts can be stored in an MSN Favorite Places folder or anywhere on the members' systems. Because shortcuts are OLE objects, they can be moved around as easily as files. For example, if members find interesting information in a particular location, they can share the "find" with other members by sending a shortcut to the information by e-mail or even by posting the shortcut on a bulletin board.

E-Mail

In line with The Microsoft Network's close integration with Windows 95, MSN uses the Microsoft Exchange client—the universal e-mail client included with Windows 95. MSN e-mail messages appear in the same mailbox as other e-mail, such as LAN e-mail. Because MSN uses the Microsoft Exchange client to manage its e-mail, users need to learn only one e-mail application. MSN's e-mail supports file attachments, so members can attach spreadsheets, graphics files, word processing documents, or almost any other kind of electronic file.

Multitasking

The Microsoft Network takes advantage of the multithreaded multitasking capabilities provided by Windows 95 so that several different MSN tasks can run at the same time. Multitasking capabilities are particularly useful when downloading files. For example, while a file is being downloaded, members can still browse around, read e-mail, participate in a chat room, or do anything else on MSN without waiting.

Worldwide Access

The Microsoft Network will be available around the world when Windows 95 is released. Local dial-up access will be available in 35 countries, and the MSN application will be localized into many different languages.

Getting Started with MSN

In the Welcome to Windows 95 dialog box, an Online Registration button gives the opportunity to register Windows 95 electronically. (If the initial Welcome to Windows dialog box is disabled, users can still run Online Registration by clicking the Start button, choosing Programs and then Accessories, and selecting Online Registration.) After filling out their registration information, users are asked whether they want to learn about The Microsoft Network. Selecting "Yes" starts MSN Signup. (If a user's modem isn't already configured automatically by Windows 95, the user can do so manually by clicking the Modem icon in the Control Panel.)

If users prefer not to register Windows 95 electronically, they can obtain an MSN account by clicking the Start button, choosing Programs and then The Microsoft Network, and selecting Signup.

C H A P T E R   1 6

Multimedia Services

For the past year, the home market has been the fastest-growing segment of the PC business, and multimedia titles have been one of the fastest-growing segments of the software industry. A large and increasing percentage of the PCs purchased for home use include the equipment that makes multimedia applications possible, notably horsepower, CD-ROM drives, sound subsystems, and local-bus video.

In 1993, the installed base of multimedia-capable Windows PCs grew rapidly to become the largest multimedia computing platform in the world (see Figure 104). By Christmas of 1993, more multimedia titles were available for Windows than there were for any other computing platform (see Figure 105 on the following page).

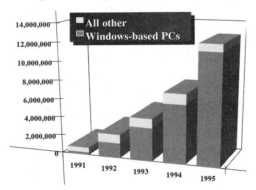

Figure 104. Estimated and forecast sales of multimedia-capable PCs (source: Dataquest)

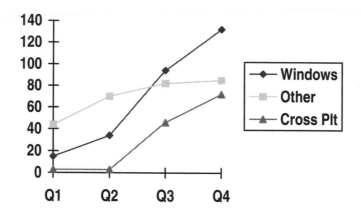

Figure 105. The number of multimedia titles sold by computer software retailers in 1993, by platform and by quarter (source: PC Data)

A Little History

It is worth dwelling for a moment on how far Windows multimedia has come in the last few years. When Microsoft Video for Windows 1.0 was released in 1992, sound cards and CD-ROM drives were relatively rare. Graphics subsystems were universally ISA-based, and software codec (compression/decompression) technology was in its infancy. The standard size for a digital video clip was 160 pixels by 120 pixels—one-sixteenth of a VGA resolution screen. Technologists, who understood the difficulties of this accomplishment, cheered wildly and proclaimed the dawn of the multimedia computing era. Customers shrugged. What was so great about a video clip the size of a "dancing postage stamp"?

In 1993, hardware and software makers began to deliver equipment and technology that offered better-than-postage-stamp performance at reasonable consumer prices. Double-speed CD-ROM drives and local bus video offered more bandwidth to support the massive data requirements of digital video and quality sound. A second generation of software codecs made more effective use of the data available. Prices on 16-bit sound cards dropped into consumer range. With Microsoft Video for Windows 1.1, the size of a digital video clip that a mainstream computer could display reliably increased to 320 pixels by 240 pixels—one-quarter the size of the screen. Critics labeled these digital video clips "dancing credit cards," but consumers found digital video of this size compelling enough that it spurred a virtual tidal wave of multimedia title development. Retail software store shelves are now crowded with multimedia titles and games, and progress marches on.

Installing Windows 95 provides today's multimedia PCs with an overnight upgrade in multimedia capabilities. Based on the capabilities of high-end PCs in 1994, the mainstream PC of 1995 will be able to play digital video segments that are larger, smoother, and better-looking than ever before—even up to 640 pixels by 480 pixels (full screen) and beyond (see Figure 106). We are now able to look forward quite realistically to a time when the amount of data that can be stored on a CD-ROM, rather than the speed of the video subsystem, is the most relevant factor limiting the richness of a consumer's experience with a multimedia title or game.

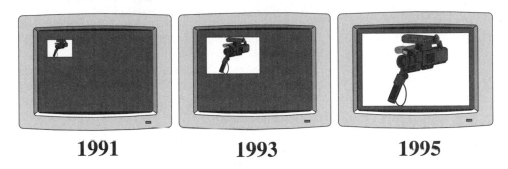

1991   **1993**   **1995**

Figure 106. Digital video, evolving through the dancing postage stamp (1991) and dancing credit card (1993) eras to full screen

A New High-Performance Multimedia Platform

Windows 95 delivers a new high-performance platform for PC multimedia. From a "big picture" perspective, the "greatest hits" of what Windows 95 contributes to the world of multimedia computing are as follows:

- For consumers, Windows 95 makes multimedia easier, more engaging, and more fun.

  - **Easier.** Plug and Play makes the successful installation of multimedia devices far easier for consumers. All of the architectural support for digital video, audio, and MIDI is built into Windows 95, so that users are relieved of setup challenges. And Windows 95 is compatible with multimedia titles and tools created for Windows 3.1.

  - **More engaging.** Installing Windows 95 is an immediate multimedia upgrade that allows any PC to become a better, more exciting multimedia playback machine. Authors creating titles and games for Windows 95 can make their products faster and more exciting to play.

  - **More fun.** Windows 95 is a much better platform for computer games than any earlier version of Windows and includes support for fast, intensely graphical games.

- For developers, Windows 95 offers a powerful platform for professional multimedia authoring.

  - **Power.** The new 32-bit architecture in Windows 95 squeezes vastly improved multimedia performance out of PCs, so developers can capture digital video and sound that is bigger and bolder than ever before. The multitasking architecture of Windows 95 makes it a much more convenient working environment for multimedia authors.

  - **Professional quality.** The streamlined architecture of digital video, digital audio, MIDI, and file handling subsystems in Windows 95 enables authors and toolmakers to create high-quality sound, video, and animation effects. Windows 95 is an attractive platform for the professional development of multimedia effects and footage beyond the realm of the PC— for example, TV commercials.

- For hardware makers, Windows 95 offers exciting new opportunities.

  - **Graphics.** A display driver technology called Display Control Interface (DCI) offers ways for Windows 95 to take advantage of hardware assistance for several graphical operations, such as image stretching.

  - **Sound.** A new technology called Polymessage MIDI offers sound card manufacturers a way to play complex MIDI sequences with virtually no CPU use. Sound cards are improving rapidly, and competition based on features is increasing.

Making Multimedia Easier

Microsoft is committed to making Windows the leading force in multimedia technologies and systems for PCs. This commitment takes many forms, the most important being an ongoing investment in multimedia-related research and development. Some of the results of the last few years of research and development are described in this chapter. Multimedia technologies are evolving rapidly, and Microsoft will continue to press ahead in providing tools and architectural enhancements to enable developers and consumers to take advantage of new innovations.

Plug and Play Support

As multimedia applications, titles, tools, and games have become more and more compelling, consumers have begun buying add-on multimedia components, such as CD-ROM drives and sound cards. Buying these devices has been cheap and easy; installing them has been a different matter. To put it mildly, installing a CD-ROM in a PC has required...patience.

Support of Plug and Play in Windows 95 makes the prospect of adding a new multimedia device to a PC considerably less daunting. Just plug in a Plug and Play–enabled sound card and, literally, it plays. In fact, Windows 95 even makes the prospect of installing *old* multimedia devices less daunting because it includes tools that make identifying and resolving conflicts between legacy devices that are not Plug and Play–enabled vastly easier. To make this process as painless as possible, Windows 95 includes built-in drivers for the most popular sound cards.

It is difficult to overstate the importance of Plug and Play for multimedia. For the multimedia market, Plug and Play will have the following three effects:

- It will allow the base of multimedia-capable PCs to grow through Plug and Play upgrade kits, rather than placing so much of the growth burden on the purchase of new CPUs. Because Windows 95 includes the basic architecture for handling sound, MIDI, and digital video, every PC running Windows 95 can easily be made into a multimedia PC by plugging in a sound card and/or a CD-ROM drive.

- It will substantially decrease the cost of installing and supporting multimedia devices, which will help speed their adoption for business use.

- As multimedia standards, such as CD-ROM speed, continue to improve, Plug and Play will allow consumers to conveniently upgrade multimedia components without replacing their entire PC. Plug and Play support will be vital to the adoption of new multimedia devices, such as MPEG cards.

AutoPlay

In various ways, titles and games that run off a CD-ROM feel different from other applications. First, starting CD-ROM programs differs from starting hard-disk–based applications. First, users have to open a drawer, extract the right disk, and place it in the CD-ROM drive before they can run the program like any other program—assuming, of course, that they can find the icon they created when they first installed the program. A second difference between CD-ROM programs and hard-disk–based applications is that CD-ROM products may be used irregularly.

While watching users run multimedia applications, Microsoft realized that the act of placing a disk in a CD-ROM drive is loaded with information. If the CD-ROM is a program that the user has never run before, the act of putting the CD-ROM in the drive means that the user intends to install the program. If the program has already been installed, the act of putting the CD-ROM in the drive means that the user intends to run the program.

In Windows 95, a feature called AutoPlay allows software developers to make their products easier for users to install and run. When the user puts a disk in a CD-ROM drive, Windows 95 automatically spins it and looks for a file called AUTORUN.INF. If this file exists, Windows 95 opens it and follows the instructions. This new feature makes the setup instructions for a Windows 95–based multimedia game or title almost absurdly easy, reducing them to something like the following:

1. To play this program, insert the disk in your CD-ROM drive.

2. Have a nice day!

Built-In Support for Digital Video

For the past several years, Microsoft has been developing a high-performance architecture for digital video: Microsoft Video for Windows. (For more details, see the section titled "Multimedia Graphics Architecture" later in this chapter.)

In the past, Video for Windows was distributed separately (principally as a Software Developers Kit), but with the release of Windows 95, Video for Windows is now built into every copy of Microsoft Windows, including Windows NT. The widespread ability to play digital video has the following implications:

- Users and ISVs can use the .AVI file format to distribute digital video files with the same confidence that they distribute files of other Windows–supported formats, such as .TXT, .WRI, .BMP, .PCX, and .WAV.

- The barriers to entry for would-be multimedia title and tool developers are further lowered because the issues of licensing and installing Microsoft Video for Windows disappear.

Built-In Support for Sound and MIDI

MIDI is the computer equivalent of sheet music. Using sheet music, an arranger can describe how to play Beethoven's *Moonlight Sonata* in a few pages, but to actually play the piece, a person who knows how to read sheet music needs a piano. The music performed from the sheet music varies in sound depending on the circumstances—for example, when played on an expensive grand piano, the sonata sounds better than when played on an old upright.

Similarly, a MIDI file can contain the electronic instructions for playing the *Moonlight Sonata* in just a few kilobytes, but playing the piece requires a device, such as a sound card, that knows how to "read" MIDI instructions and can produce a piano sound. And just as the sound of real pianos varies somewhat, so does the piano sound produced by sound cards.

At the high end, MIDI is used as a development tool for musicians. Virtually all advanced music equipment today supports MIDI, and MIDI offers a convenient way to control the equipment very precisely. At the low end, MIDI is becoming an increasingly popular tool for multimedia product developers because it offers a way to add music to titles and games with a tiny investment of disk space and data rate. The majority of sound cards today have on-board MIDI support built in.

Windows 95 includes built-in support for both MIDI and waveform audio (.WAV).

The CD Player

Many people like to play audio CDs in their CD-ROM drives while working, so Windows 95 includes the CD Player. As Figure 107 shows, the controls on this player look just like those on a regular CD player, and the Windows 95 CD Player supports many of the same features found in advanced CD players, such as random play, programmable playback order, and the ability to save programs so that users don't have to re-create their playlists each time they pop in a CD.

Figure 107. The CD Player, which will play, uninterrupted, in the background

Making Multimedia More Engaging

With Windows 95, users' PCs become a better multimedia machine, so software developers can produce faster and more engaging titles and games.

Built-In CD+ Support

In addition to making it easy for users to play their favorite audio CDs from their current collection, Windows 95 is helping to define a standard for music CDs of the future. Windows 95 is the first operating system to announce support for the new Sony/Phillips CD+ format, which will enable audio CD players and multimedia PCs to easily play the same compact discs. This new format allows both audio and data to be integrated on the same CD, in a manner conducive to users of both audio CDs and PC–based CD-ROM titles.

The CD+ format uses new technology, called "stamped multisession," that solves the "track one" problem that has prevented easy use of CD-ROMs in audio CD players. Until now, CD-ROM titles have used the first track of a compact disc for data, thus producing static—and potential speaker damage—when played on audio CD players. Sony and Phillips are implementing stamp multisession under the brand name CD+. Other music-industry companies can license the CD+ brand from them or create their own implementations of stamp multisession. Microsoft Windows 95 will accommodate all compatible implementations of the technology.

Because data and audio information can be combined on the same CD, the new CD+ format will open up a broad, new category of CD titles that can be enjoyed fully as audio discs and, when inserted into a PC running Windows 95, can also provide digital information in the form of music videos, song lyrics, biographies, and other text, and even promote online exchanges with musicians.

The new format leverages a range of new features being included exclusively in Windows 95 to help make multimedia more engaging. The AutoPlay feature, for example, enables users to insert a compact disc in their CD-ROM drive and have it automatically play. Also, the 32-bit multimedia subsystems in Windows 95 enable unprecedented playback performance. The new CD file system further facilitates multimedia use, while Plug and Play support makes installing and using CD-ROM drives and related hardware simple for consumers.

Bigger, Faster, Better-Looking 32-Bit Digital Video Playback

Displaying digital video involves moving and processing huge streams of data continuously and efficiently. The new digital video implementation in Windows 95 offers some exciting new efficiencies, allowing software developers to confidently create multimedia titles that are more compelling and better-looking than ever before.

Multimedia title and game developers are business people. When they create a product, they do so with the hope of turning a profit. To maximize the number of PCs that can run a title, most developers tend to include lowest-common-denominator digital video. As a result, video windows the size of postage stamps with low frame rates (which make movement look "jerky") and extreme compression (which makes the video look "blocky") have tended to be the norm. However, Windows 95 raises the lowest common denominator significantly.

In the past, the process of displaying digital video has relied on a series of 16-bit systems that read data from the disk, decompress the video data, and display it on screen. One key design goal of Windows 95 was to enable this architecture to make the transition to 32 bits, and the difference is eye-popping. For multimedia users, installing Windows 95 is the quickest and cheapest multimedia upgrade available. Without adding any hardware, Windows 95 enables users to display bigger, smoother, more colorful digital video than ever before.

This improvement does not come at the expense of compatibility. Multimedia in Windows 95 is fully compatible with 16-bit multimedia titles. Early testing has shown that the 32-bit improvements in file access speed and stream handling results in performance improvements even for 16-bit multimedia applications. However, the biggest improvements will obviously be realized in the new generation of fully 32-bit titles that will be designed for Windows 95.

For users who upgrade their PCs to Windows 95, one easy-to-overlook source of performance improvements is the display driver. Many display drivers are updated more or less continuously, whether to fix problems, enhance performance, or incorporate new features such as DCI. Most users, however, don't update drivers on their system unless they are having a problem. Upgrading to Windows 95 ensures that they have the latest and greatest.

Multitasking and Threading

Multimedia applications don't take well to interruption. When watching a video clip or listening to a sound file, users really don't want it to stop in the middle. Because of multitasking, interruption is less likely. The multitasking in Windows 95 is quite different from earlier versions of Windows because it is preemptive. In Windows 95, multiple 32-bit processes can share the CPU at the same time, whether those processes have been initiated by different applications (multitasking) or by one application (threading).

Threading has a very important implication because it allows multimedia titles and games to have a smoother, more finished feel to them. A game might have one thread that plays background music continuously during game play to help smooth out the breaks between scenes while another thread is loading new data.

As applications, tools, and codecs are gradually rewritten to 32 bits, video and other multimedia processes will become less and less likely to be interrupted by other applications. For example, in Windows 95 you can move a video window while it is playing without interrupting it.

Built-In Support for Fast CD-ROMs

The development of faster CD-ROM drives (double and triple speed) has been essential for the growth of multimedia computing because faster reading of CD-ROM data helps make video and audio playback from CD-ROM drives look and sound better.

To get the best possible performance from these new devices, Windows 95 includes a new 32-bit CD-ROM file system (CDFS) for reading files from CD-ROM drives as quickly and efficiently as possible. (The Windows 3.1 system for reading files from CD-ROM drives [MSCDEX.DLL] is also included in Windows 95 for compatibility with products that rely on it.) CDFS is an important component of the overall performance enhancements to multimedia in Windows 95.

Windows 95 also extends its support for CD-ROM to drives that read XA-encoded disks, such as Kodak PhotoCD and video CDs.

Hardware Support for TV-Like Video

Digital video and stereo audio can be squeezed into an incredibly small data stream using a complex codec called MPEG. For example, with MPEG compression most feature movies can fit on two CD-ROMs. Because MPEG is so complex, displaying video from an MPEG file is a calculation-intensive process—so calculation-intensive, in fact, that the most appealing way to display MPEG video on today's PCs is by using hardware assistance.

Together with the Open PC MPEG Consortium, Microsoft has defined an industry standard for MPEG board and chip manufacturers who want to ship MPEG devices for Windows 95. This standard allows applications to incorporate MPEG video without worrying about precisely which vendor's MPEG device is present to decompress it.

Making Windows More Fun

In 1994, the home market was the fastest-growing segment of the PC business, and more and more users have been demanding games for Windows. Games are already the largest category of multimedia application, but most computer games are designed to run on MS-DOS (see Figure 108). Windows 95 is a much better platform for computer games than any earlier version of Windows because it includes support for fast, intensely graphical games. It also has built-in joystick support, so users don't need to load external drivers.

1993 Computer Game Sales by Platform

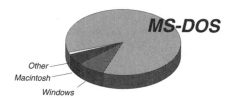

Source: PC Data 1993 Annual Report

Figure 108. At the end of 1993, computer games were one of the last remaining software categories for which Windows product sales trailed MS-DOS product sales

Fast DIB Drawing

The speed of graphics (or, more accurately, the lack of it) in Windows has been one of the biggest obstacles that prevented game developers from choosing the Windows platform for their games. Windows 95 addresses this issue head-on in a way that provides substantially improved speed while preserving the device independence that makes Windows appealing in the first place.

A new 32-bit call, CreateDIBSection, has been added to the Win32 API for Windows 95 and Windows NT. This new feature allows developers to quickly get bitmaps onto the screen. If nothing fancy (such as clipping or stretching) is involved, the CreateDIBSection call actually allows applications to send DIBs more or less directly to the video frame buffer. (For more information, see the diagram in the section titled "Multimedia Graphics Architecture" later in this chapter.)

Because this kind of graphic speed is critically important to quality games, Microsoft has moved a portion of the CreateDIBSection improvements of Windows 95 into a tool for Windows 3.1 called the WinG (pronounced *Win Gee*; the *G* stands for *games*) libraries. The WinG libraries allow game developers to create fast, graphical games for Windows 3.1 with the assurance that the game will be fast and compatible with Windows 95. Figure 109 shows such a game.

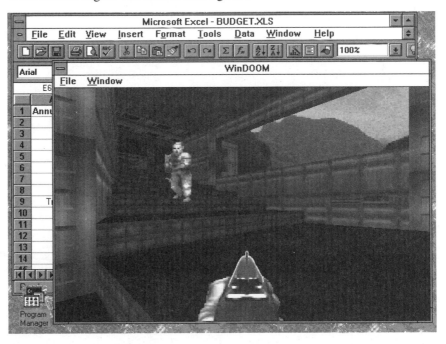

Figure 109. The graphics core of DOOM for Windows was ported from MS-DOS to the WinG library in two days. Id Software is scheduled to ship a full version of the product towards the end of 1994

A Powerful Development Environment

Because of its new 32-bit, multitasking architecture, Windows 95 is an attractive platform for the professional development of multimedia titles.

Sound Compression for CD-Quality Sound

Sound can take up a lot of disk space. Full CD-quality, uncompressed stereo audio contains a lot of data—about 176 KB for every second of sound! An entire CD-ROM can contain only a little over an hour of music. Sound can also eat up a fair-sized chunk of the data rate that a CD-ROM drive is capable of sustaining.

To lessen the burden of storing and playing sound from an application, Windows 95 includes a family of sound compression technologies. These codecs can be divided into the following two groups:

- Music-oriented codecs, such as IMADPCM, allow close to CD-quality sound to be compressed to about one-quarter of its original size.

- Voice-oriented codecs, such as TrueSpeech, allow extremely efficient compression of voice data.

This support for compressed sound is two-way: Sound can be played from a compressed sound file, or a sound file can be compressed using the built-in sound recording and editing utility. If users have microphones, they can turn on voice compression when recording so that the file is compressed in real time.

In addition to the codecs that come with Windows 95, the audio architecture of Windows multimedia is designed to be extensible through other installable codecs. (The Windows 95 video architecture can be extended in the same way.)

Polymessage MIDI Support for Better Sound

Windows 95 comes with Microsoft's best-ever implementation of MIDI, including a new technology called "polymessage MIDI support." This enhancement allows Windows 95 to communicate multiple MIDI instructions simultaneously within a single interrupt. As a result, playing MIDI files requires even less computing power than it did before and allows developers to process MIDI instructions alongside graphics and other data even more successfully.

Multitasking

Multitasking makes Windows 95 a much more attractive platform for multimedia authoring. Creating multimedia content is very CPU-intensive work that can take a long time to complete. For example, compressing a digital video file could take hours, depending on the complexity of the file and what type of system is doing the compression. Moreover, digital video files had to be compressed one at a time. As a result, video authors were virtually chained to their desks until their work was done.

Because of the Windows 95 multitasking capabilities, authors retain control of their PCs, even when an enormous compression operation is underway. Digital video authors can initiate several compression operations at once—and then head home.

Professional Quality

The digital video, digital audio, MIDI, and file handling subsystems in Windows 95 make it an ideal platform for developing high-quality video, sound, and animation effects.

Capture and Compression of Bigger Digital Video

The grim reality is that video contains an enormous amount of data. Capturing digital video is even more data-intensive than playing it back, because raw digital video footage is uncompressed. A single frame of full-color video at 640 pixels by 480 pixels contains close to a megabyte of data. At 30 frames per second, you can fill up a 1 GB hard drive with uncompressed video data in less than a minute. This data can be compressed to make storage go further, but for multimedia developers, the rate at which they can write data to disk is still an important concern.

The 32-bit file access of Windows 95 is every bit as important to digital video authors as it is to digital video users. Because data can be written to disk more quickly in Windows 95, authors can capture better-looking video—bigger, more frames per second, and more colorful. After the raw footage is captured, the potentially time-consuming process of compression begins. Both Cinepak and Indeo will be available in 32-bit versions for Windows 95 to make the compression process considerably more efficient.

General MIDI for Specific Sounds

One of the early challenges for MIDI was that it was, in a way, too flexible. Any instrument can be "connected" to any MIDI channel so that a "sequence" (song) written for a piano might accidentally end up being played on a tuba. Windows 95 supports the General MIDI specification, an industry-standard way for MIDI authors to request particular instruments and sounds.

Built-In Support for Multimedia Devices

Windows 95 includes built-in support for common multimedia authoring devices, such as laser disks and VCRs. This support simplifies the process of setting up a system for "step capture," a process in which the author captures digital video data one frame at a time, usually to be compressed later. Step capture is a slow process, but it is the best way to capture the highest quality digital video. Frame-accurate control of the VCR is also important for recording broadcast-quality special effects for use in commercials, movies, television programs, music videos, and so on.

Multimedia PCs for 1995

All things being equal, installing Windows 95 upgrades any PC into a more capable multimedia tool. However, all things are *not* equal. The quality and capability of multimedia PCs and devices varies a great deal.

Microsoft is publishing the *Microsoft PC 95 Hardware Design Guide* to help IHVs and OEMs identify opportunities to take advantage of new capabilities in Windows 95. This guide makes the following five high-level recommendations to OEMs:

- **Balance beats horsepower.** Multimedia playback places heavy demands on many parts of the system, from the CD-ROM (reading) to the hard disk (writing) to the CPU (decompressing) to the video and audio subsystems (playing). A fast CPU does not guarantee a great playback system. In fact, multimedia playback on most high-end PCs is not constrained by the CPU.

- **Local bus video is indispensable.** Even OEMs creating non-multimedia systems should use local bus video because doing so gives consumers the option of using Plug and Play to create a multimedia system later. Without local bus video, a PC cannot keep up with the amount of video data that 1995's consumer multimedia titles and games will want to display continuously.

- **CD-ROM drives must be double-speed or better.** Titles in 1995 will assume double-speed data rates.

- **Displays must be SVGA (800 x 600) or better with 16-bit color**. Why are more than 256 colors required? Because multimedia applications use a lot of colors and tend to compete for access to the system palette. For example, if a multimedia presentation includes a digital video clip of an underwater scene on a slide with a smooth-shaded maroon background, a 256-color palette doesn't have enough colors to make both the slide background and the underwater scene look good.

- **Audio must be 16-bit**. The installed base of sound cards that can interpret MIDI is now large enough to be tempting to game and title developers. Not all sound systems are equal: Some sound great (16-bit with sampled sounds), and some sound like *Star Trek* reruns. The differences are significant, and consumers will be able to tell the difference.

New Opportunities for Great-Sounding Audio

The quality of audio cards and sound systems varies a great deal. Sound cards have generally been used for their ability to play waveform audio—the equivalent of recorded sound. For some uses, such as voice-overs, recorded waveforms have no realistic alternative. However, recorded sound is very resource-intensive for both the CD-ROM and the CPU.

In Windows 95, enhancements to the handling of MIDI make it an even more appealing alternative to .WAV for playing music within games and multimedia titles. Makers of audio cards and systems can provide the following features to distinguish themselves in the marketplace:

- **Polymessage MIDI support.** This highly efficient new technology is included in Windows 95 to make using MIDI easier for application and game writers. When a sound card supports polymessage MIDI, the CPU use required to play even a very complex song is quite small.

- **16-voice-or-better polyphony.** Polyphony is the ability to play multiple sounds at once. Support for more concurrent sounds means fuller-sounding playback.

- **Sampled sound rather than waveform synthesis.** Waveform synthesis uses a mathematical approximation of a sound such as a piano. Sampled sound is an actual recording of the piano, and it sounds considerably better. Including samples of at least the most common general MIDI instruments helps ensure that music in games and titles doesn't sound synthetic.

Taking Advantage of New Video Card Features

In the summer of 1994, Microsoft released the new DCI display driver development kit. The DCI technology was developed in partnership with Intel and other makers of advanced video display cards.

DCI is a device driver level interface that allows Windows to take advantage of the following hardware features when they are built into advanced display adapters:

- **Stretching.** Speeds up the rendering of images that are stretched or distorted.

- **Color-space conversion.** Assists in playback of compressed digital video by accepting YUV data instead of requiring RGB.

- **Double buffering.** Allows faster, smoother block transfers (BLTs) of images by providing memory space for off-screen drawing.

- **Chroma key.** Facilitates the merging of video data streams, allowing a particular color to be treated as "transparent" in the merge operation.

- **Overlay.** Speeds display of partly concealed objects.

- **Asynchronous drawing.** Along with double buffering, provides a faster method for "drawing" into offscreen memory space.

Most of these hardware features relate to the fast, efficient decompression and playback of digital video. Applications that use the Microsoft Video for Windows architecture will benefit from these features automatically and substantially.

The Multimedia Architecture

The Multimedia Graphics Architecture

The Windows 95 graphics architecture is illustrated in Figure 110. As the figure shows, an application might want to "draw" the following four kinds of graphics on the screen, and it can use four APIs to do so:

- **"Productivity application" graphics**. Applications that want the system to help them draw scroll bars, fonts, buttons, and so on use GDI, the basic Windows graphics API.

- **Digital video**. Applications that want to play digital video use the Video for Windows API. (More details about the Video for Windows architecture are provided in the next section.)

- **Game graphics**. Games draw their own graphics (in memory) and use WinG when they want bitmaps blasted to the screen as fast as possible. WinG is available for Windows 3.1, and provides many of the same benefits as the CreateDIBSection function in Windows 95, as well as fast access to the frame buffer through DCI.

- **3D engineering graphics**. Applications that want the system to help them draw 3D solids use OpenGL. OpenGL is Microsoft's strategic choice for a 3D application programming interface, and Microsoft has a long-term commitment to deliver an implementation of OpenGL as part of the broader Win32 API. Microsoft's first OpenGL implementation shipped in Windows NT 3.5.

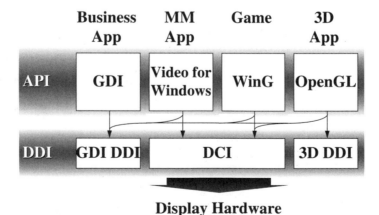

Figure 110. The Windows 95 graphics architecture

The device driver interface in Windows 95 has the following three parts, and the APIs described earlier are designed to take advantage of whichever part provides the best performance:

- **GDI-DDI.** The basic graphics device driver interface for Windows. It is optimized for the flexible graphics requirements described earlier for the GDI API.

- **DCI.** The new device driver interface created jointly by Microsoft and Intel. DCI drivers provide a fast, direct way for games and digital video to write to the video frame buffer. They also enable digital video playback to take advantage of several specific kinds of hardware support included in advanced graphics adapters. For example, stretching hardware can allow users to scale up the size of a digital video clip with virtually no additional strain on the CPU. Color space conversion support in hardware can reduce the amount of work a codec must perform by up to 30 percent, allowing substantially better video playback.

- **3D-DDI.** Enables applications that use OpenGL to take advantage of accelerated 3D support in hardware.

Multimedia Data Routing

The diagram in Figure 111 illustrates (in simplified form) the path that synchronized multimedia data travels from storage to playback.

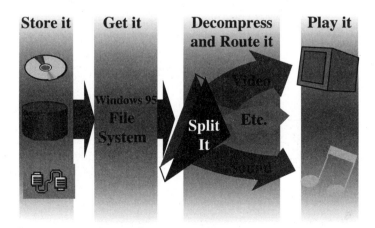

Figure 111. Multimedia data routing

To start with, the data—usually an .AVI file—must be stored somewhere, such as a CD-ROM, a local hard drive, or a network file server. The quality of the eventual playback will be constrained by the amount of data that the storage medium can supply continuously to the file system.

A command—for example, Play—that is usually issued through the Media Control Interface (MCI) causes the relevant part of the file system in Windows 95 to retrieve the stored data. Obtaining this data swiftly and steadily is vital to the success of overall playback performance, and the 32-bit protected-mode enhancements in the new file system (and CDFS) in Windows 95 make a big contribution to the overall performance enhancements of multimedia in Windows 95.

A multimedia data stream, such as an .AVI file, generally contains multiple components, such as digital video data, audio data, text, and perhaps other data such as hot spot information, additional audio tracks, and so forth. As multimedia information comes off the CD-ROM, the first job of the Video for Windows architecture is to figure out what the data stream contains and to separate and route it accordingly.

In most cases, digital video and digital audio are stored in a compressed form, and before it can be seen or heard, it must be decompressed. Frequently, this function is performed in software. However, if hardware support is available on the graphics adapter or sound card for all or part of the decompression work, Video for Windows can tap into it.

Windows 95 ships with a set of useful software-only codecs for both video and audio. However, the Video for Windows architecture has been created in a way that allows additional codecs to be installed. As new codecs become available for particular audio and digital video needs, they can be plugged into the Video for Windows architecture. For example, motion JPEG, which is not included in Windows 95, is a useful codec for multimedia authoring, and capture cards that support JPEG compression and decompression are easily available.

C H A P T E R   1 7

Installation and Setup

The very first contact that users have with Windows 95 is during initial installation on their computer. If the installation process is not easy, or if novice or intermediate users are confronted with a series of configuration-related questions that they don't know how to answer, their initial experience with the operating system will be bad, and that tone will be set for their first trial of the system itself. Advanced users can overcome difficult installation procedures, but their frustration level still has a finite threshold.

For Windows 95, the Setup program has been completely rewritten to offer greater flexibility and better customization than Windows 3.1. In addition, Setup in Windows 95 is more modularized than Setup in Windows 3.1, allowing the easy customization of individual Setup steps, as well as the easy installation of new custom components.

Summary of Improvements over Windows 3.1

The installation of Windows 95 has been improved over Windows 3.1 in a number of areas, including the following:

- A modular setup architecture that provides increased customization and flexibility

- An entirely GUI-based approach and improved interaction with the user, including better visual feedback of progress during setup

- Improved hardware device detection and configuration support

- Better customization of components to install

- Built-in smart recovery mechanisms for failed setup

- Built-in verification of installed components for easy correction and replacement of corrupted or deleted files

- A network setup process that is well integrated with other setup components and that provides support for a number of network installation configuration scenarios

- Support for an automated batch installation procedure, allowing Windows 95 to be installed with little or no user intervention

- Better flexibility so that PC installers, VARs, and MIS organizations can customize Setup by adding components to be installed at setup time, such as custom in-house applications

A Modular Setup Architecture

In MS-DOS, Setup is responsible for installing the basic disk operating system on the PC. In Windows 3.1, Setup is a combination of components and installation procedures inherited from prior versions and is responsible for installing the GUI on the PC. In Windows for Workgroups, the Setup functionality of Windows 3.1 was extended to install networking components on top of the GUI and disk operating system. Because Windows 95 is a complete, integrated operating system, it is now responsible for installing the disk operating system, the GUI, and the networking functionality on the PC. These responsibilities posed some interesting problems when the Windows 95 development team first approached the daunting task of writing Setup for Windows 95.

The original Setup written for Windows was not flexible enough to easily add components without making the installation procedures unwieldy. To make the installation process easier, modularized, and more flexible, the Windows 95 development team for Setup completely rewrote the installation code. As a result, Windows 95 uses more intelligent defaults and mechanisms for automatically configuring or installing key components while requiring only minimal user intervention, furthering the ease-of-use of the operating system.

For end-users, Setup in Windows 95 provides a simple, easy way to initially install and configure Windows 95. For MIS organizations, Setup in Windows 95 provides greater control and flexibility over components that are installed and offers support for automated batch installation to further simplify the setup procedure.

A GUI-Based Setup Program

Setup in Windows 95 differs from that in Windows 3.1 by featuring an entirely GUI-based setup process. Using a GUI-based setup simplifies the interaction with the user by providing better visual feedback of configured options and greater flexibility for navigating through the setup process. To support a GUI-based setup, Windows 95 features a Setup program that runs entirely from within the Windows environment. Users who already have either Windows or Windows for Workgroups on their PCs can run Windows 95 Setup the same way that they would run an installation program for any Windows–based application. For new installations, Windows 95 Setup includes the necessary components to install a minimal version of Windows to support the GUI-based setup process.

The GUI-based Setup provides better visual feedback to users throughout the installation process. Users are constantly shown where they are in the setup process and are given a number of visual cues that the system is engaged in the setup process.

The Leveraging of Detection Code

Setup's modular architecture allows the leveraging of detection and installation procedures beyond the initial setup process. The same procedures and detection mechanisms used by Setup to detect and initially configure hardware devices and peripherals during the setup process are also used for maintaining or detecting devices after installation. For example, the same code base used during the setup process for the detection of Plug and Play or legacy hardware devices is also used to detect or configure new devices after Windows 95 is up and running.

Customization Improvements

For system administrators, Windows 95 makes customization easier than Windows 3.1, which provided few mechanisms for easily customizing the setup process. Customization of Setup allows for better control over components installed into an existing environment. MIS organizations can now easily tailor the existing configuration options for Setup components, such as supported network interface cards or supported printers. Windows 95 also offers the flexibility for system administrators to add components to be installed during the setup process or to run additional procedures during the final phases of Setup.

Hardware Detection Improvements

During the setup process, Windows 95 detects the hardware devices and components configured on the computer and uses this information to install drivers and set the appropriate entries in the Registry. Unlike the simple hardware detection mechanisms used in Windows 3.1, which identified the PC configuration for a narrow group of devices, Windows 95 provides more versatile hardware detection and configuration mechanisms and provides detection support for a wider range of devices.

Windows 95 provides straightforward detection support for the base computer components, such as communication ports and processor type, but provides more robust detection of system devices, including video display adapters, pointing devices, hard disk controllers, floppy disk controllers, and network interface cards.

Hardware resources, such as IRQs, I/O addresses, or the DMA address, that are in use by more than one device can cause havoc when initially installing an operating system and may prevent the system from starting properly. Windows 95 Setup helps detect any hardware resource conflicts early in the setup process.

Windows 95 detects hardware components and devices one of two ways:

- It leverages Plug and Play detection to identify Plug and Play devices and peripherals.
- It uses a manual query detection mechanism for legacy devices and peripherals.

After Setup detects a device, Windows 95 installs the appropriate device drivers and configures the system.

The Setup Process

Setup in Windows 95 provides options to support the following four common scenarios and is designed to make installing Windows 95 to meet users' needs easy:

- **Typical.** Most users will select this the option to perform a "typical" installation of Windows 95.

- **Compact.** This option performs a "compact" installation of Windows 95, installing the minimal files needed for proper operation.

- **Laptop.** This option installs the components of Windows 95 that are useful for laptop or mobile computer users.

- **Custom.** This option provides full customization of the Windows 95 setup process, allowing users to install all or selected components.

Windows 95 Setup is quite a bit simpler than Windows 3.1 Setup and is divided into the following four logical phases:

- Detecting hardware
- Asking configuration questions
- Copying component files for Windows 95
- Configuring the final system

The following sections describe what happens in each of these phases.

The Hardware Detection Phase

During the hardware detection phase, Setup analyzes installed system components, detects installed hardware devices, and detects connected peripherals. During this phase of Setup, Windows 95 analyzes the system to identify the hardware resources that are available—for example, IRQs, I/O addresses, and DMA addresses—identifies the configuration of installed hardware components—for example, IRQs in use—and builds the hardware tree in the Registry.

Windows 95 uses a number of mechanisms to detect installed hardware devices during setup. For legacy PCs, Windows 95 maintains a database of known hardware devices and performs a manual detection to check I/O ports and specific memory addresses to attempt to identify whether they are being used by recognized devices. Windows 95 also checks for Plug and Play peripherals connected to legacy PCs, which return their own device identification codes. For PCs that contain a Plug and Play BIOS, Windows 95 queries the PC for installed components and the configuration used by these components. (Windows 95 also checks for Plug and Play peripherals connected to Plug and Play PCs.)

During the hardware detection phase of Setup, Windows 95 tries to identify hardware conflicts and provides a mechanism to resolve conflicts early in the installation process to overcome the hardware configuration issues that Windows 3.1 users encounter.

When the hardware detection phase is complete, a dialog box allows users to proceed with Setup or to review the hardware devices that were detected and the system components that Windows 95 will install.

The Configuration Questions Phase

Windows 95 uses information found in the first phase to determine which system components it should install. During the Windows 3.1 setup process, users were constantly asked for system configuration information and confirmations. By contrast, Windows 95 consolidates the configuration and customization phase of Setup into a single procedure at the beginning of the setup process. Users can review the components Windows 95 will install and remove or add any components.

The Copying Files Phase

This phase of Setup is the most straightforward. After users have identified or confirmed which components Windows 95 should install, Setup begins copying files from the Windows 95 installation disks (or from a network server, if specified). When the necessary files have been copied to the PC, Setup prompts users to remove any disks in floppy drives and then reboot the system to proceed with the final phase of Setup.

The Final System Configuration Phase

During the final system configuration phase, Setup upgrades the existing configuration of Windows and replaces the existing version of MS-DOS with the new Windows 95 operating system. After files are updated and the system is configured, Setup guides users through a process to configure peripheral devices, such as modems or printers, that are connected to the system. When this configuration is complete, Windows 95 is ready to use.

Better Control over Installed Components

Users now have greater control over components and parts of Windows 95 that are installed during the Setup process. Based on the modular architecture of Windows 95, users will be able to selectively choose the options that Windows 95 will install for the given functionality that they desire.

Setup's Smart Recovery Mechanism

During setup of Windows 3.1, if the system hung during device detection or if the setup process ended abnormally, a flag would be set disabling hardware detection for the next time that Setup was run. This mechanism provided a means for users to bypass a section of Setup that would otherwise fail. However, they were required to rerun the entire setup process and manually identify hardware devices.

Windows 95 supports a far better recovery mechanism in the case of Setup failure. During the setup process, Windows 95 creates and maintains a log as the setup operations are performed and the hardware devices are detected. If Setup fails—for example, because of a hang during hardware detection—the last entry in the Setup log identifies where the process was interrupted. To recover and resume, users simply rerun Setup. The Setup program recognizes that it was run before and begins from where it left off. In the case of a hang during a hardware detection procedure, the system actually bypasses the detection module where the hang occurred and allows users to manually select the correct device installed in or connected to the system.

Built-In Verification of System Files

Under Windows 3.1, if a component file was accidentally deleted or a system file was corrupted, users had no easy way to recover the given file. They needed either to use the Expand utility to recopy a known file or to completely reinstall Windows 3.1 to reinstate a lost file.

Windows 95 provides some flexible solutions to this problem. During the setup process (and during subsequent maintenance of the Windows 95 system), Windows 95 creates and maintains a log of the installed components. This information is used as part of Setup's smart recovery support and is also used to verify the integrity of installed components.

If users run Setup after Windows 95 is already installed, Setup asks them whether to reinstall Windows 95 or simply to verify installed components. If they want to verify installed components, Setup examines the setup log and runs through the setup process *without* copying all system components. Instead, it verifies the integrity of the files that were installed during Setup against the files provided on the Windows 95 installation disks. If the integrity check fails because of either a missing or corrupted file on the Windows 95 computer, Setup automatically reinstalls the missing or corrupted file.

This capability in Windows 95 greatly simplifies and reduces the time required to resolve missing files or corrupted configurations, thereby helping to reduce the time and money required to support desktop configurations.

Network Setup Improvements

Windows 95 provides improved support for installation and use in network environments. Windows 95 can be installed on a network to upgrade existing Windows users, or it can be used to convert existing MS-DOS PCs. Windows 95 offers the same capabilities for running Windows from a network but also provides additional functionality to better address the requests of MIS organizations.

In addition to basic support for stand-alone computers, Windows 95 includes Setup provisions for better supporting the following:

- Installing and running Windows 95 from a local computer on a network

- Installing and running Windows 95 from a network server instead of installing it on the local computer

- Installing Windows 95 on a network server and supporting diskless computers that RIPL boot from the network server

- Installing Windows 95 on a network server and supporting computers with a single floppy drive that run Windows 95 from the network server

Additional information about network support in Windows 95 is given in Chapter 9, "Networking."

Network Installation Location Remembered

When users modify the configuration of their PCs in a networked environment, the Windows 95 Setup program makes the installation of new drivers easy by remembering the location on the network from which Windows 95 was installed. Any user that has been prompted for the insertion of a diskette containing needed files for Windows or Windows for Workgroups will appreciate this new functionality. Whether the server is a NetWare server or a Windows NT server, when users add a device or require additional driver support files to properly run Windows 95, Setup automatically attempts to get the files from the network server. Setup stores a UNC pathname in the Registry, eliminating the need to maintain a permanent network connection on the PC.

Batch Installation Support

Windows 95 features a batch installation option that permits the use of an installation script to automate the installation process. MIS organizations or VARs can simplify the installation procedure for users by specifying answers to questions that Setup asks, as well as specifying defaults for installing and configuring devices such as printers.

System administrators can use the NetSetup tool provided with Windows 95 to create a batch script that specifies all of the options that Setup needs, thereby providing support for hands-free installation. The batch installation capability of Windows 95 is more flexible and customizable than that provided with Windows 3.1 or Windows for Workgroups 3.11.

Windows or Windows for Workgroups Configuration Preserved

Windows 95 can easily be installed as an upgrade on a PC where Windows or Windows for Workgroups already exists. During the upgrade process, Windows 95 uses existing configuration information to set installation defaults and examines the contents of specific .INI files to further determine the appropriate Setup options.

Windows 95 preserves configuration information, such as the Program Group definitions created by the user, and maps user interface-related features or functionality from Windows 3.1 or Windows for Workgroups to that of the interface used by Windows 95.

C H A P T E R   1 8

International Language Support

With the growth of the worldwide PC market, Microsoft Windows and Windows–based applications have made PCs easier to use around the globe. The fact that Windows and Windows–based applications are sold and used worldwide poses some unique problems for both Microsoft as an operating-system vendor and ISVs as application developers.

When a new software application or operating system intended for a world market is developed, efforts must be made to localize the software to the countries and written languages in which it will be used. In many cases, localization is a simple matter of translating the names of menus, menu items, and strings displayed by the software into the language used in the locale. However, as the features and functionality of a software product grow, so does the complexity required to tailor the application to characteristics of the native country. Since the start of the design work for the Windows NT operating system, Microsoft has been adding to the level of support for international languages and cultural conventions in the 32-bit editions of the Windows family of operating systems.

This section discusses the localization plans for Windows 95, the built-in international support for using Windows 95 on a worldwide basis, and the special provisions that Windows 95 includes for enhancing existing or developing new applications that can be used in different parts of the world.

Summary of Improvements over Windows 3.1

Support for using the Windows operating system on a global basis is improved in Windows 95. The benefits for both users and software developers are summarized on the following page.

The benefits for users include the following:

- **Easy switching from one language to another.** Windows 95 makes both the use of multiple language fonts and character sets, and switching among the different keyboard layouts required to support them, easy.

  With the Eastern European version of Windows 3.1, users can directly switch between only two keyboard layouts—for example, Russian and English. With the standard Latin versions of Windows, users cannot easily switch between different keyboard layouts; they have to go to the Control Panel for each language switch. With Windows 95, users can easily switch among all available languages and corresponding keyboard layouts configured on their system by using the ALT+SHIFT key combination, making the integration of information in a multilingual document easy.

- **Font substitution.** Windows 95 substitutes fonts when switching among different languages if the original font is not present on the system. When switching among different languages, matching fonts for the new language are substituted if the original font is not available. As a result, users can read and use the text for a similar character set, even if they don't have the font that the original information was created in.

- **Correct sorting and formatting rules.** Different locales and cultures have different rules for interpreting information. For example, cultures use different sequence algorithms for sorting information, use different comparison algorithms for finding or searching for information, and use different formats for specifying time and date information. Win32–based applications that use the National Language Support (NLS) APIs allow users to easily exchange information on a global basis, while preserving the integrity of the information.

The benefits for developers include the following:

- **Easy addition of international language support to applications.** Developers can now use the Win32 NLS APIs for sorting, searching, and manipulating information in a locale-independent way. NLS services in Windows 95 ensure that information is handled correctly for the given culture or locale. The correct national format is automatically supplied based on the international settings specified by the user in the Control Panel. For example, to obtain the current date format information to match the current locale, the application calls an NLS API, and the system returns the correct format. Likewise, to sort information in the proper sequence in French, Norwegian, or Spanish, the application calls a corresponding culture-independent NLS API.

- **Automatic switching of fonts and keyboard layouts.** Windows 95 provides services that application developers can use to ensure that as users move through a multilingual document, the correct fonts and keyboard layouts are used. For users who create or edit multilingual document content—for example, translators—a Win32–based application that uses the international services in Windows 95 automatically activates the correct fonts and corresponding keyboard layouts for the edit point in the text. This feature allows easy editing of information contained within multilingual documents.

- **Preservation of language-specific attributes on the Clipboard.** Windows 95 provides additional services for application developers so that information can be passed through the Clipboard to easily exchange information between internationally-aware applications, while preserving all language formatting characteristics.

- **Switching of languages by multilingual-aware applications.** Windows 95 provides services that application developers can use to automatically switch the language that the system uses to match attributes in a document. For example, as users scrolls through a multilingual document, the application can automatically switch the system language to match the format of the information contained within the document.

- **Storage of international language information in RTF format.** Extensions have been provided to the RTF specification to support saving language-relevant information in Rich Text Format (RTF) from a multilingual-aware application.

The Localization of Windows 95

As a result of the success of Microsoft Windows around the world, Windows and Windows–based applications have been localized into many different languages. Microsoft Windows 3.1 was localized into more than 25 major languages, a process that took as long as 18 months and delayed the availability of Windows 3.1 for some language versions. With Windows 95 international localization, issues have been worked on concurrently with the development of the domestic U.S. version of the operating system. To better support a global market, Microsoft plans to localize Windows 95 into at least 29 different language versions, including German, French, Spanish, Swedish, Dutch, Italian, Norwegian, Danish, Finnish, Portuguese, Japanese, Chinese, Korean, Russian, Czech, Polish, Hungarian, Turkish, Greek, Arabic, Basque, Hebrew, Thai, Indonesian, and Catalan (as well as several variations of these languages). The localized versions of Windows 95 will be released on a planned development schedule that does not exceed 120 days.

International Language Issues

Localization is only a small part of the effort that goes into ensuring that an operating system can be used effectively in a worldwide environment. A worldwide operating system must also provide services to support the use of international applications and to support the global market by making the application developer's job easier. This section discusses some of the language issues that international users and application developers face:

- **From the user's perspective.** Some users need to include more than one language in a document. For example, they might be translating from English into Russian or they might be writing a product instruction manual in many different languages. When using more than one language, users must deal with a series of obstacles. For example, they must repeatedly switch to another keyboard layout on-the-fly so that they can continue writing in a different language. When using a database, users faces the problem of sorting the information in the correct order for a given language.

- **From the developer's perspective.** When localizing a product into different languages, developers are faced with several questions, such as the following: "What is the correct sorting order for French?" "How is a date represented in Germany?" "Do the Swedes really need to have the ability to use the characters Å, Ä, and Ö?" "If a document contains text in more than one language, is there some way for the software to know which part of the document is in which language?" "Can information in a multilingual document be passed to another application via the Clipboard?" Many developers try to address these issues in their applications and fall short, creating problems for the users, their support organization, and their own development team.

Because the mainstream Windows platform has not previously offered international language support as an operating system service, many application vendors have hard-coded global characteristics into their applications. Hard coding allows their applications to be used in a given locale, but prevents the applications from being used easily in a different cultural environment. As a result, users depend on application developers to provide a version of the application that matches their locale attributes.

In Windows 95, Microsoft has set out to offer international language support at the operating system and API level. This support adds functionality that provides solutions for using software and exchanging documents around the world. Providing international language support services in Windows 95 makes it easier for application developers to solve international language issues related to presenting or manipulating information in their applications. This section discusses those issues.

Date and Time Formats

Date and time information needs to be represented in different formats depending on the locale where the information is being used. For example, date information presented in American English places the day between the month and year, as in "March 9, 1994," whereas a different locale may represent the same date as "9 March 1994."

Sorting and Searching

International language issues are much more complex than simply representing date and time information in the correct format. Sorting and searching algorithms in applications must correspond to the proper language rules for the locale in which the information is being used and manipulated. The following examples illustrate the subtle differences between language rules:

- In French, diacritics are sorted right to left instead of left to right, as in English.

- In Norwegian, some extended characters follow the Z character because they are considered unique characters rather than characters with a diacritic.

- In Spanish, CH is a unique character between C and D, and Ñ is a unique character between N and O.

As a further example, if a database in Swedish is sorted with an English-language sort algorithm, the names would be sorted as shown in the left column of this table:

How Are Names Sorted?	
English sorting	**Correct Swedish sorting**
Andersson	Andersson
Åkesson	Karlsson
Ärlingmark	Magnusson
Karlsson	Turesson
Magnusson	Åkesson
Turesson	Ärlingmark

The system treats the Å and Ä as an A and therefore sorts them after A at the top of the list. However, in the correct Swedish sort order, the Å and Ä are sorted after Z because they are separate vowels that occur at the very end of the alphabet. A Swede looking for "Ärlingmark" would be confused to find it near the beginning, instead of at the end, of a list of names.

With Windows 3.1, many developers came up with their own sorting routines for different languages and hard-coded this functionality into their applications. Their applications are too inflexible to support the numerous right sorting tables required for all the languages into which they might want to localize their applications.

National Character Sets, Keyboards, and Fonts

In standard Windows 3.1, fonts native to the Eastern European countries, such as Greece, Russia, and Turkey, cannot be used. For example, if users tried to install a Russian font with an English or French version of Windows 3.1, the characters appeared unintelligible on the screen, and users couldn't use the font. To solve this problem, a special English Eastern European version of Windows 3.1 was designed for English users who needed to use Eastern European fonts, including Russian Cyrillic or Greek. The English Eastern European version of Windows 3.1 offered the same capabilities as the true Russian or Turkish Eastern European version of Windows for displaying font and character information.

The Solution: Multilingual Content Support

Windows 95 resolves many of the problems related to international language issues by integrating multilingual content support in the core of the operating system. Windows 95 also offers national language support to application developers as a series of APIs that are part of the Win32 API set.

Multilingual content support is the ability to display and edit text of various languages and scripts in a single document. Multilingual content support is a core feature of Windows 95 and will be also be provided in the next major release of Windows NT (code-named Cairo).

Multilingual content support in an application provides the following two major benefits:

- Users can create and edit documents with content in multiple languages and scripts and exchange these documents with users of other language systems. This feature is important within the European Union, for example, where Greek and Latin–based languages must coexist in documents.

- An application that supports multilingual content supports the native content of any market into which it is sold.

Easy Switching Among Languages and Keyboards

Windows 95 allows users to add support for multiple keyboard layouts to match different international conventions. In the Control Panel, the Keyboard icon provides the ability to configure the system to support the preferred keyboard layouts, as shown in Figure 112.

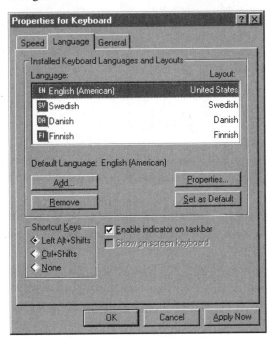

Figure 112. The Keyboard property sheet, showing international layout support

To change the keyboard layout in Windows 3.1, users had to go to the Control Panel each time they wanted to switch to a different keyboard layout. In Windows 95, switching keyboard layouts is much easier. Figure 113 on the following page shows a sample legacy word processing document that illustrates the ability to integrate text by using the Arial font in different languages within the same document. The language identifier in the status area of the Taskbar allows users to easily switch the system language among the available language options. A Windows 95 application that uses NLS APIs would incorporate the ability to switch the preferred language directly on the Toolbar of the application.

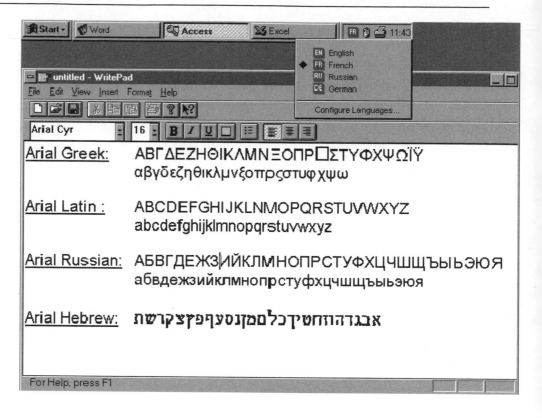

Figure 113. Switching among different languages to create a multilingual document

Multilingual Extensions to the ChooseFont Dialog Box

The ChooseFont common dialog box has been enhanced to include a list box showing the character set scripts supported by a particular font. This mechanism ensures the correct representation of fonts for a given language.

Figure 114 shows an early representation of the new ChooseFont common dialog box, illustrating the integration of font script selection options. The Font Script list shows the script names for each of the character sets covered by the font selected in the Font list. The Sample box displays a font sample that is dependent on the script selected, as well as the other font attributes. The sample preview string, which is specific to the selected character set, shows what each of the different scripts looks like.

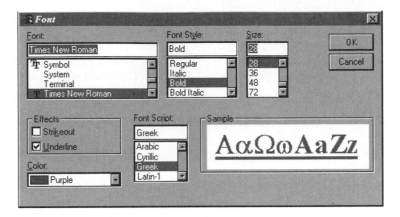

Figure 114. The Font dialog box, showing the new Font Script list

Internationally aware applications can support multilingual font selection by allowing users to select fonts via the ChooseFont common dialog box and by recognizing the extensions to the ChooseFont data structures in Windows 95. Even Windows–based applications—which, though not originally designed for Windows 95, support formatted text but not multilingual messages—can gain some basic level of support for multilingual content. If an application uses the ChooseFont common dialog box, it benefits from the enhancements, allowing users to select from the full range of character sets and fonts configured in the system. As long as the application saves the complete logical font data structure representation for fonts, an existing Windows–based application can get by without being aware that the font selected by the user includes a possible change of character set. (Applications generally do save this data when saving text in their native format, but not all save this data when writing to interchange formats, such as RTF.)

Multilingual Support for Exchanging Information via the Clipboard

A good multilingual-aware application can exchange multilingual content with other aware applications and can exchange appropriate flat text with unaware applications, within the limitations of the ASCII text formats. Windows 95 provides special support in the data exchange APIs to pass language information along with the rich text data.

Try It!

Test Multilingual Content Support

1. In the *Control Panel*, open the *Keyboard* tool and click the *Language* tab. Add a couple of keyboards—for example, Swedish and French—and then click *OK*. At the right end of the *Taskbar*, notice that a small square is displayed in the status area to represent the active keyboard layout. Two letters in the square represent the language—for example, "EN" for "English."

2. Start a word processing application and create a document in which to test the multilingual content support.

3. Hot-switch among different input languages by pressing ALT+SHIFT, toggle through the available configured languages, and select one.

4. After you have switched to a new input language, type something. A multilingual-aware application automatically switches the font if necessary. (Of course you have to know where the keys are on that country-specific keyboard layout.)

5. Switch to a different language and type something.

6. Move the insertion point through the text. A true multilingual-aware application automatically switches the input language to match the current language format when you move through different languages in the text.

The Win32 National Language Support APIs

When users install Windows 95, they specify a locale preference. (This preference can be changed later via the Control Panel.) The Win32 NLS APIs can use either this default locale setting or a specific locale setting. Using the Win32 NLS APIs offers the following benefits to developers:

• They can easily integrate international language support into their Win32–based applications. These APIs, which are supported on both the Windows 95 and Windows NT platforms (with limited support available for Win32–based applications under Windows 3.1) allow applications to correctly retrieve regional and language settings, format date and time, sort lists according to cultural rules, compare and map strings, and determine character type information. Application developers in the U.S. can be sure that the sorting order and date formats that Microsoft provides with the operating system are correct, so all they have to do to sort or display information is use the appropriate Win32 NLS APIs.

• They can more easily develop applications for new global markets. Using this API set lowers development costs by eliminating the need for proprietary sorting methods, parsing the WIN.INI file or Registry, and locale-specific coding.

• Perhaps more important for developers, the API set provides a mechanism for accurate and consistent behavior on all 32-bit Windows platforms.

Users benefit because the API set ensures that information is handled and displayed correctly for a given locale-specific format. In addition, users don't have to worry about whether their international text is being sorted properly.

CHAPTER 19

Accessibility

Microsoft is committed to making computers easier to use for everyone. Personal computers are powerful tools that enable people to work, create, and communicate in ways that might otherwise be difficult or impossible. The vision of making computers easier to use for everyone can be realized only if people with disabilities have equal access to the powerful world of personal computing.

The issue of computer accessibility in the home and workplace for people with disabilities is becoming increasingly important. Seven to nine out of every ten major corporations employ people with disabilities who may need to use computers as part of their jobs. In the U.S. alone, an estimated 30+ million people have disabilities that can potentially limit their ability to use computers. Additionally, as the population ages, more people experience functional limitations, causing the issue of computer accessibility to become important to the population as a whole.

Legislation, such as the Americans with Disabilities Act (which affects private businesses with more than 15 employees) and Section 508 of the Rehabilitation Act (which addresses government spending), also brings accessibility issues to the forefront in both the public and private sectors.

Microsoft already offers a number of products specifically for users with disabilities and includes features in its mainstream software products to help make them more accessible. Microsoft's two most prominent accessibility products are Access Pack for Microsoft Windows and AccessDOS. Both were developed by the Trace Research and Development Center at the University of Wisconsin–Madison using research funded by NIDRR. Also available is Access Pack for Microsoft Windows NT. These products enhance the Windows, MS-DOS, and Windows NT operating systems by adding a variety of features that make the computer more accessible for users with limited dexterity or hearing impairments. Microsoft distributes these utilities at no charge to customers and announces their availability in each of its new products.

Windows 95 offers several enhancements designed to make the system more accessible and easier to use for people with disabilities. In recent years Microsoft has established close relationships with users who have disabilities, organizations representing disabled people, workers in the rehabilitation field, and software developers who create products for this market. Based on their combined input, the following specific design goals were defined for Windows 95:

- Integrate and improve the features from Access Pack that compensate for the difficulties some people have using the keyboard or the mouse.

- Make the visual user interface easier to customize for people with limited vision.

- Provide additional visual feedback for users who are deaf or hard of hearing.

- Provide new APIs and "hooks" for ISVs developing third-party accessibility aids, including those that allow blind people to use Windows.

- Make information on accessibility solutions more widely available and increase public awareness of these issues.

Enhancements designed to meet these goals are included throughout Windows 95. This chapter describes these enhancements, which will make computing easier for people who have disabilities.

Summary of Improvements over Windows 3.1

The primary improvements in accessibility for Windows 95 are the following:

- Make UI elements scaleable

- Compensate for difficulties using the keyboard

- Emulate the mouse with the keyboard

- Support alternative input devices that emulate the keyboard and mouse

- Provide visual cues to tell users when an application is making sounds

- Advise applications when the user has limited vision

- Advise applications when the user needs additional keyboard support due to difficulty using a mouse

- Advise applications when the user wants visual captions displayed for speech or other sounds

- Advise applications when they should modify their behavior to be compatible with accessibility software utilities running in the system

- Optimize keyboard layouts for users who type with one hand, one finger, or a mouthstick

- Include audible prompts during Setup for users who have low vision

- Optimize color schemes for users with low vision

- Include accessibility information in Microsoft product documentation

General Features of Accessibility Enhancement

To provide information about accessibility features and to provide ways of controlling the features, Windows 95 includes several enhancements.

Online Help

An Accessibility section in the Windows 95 contents and index of online Help provides a quick reference and pointer to topics that can help adjust the behavior of the system for people with disabilities.

Controlling the Accessibility Features

In Windows 95, most of the accessibility features described in this chapter are adjusted through the Accessibility Options icon in the Control Panel. Clicking this tool displays the property sheet shown in Figure 115 on the following page, which enables users to turn the accessibility features on or off and customize timings, feedback, and other behavior for their particular needs.

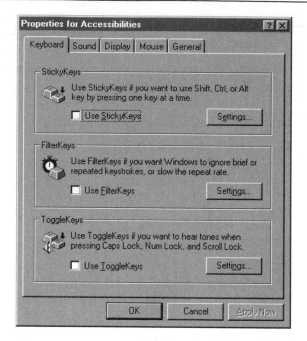

Figure 115. The Accessibilities property sheet

Emergency Hotkeys

Most of the accessibility features described in this chapter are adjusted through the Control Panel. But if users can't use the computer until an accessibility feature is turned on, how can they use the Control Panel to activate it? This chicken-and-egg problem is solved by providing emergency hotkeys with which users can temporarily turn on the specific feature they need. Then, after a feature is turned on, users can navigate to the Control Panel and adjust the feature to their own preferences or turn it on permanently.

If a feature gets in the way or if another person needs to use the computer, the same hotkey can be used to temporarily turn off the feature.

Microsoft has worked hard to ensure that the emergency hotkeys don't get in the way of users who don't need them. Each hotkey is an obscure key combination or key sequence that should not conflict with applications. If a conflict does arise, the hotkeys can be disabled, and the features will still be available as needed.

As an additional precaution, each emergency hotkey plays a rising tone and displays a confirmation dialog box that briefly explains the feature and how it was activated. If users pressed the hotkey unintentionally, this notification allows them to deactivate the feature. It also provides a quick path to a more detailed Help topic and the Control Panel settings for that feature, allowing users to disable the hotkey permanently.

The Accessibility TimeOut

The Accessibility TimeOut turns off Access Pack's functionality after the system has been idle for a certain period of time. It returns the system to its default configuration. This feature is useful on machines shared by multiple users. The Accessibility TimeOut can be adjusted using the Control Panel.

The Accessibility Status Indicator

Windows 95 provides an optional visual indicator, shown in Figure 116, that tells users which accessibility features are turned on, helping users unfamiliar with the features to identify the cause of unfamiliar behavior. The indicator also provides feedback on the keys and mouse buttons currently being "held down" by the StickyKeys and MouseKeys features (discussed later in this chapter). The status indicator can be displayed on the Taskbar or as a free-floating window and can be displayed in a range of sizes.

Figure 116. The Accessibility status indicator

Features for Users with Low Vision

Windows 95 offers several enhancements designed to make the system more accessible and easier to use for people with low vision.

Scaleable User Interface Elements

Users who have limited vision or who suffer eyestrain during their normal use of Windows can adjust the sizes of window titles, scroll bars, borders, menu text, and other standard screen elements. These sizes are completely customizable through the Control Panel in Windows 95. Users can also choose between two sizes for the built-in system font.

A Customizable Mouse Pointer

Users who have difficulty seeing or following the mouse pointer can now choose from three sizes: normal, large, and extra large. They can also adjust the color or add animation, both of which can increase the pointer's visibility.

High-Contrast Color Schemes

The Windows color schemes allow users to choose from several well-designed sets of screen-color options designed both to match users' individual tastes and to meet their visual needs. The new color schemes in Windows 95 include high-contrast colors designed to optimize the visibility of screen objects, making it easier for users with visual impairments to see them.

High-Contrast Mode

Many users with low vision require a high contrast between foreground and background objects to be able to distinguish one from the other. For example, they may not be able to easily read black text on a gray background or text drawn over a picture. Users can set a global flag to advise Windows 95 and applications that they need information to be presented with high contrast.

Windows 95 also provides an emergency hotkey that allows users to set the computer into high-contrast mode when they can't use the Control Panel or when the current color scheme makes the computer unusable for them. Pressing this hotkey—Left ALT, Left SHIFT, and PRINT SCREEN keys simultaneously—allows them to choose an alternate color scheme that better meets their needs.

Try It!

Take a New Look

1. Imagine you can't read black text on a gray background because all the lines blur together.

2. Press Left ALT + Left SHIFT + PRINT SCREEN until you find a text/background combination that's more suitable to your needs.

Features for Easier Keyboard and Mouse Input

Windows 95 offers several enhancements designed to make inputting information via the keyboard and mouse easier.

StickyKeys

Many software programs require users to press two or three keys at one time. For people who type with a single finger or a mouthstick, that just isn't possible. StickyKeys allows users to press the keys of a key combination one at a time and instructs Windows to respond as if the keys had been pressed simultaneously.

When StickyKeys is turned on, pressing any modifier key—that is, CTRL, ALT, or SHIFT—latches that key down until either the mouse button or a non-modifier key is released. Pressing a modifier key twice in a row locks it down until it is pressed a third time.

The functionality of StickyKeys is adjusted using the Control Panel, or it can be turned on or off using an emergency hotkey, by pressing the SHIFT key five consecutive times.

SlowKeys

The sensitivity of the keyboard can be a major problem for some people, especially if they often press keys accidentally. SlowKeys instructs Windows to disregard keystrokes that are not held down for a minimum period of time, allowing users to brush against keys without any ill effect. When users put a finger on the correct key, they can hold the key down until the character appears on the screen.

The functionality of SlowKeys is adjusted using the Control Panel, or it can be turned on or off using an emergency hotkey, by holding down the Right SHIFT key for eight seconds. (This hotkey also turns on RepeatKeys.)

RepeatKeys

Most keyboards allow users to repeat a key just by holding it down. This feature is convenient for some but can be a major annoyance for people who can't lift their fingers off the keyboard quickly. RepeatKeys lets users adjust the repeat rate or disable it altogether.

The functionality of RepeatKeys is adjusted using the Control Panel, or it can be turned on or off using an emergency hotkey, by holding down the Right SHIFT key for eight seconds. (This hotkey also turns on SlowKeys.)

BounceKeys

For users who "bounce" keys and produce double strokes of the same key or similar errors, BounceKeys instructs Windows to ignore unintended keystrokes.

The functionality of BounceKeys is adjusted using the Control Panel, or it can be turned on or off using an emergency hotkey, by holding down the Right SHIFT key for 12 seconds. Users hear an up-siren after eight seconds, and another double-tone after 12 seconds. Releasing the SHIFT key after the double-tone activates BounceKeys.

MouseKeys

The MouseKeys feature lets people control the mouse pointer using the keyboard. Users don't need to have a mouse to use this feature. Windows 95 is designed to allow users to perform all actions without needing a mouse, but some applications may require one, and a mouse can be more convenient for some tasks. MouseKeys is also useful for graphic artists and others who need to position the pointer with great accuracy.

When MouseKeys is turned on, the following keys navigate the pointer on the screen:

- Press any number key except 5 on the numeric keypad—these keys are also called the direction keys—to move the pointer in the directions indicated in Figure 117.

- Press the 5 key for a single mouse-button click, and press the + key for a double-click.

- To drag an object, point to the object, press INS to begin dragging, move the object to its new location, and press DEL to release it.

- Select the left or right mouse button or both mouse buttons for clicking by pressing the /, -, or * key, respectively.

- Hold down the CTRL key while using the direction keys to "jump" the pointer in large increments across the screen.

- Hold down the SHIFT key while using the direction keys to move the mouse a single pixel at a time for greater accuracy.

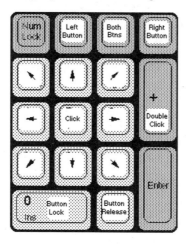

Figure 117. The keys on the numeric keypad that control the mouse pointer

The functionality of MouseKeys can be adjusted using the Control Panel, or it can be turned on or off using an emergency hotkey, by pressing the Left ALT, Left SHIFT, and NUM LOCK keys simultaneously.

ToggleKeys

ToggleKeys provide audio cues—high and low beeps—to tell users whether a toggle key is active or inactive. It applies to the CAPS LOCK, NUM LOCK, and SCROLL LOCK keys.

The functionality of ToggleKeys can be adjusted using the Control Panel, or it can be turned on or off using an emergency hotkey, by holding down the NUM LOCK key for eight seconds.

Try It!

Type with a Pencil

1. Suppose you could only type with a single finger, or with a pencil held between your teeth. How would you press ALT+TAB? Start by pressing SHIFT five times to turn on StickyKeys. (Notice the status indicator on the Taskbar.)

2. Now press ALT and see what happens. Press TAB and you'll have just typed two keys at once with a single finger.

3. Press ALT twice and then press TAB a few times to see the ALT+TAB window and to cycle through all the tasks you have running.

4. When the name of the task you want to switch to is displayed, press ALT one more time to release it.

5. Turn off StickyKeys by pressing two keys at the same time.

Don't Touch That Mouse

1. Press the Left ALT, the Left SHIFT, and the NUM LOCK keys simultaneously.

2. Try dragging and dropping a selection and clicking or double-clicking both the left and right mouse buttons by using your keyboard's numeric keypad. (For details, see the section titled "MouseKeys.")

Test Support for MS-DOS–Based Applications

1. Start an MS-DOS–based application.

2. Try StickyKeys or MouseKeys. All of the accessibility features are available when you are running an MS-DOS–based application. They are available any time you need them, whatever you may be doing.

Features for Users Who Are Hearing-Impaired

Windows 95 offers several enhancements designed to make the system more accessible and easier to use for people who are hearing-impaired.

ShowSounds

Some applications present information audibly, as waveform files containing digitized speech or through audible cues that each convey a different meaning. These cues might be unusable by a person who is deaf or hard of hearing, or someone who works in a very noisy environment, or someone who turns off the computer's speakers in a very quiet work environment. In Windows 95, users can set a global flag to let applications know they want visible feedback, in effect asking the applications to be "close captioned."

SoundSentry

SoundSentry tells Windows to send a visual cue, such as a blinking title bar or screen flash, whenever the system beeps. Turning on this feature allows users to see messages that they might not have heard.

Support for Alternative Input Devices

Windows 95 provides support for the use of alternative input devices, such as head-pointers or eye-gaze systems, with which users can control the computer.

SerialKeys

The SerialKeys feature, in conjunction with a communications aid interface device, allows users to control the computer using an alternative input device. These devices can send coded command strings through the computer's serial port to specify keystrokes and mouse events that are then treated like normal keyboard and mouse input.

Support for Multiple Pointing Devices

The Plug and Play architecture in Windows 95 inherently supports multiple cooperating pointing devices. This capability allows seamless addition of alternative pointing devices, without requiring users to replace or disable the normal mouse.

Features for Software Developers

Windows 95 contains many built-in features designed to make the computer more accessible to people with disabilities. To make a computer running Windows 95 truly accessible, application developers must provide access to their applications' features, taking care to avoid incompatibilities with accessibility aids.

Accessibility Guidelines for Software Developers

As part of the *Windows 95 Software Development Kit* and the *Windows 95 User Interface Design Guidelines*, Microsoft provides developers with documentation that not only outlines these important concepts, but also provides technical and design tips to help ISVs produce more accessible applications. Most of these tips involve very little additional work for developers, as long as they are aware of the issues and incorporate accessibility into application designs at an early stage. By providing this information to application developers, Microsoft hopes to increase the general level of accessibility of all software running on the Windows platform.

Methods for Simulating Input

Windows 95 now allows developers of voice-input systems and other alternative input systems to easily simulate keyboard and mouse input using fully documented and supported procedures.

Chaining Display Drivers

Some accessibility aids, such as screen review packages for low-vision users, need to detect information as it is drawn to the screen. Windows 95 supports chaining display drivers that allow these utilities to intercept text and graphics being drawn, without interfering with the normal computer operation.

New Common Controls

Many accessibility aids have difficulty working with applications that implement nonstandard controls. Windows 95 introduces a whole new set of controls for mainstream software developers, and these standardized implementations are designed to cooperate with accessibility aids.

CHAPTER 20

Applications and Utilities

Windows 95 includes a set of applications and utilities designed to take advantage of new areas of the operating system, including 32-bit preemptive multitasking, long filenames, new visual elements and common dialog boxes, OLE, TAPI, MAPI, and other Win32 API features. This chapter describes some of the new applications and utilities.

The applications and utilities listed in this chapter have been either completely redesigned or designed from scratch so that novice users' first experiences of using the applications will be good ones. Experienced users will find the applications both powerful and flexible, but the applications were not necessarily designed to satisfy all the needs of advanced users. Many of the applications and utilities will help to inspire third-party developers to further utilize technology included in Windows 95.

The Quick Viewers

The Quick Viewers included in Windows 95 provide a new capability, allowing users to view files in most popular file formats without opening the application used to create the files. The Quick Viewers are really convenient for looking at attachments sent in e-mail messages or browsing files on a network. Figure 118 on the following page shows the right-click context menu with the Quick View command chosen and the resulting Quick View window showing the contents of a Microsoft Excel worksheet.

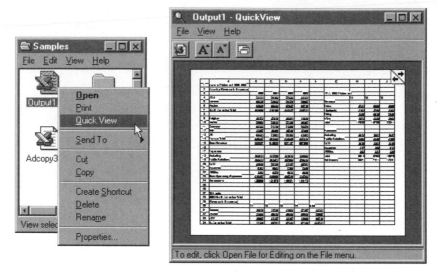

Figure 118. A Microsoft Excel worksheet in a Quick View window

The Quick Viewers also support the ability to drag and drop a file from the Windows Explorer or desktop into an open Quick View window. If the extension of a file is not associated with a known application, the Open With dialog box is displayed so that users can specify whether they want to view the file in a Quick View window or open the selected file with an application.

Users can choose Options from the Window Explorer's View menu and specify the default Open command for any file type to be quick-viewed, which is convenient for users who often view a particular file type but do not have the corresponding application on their hard disk. Users can also assign extensions to applications to view files with those extensions in a specific file format.

Users can customize the Quick View window in the following ways:

- They can view files in standard view or page view, in both landscape and portrait modes.
- They can view files in different fonts and font sizes.
- They can rotate bitmap files so that documents such as fax messages are oriented correctly.

Jointly developed by Microsoft and Systems Compatibility Corporation (SCC), the Quick Viewers are available for most popular file formats. SCC offers additional viewers and features in their Outside In for Windows product. In addition, ISVs are encouraged to include Quick Viewers for the file formats they support in future releases of their software. Windows 95 provides Quick Viewers that support the following file formats:

.ASC	ASCII files
.BMP	Windows Bitmap Graphics files
.CDR	Corel Draw files
.DOC	Files created by Word for MS-DOS versions 5 and 6; Word for Windows versions 2 and 6; and WordPerfect versions 4.2, 5, 6, and 6.1
.DRW	Micrographix Draw files
.EPS	Encapsulated PostScript files
.GIF	CompuServe GIF files
.INF	Setup files
.INI	Configuration files
.MOD	Files created by Multiplan versions 3, 4.0, and 4.1
.PPT	PowerPoint version 4 files
.PRE	Freelance for Windows files
.RLE	Bitmap files (RunLengthEncoding)
.RTF	Rich Text Format files
.SAM	AMI and AMI PRO files
.TIF	TIFF files
.TXT	Text files
.WB1	Quattro Pro for Windows spreadsheet files
.WK1	Lotus 1-2-3 Release 1 and 2 files
.WK3	Lotus 1-2-3 Release 3 files
.WK4	Lotus 1-2-3 Release 4 spreadsheet and chart files
.WKS	Lotus 1-2-3 files and Microsoft Works version 3 files
.WMF	Windows Metafiles
.WPD	WordPerfect demo files
.WPS	Works Word Processing files
.WQ1	Quattro Pro for MS-DOS files
.WQ2	Quattro Pro version 5 for MS-DOS files
.WRI	Windows 3.x Write files
.XLC	Excel 4 chart files
.XLS	Excel 4 spreadsheet and Excel 5 spreadsheet and chart files

WordPad

WordPad is a 32-bit editor that replaces the Write and Notepad applications provided with Windows 3.1. Although it is not a full-blown word processor, WordPad makes creating simple documents and memos easy for users. The WordPad window is shown in Figure 119.

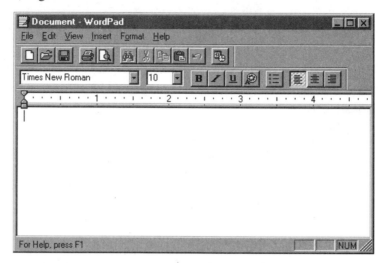

Figure 119. The WordPad application

WordPad was written from scratch as a good example of the user interface style that applications written for Windows 95 should use. It utilizes the new common dialog boxes for opening, saving, and printing files, which makes it easy for users to use long filenames.

As an OLE server and client application, WordPad provides easy integration with other OLE-enabled applications provided with Windows 95 or available from third parties. WordPad uses the same native file format as Microsoft Word for Windows version 6, but also supports the reading and writing of rich text files (RTF) and text files, and the reading of Write (.WRI) files.

WordPad is MAPI-enabled, so it is easily integrated with Microsoft Exchange to allow users to send files over electronic mail, or by fax, directly from within WordPad.

Paint

Like WordPad, Paint is a new 32-bit Windows 95 application. It replaces its Windows 3.1 counterpart, Paintbrush. The Paint window is shown in Figure 120.

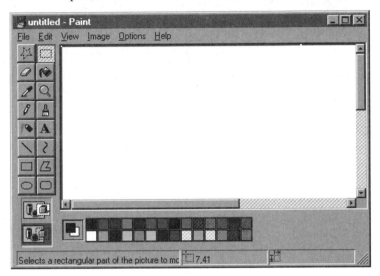

Figure 120. The Paint application

Paint is an OLE server, allowing the creation of OLE object information that can be embedded or linked into other documents. Paint is also MAPI-enabled, so it is easily integrated with Microsoft Exchange for sending images as e-mail messages or as fax messages.

Using the combination of Paint and WordPad allows novice users to see the interaction of good 32-bit applications written for Windows 95.

Backup

Backup is a new 32-bit application for Windows 95 that makes it easy for users to back up information from their computer to another storage medium, such as floppy disk or tape. As shown in Figure 121, the Backup user interface takes full advantage of the Windows 95 user interface. To make understanding and using the Backup user interface easy, it uses standard controls, such as the tree and list view controls, so that both novices and users familiar with these controls in the Windows Explorer can perform backups quickly and simply.

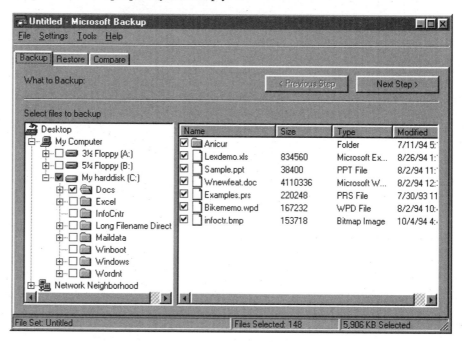

Figure 121. The Backup application, which can back up the local hard disk, floppy disks, or network drives

Backup includes the ability to drag and drop file sets and backup sets onto a link to the Backup application, which can be placed on the desktop to make starting a backup operation a simple "click and drag" procedure. The Backup application can also be run in the usual way, or users can select the Backup option on the Tools tab of the Disk property sheet.

Backup is extremely flexible and allows backing up, restoring, and comparing of files on the following:

- Hard disks

- Network drives

- Floppy disks

- QIC 40, 80, 3010, and 3020 tape drives connected to the primary floppy disk controller

- QIC 40, 80, and 3010 tape drives, manufactured by Colorado Memory Systems, which connect to the parallel port

Backup also supports compression of files to maximize storage space. The on-tape format is the industry-standard QIC-113 format. The Backup application can read tapes created with other backup applications that use this standard, both with and without file compression.

Other standard options include differential and full backup, redirection of files on restore, and always erasing floppies or tapes before a backup. Backup includes a full-system backup/restore feature that allows users to simply select the full-system backup file set (which is automatically created when Backup is first launched), perform the backup, and then restore files later. This feature works even if users replace their hard disk with a completely different type of hard disk. The Backup application does all the necessary merging of Registry settings and manages the replacement of files in use so that novice users don't have to understand all of the technical details associated with this fairly complex operation.

HyperTerminal

HyperTerminal is a new 32-bit communications application included with Windows 95 that provides asynchronous connectivity to host computers, such as online services, or other PCs. HyperTerminal replaces the Terminal application included in Windows 3.1, and is a completely different application, providing advanced features and functionality not supported by Terminal.

HyperTerminal represents a good communications application written for Windows 95 and is completely integrated with, and takes full advantage of, the new Telephony API and UniModem subsystems built into Windows 95. HyperTerminal uses the new 32-bit communications subsystem and provides error-free data transfer by leveraging the new architecture components in Windows 95, including multithreading and preemptive multitasking. The HyperTerminal user interface reflects the document-centric nature of Windows 95 and focuses on the communications connection that users make, rather than the main application. As with the other applications and utilities included with Windows 95, HyperTerminal uses the new common dialog boxes and supports the use of long filenames.

HyperTerminal makes connecting to remote computers easy for both novices and experienced PC users. Through the use of innovative autosensing technology, complex communications settings, such as baud rate, number of stop bits, parity, and terminal emulation type, are automatically determined by HyperTerminal so that users don't have to deal with these settings at all. The result is a significant usability improvement.

HyperTerminal provides mainstream communications program functionality, including terminal emulation and binary file transfer capability. Terminal emulation support includes emulation of ANSI, TTY, VT52, and VT100 terminals. Binary file transfer protocol support includes Xmodem, Ymodem, Zmodem, and Kermit file transfer protocols. Figure 122 shows HyperTerminal in action.

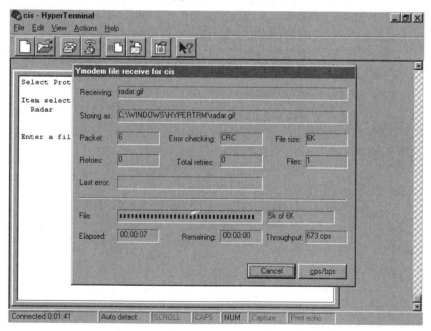

Figure 122. The HyperTerminal application, which makes connecting to host computer services and performing error-free downloading of files easy

The New MS-DOS–Based Editor

Windows 95 includes a new version of the MS-DOS–based text editor, EDIT.COM. Enhancements have been made to the editor provided with MS-DOS to make it easier for users to work with text files in case the Windows 95 shell cannot for some reason be loaded.

Users of MS-DOS will find the Edit program very familiar while at the same time benefiting from several dramatic improvements. Edit is smaller and faster than its MS-DOS predecessor. It allows users to open up to nine files at the same time, split the screen between two files, and easily copy and paste information between files. Users can also open files as large as 4 MB in size. Edit supports long filenames and allows users to open filenames and navigate through their directory structure just as they can in the Windows 95 UI. Figure 123 shows the new Edit window.

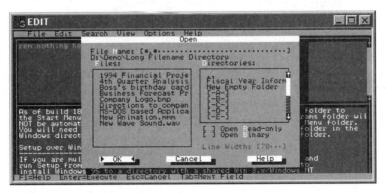

Figure 123. The MS-DOS Editor, which supports a split screen and the use of long filenames

Disk Utilities

Windows 95 includes a collection of disk utilities designed to keep the system error-free and performing optimally. In addition to the DriveSpace disk compression tool discussed in the Chapter 4, "Basic System Architecture," Windows 95 provides a disk optimizer tool and a disk checking and repair tool.

The Disk Defragmenter

The Disk Defragmenter optimizes a hard disk by rearranging information so that it is better organized. Rearranging information helps minimize the hard disk area Windows 95 needs to search to load requested information. Unlike the disk defragmenter utility provided with MS-DOS, the Disk Defragmenter is a graphical application that runs under Windows 95.

For convenience, users can defragment their disks in the background while other applications are running on their system. Additionally, users can see details of the defragmentation process and watch its progress, or they can display a minimal status, as shown in Figure 124, that simply shows the status of the defragmentation process.

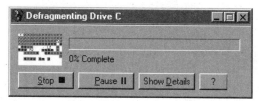

Figure 124. The Disk Defragmenter utility, which helps users optimize the performance of their disks

ScanDisk

The ScanDisk disk checking and repair tool included with Windows 95 is designed to help users check the integrity of their disks and to remedy problems that are detected. Unlike the Scandisk utility provided with MS-DOS, ScanDisk is a graphical application that runs under Windows 95. As shown in Figure 125, users can run either a standard scan, in which ScanDisk checks the files on the user's system for errors only, or a thorough scan, in which ScanDisk checks the files for errors and performs a disk surface test to check for additional errors.

As with the Disk Defragmenter, users do not need to exit any running applications to run ScanDisk. As a result, checking the integrity of a disk system and thereby preventing possible catastrophic errors in the future is easy and convenient for users.

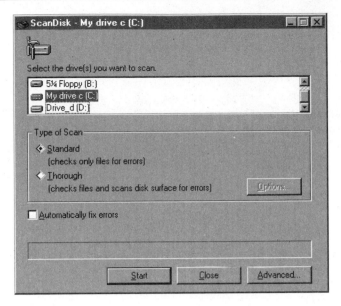

Figure 125. The ScanDisk utility, which allows users to perform a standard or thorough scan to check the integrity of their files and disk

C H A P T E R   2 1

What Makes a Great Windows 95 Application?

Although MS-DOS–based and Win16–based applications can run under Windows 95, users benefit from the additional functionality supported by Win32–based applications. This functionality includes the preemptive multitasking architecture of Windows 95 and the increased robustness and protection for running applications. In addition, the following six key contributors make a Windows 95 application great from the user's perspective:

- The Win32 Application Programming Interface (API)
- OLE functionality
- The *Windows 95 User Interface Design Guidelines*
- Support for handling Plug and Play events
- Support for quickly identifying files
- Adherence to common setup guidelines for consistent software installation

The next section discusses why these components make these applications great for users.

The Win32 Application Programming Interface

Microsoft supports the use of the Win32 API on three operating system platforms: Windows NT, Windows 95, and Windows 3.1 with Win32s. Each operating system supports a common set of Win32 APIs, allowing applications developed using a single API set to run on multiple platforms. As a result, application developers and corporate developers can learn a single API set and leverage development resources to support a broad base of hardware systems. Users benefit from being able to run the same application on multiple platforms and from increased system reliability under Windows 95 because of the improved robustness and memory protection available to 32-bit applications.

Windows 95 delivers a robust and powerful 32-bit platform on which 32-bit applications are preemptively multitasked, run in private address spaces, and can spawn multiple threads of execution. Preemptive multitasking ensures excellent system responsiveness, allowing users to run multiple applications simultaneously and integrate personal productivity and business-critical applications in a smooth manner. (This model is similar to the one used by Windows NT.) The use of a private address space for each Win32–based application ensures that multiple applications can run simultaneously without interfering with each other or the operating system itself. Windows 95 is able to provide smooth, preemptive multitasking and protected virtual memory because it is based on a redesigned 32-bit protected-mode kernel and a 32-bit protected-mode driver model.

Running 32-bit applications under Windows 95 provides the following improvements from a user perspective:

- Running multiple applications is smoother because of the preemptive multitasking architecture.

- Overall system performance is improved because of 32-bit operating system components.

- Robustness and system reliability are improved because of 32-bit memory protection and separate message queues.

- Applications have new functionality because of Win32 and other operating system services.

- File manipulation is easier because of long filename support.

OLE Functionality

Users are buying and using more applications per PC than ever before. In 1992, InfoCorp reported that the average number of applications purchased per desktop running the Windows operating system increased to more than seven programs, up from an average of 3.4 programs for customers using the MS-DOS operating system in 1986. Users who learn one Windows–based application find learning a second or third application easy, and research shows that users cite the ability to move and share information among applications as the most important reason for using Windows–based applications.

People are not only acquiring more applications, but they are also using them together, accessing several applications in order to create compound documents. The mechanism that allows applications to interoperate effectively, and thereby enables users to work more productively, is OLE. Users of OLE applications can create and manage compound documents that seamlessly incorporate data, called *objects*, of different formats. Sound clips, spreadsheets, text, and bitmaps are some examples of objects commonly found in compound documents. Each object is created and maintained by its server application, but through the use of OLE, the services of the different server applications are integrated. Users of OLE-enabled applications feel as if they are working with a single application that has all the functionality of each of the server applications. They don't need to be concerned with managing and switching between the various server applications. Instead, they can focus on the compound document they are creating and the task they are performing using OLE-based features.

The Features of OLE

With OLE, Windows 95 increases the degree of application integration available to any application that takes advantage of the services. Tight integration gives users tangible benefits, allowing them to share data and functionality across applications and combine the data as they please. Because OLE is based on an open industry standard, users can extend their applications with additional third-party products, further expanding their choices and flexibility.

OLE provides the following features to allow users to easily combine information from multiple applications:

- **Cross-application drag and drop.** Users can drag and drop graphs, tables, and pictures directly onto slides, worksheets, and documents to mix text, data, and graphics into compound documents.

- **Visual editing.** Users can double-click an object to directly edit it while remaining in the original document.

Cross-Application Drag and Drop

Drag and drop is a new, intuitive method of moving data between applications. Until recently, this method was available only for moving information *within* applications. The most widely used way of transferring data *between* applications has been to use the Clipboard, but this method involves multiple steps—using the Copy or Cut command, moving to the destination application, and using the Paste command. With the current release of OLE, drag and drop now works between applications. Users simply select an object in one application, drag it to its destination in another application, and drop it into place. Objects can also be dragged over the desktop to system resource icons, such as printers and mailboxes, making the sending, printing, and sharing of files faster and easier.

Visual Editing

Visual editing makes revising a compound document faster, easier, and more intuitive. For example, Figure 126 on the following page shows a Microsoft Excel worksheet embedded as an object in a Word document. When the user double-clicks the worksheet object, the menus and toolbars necessary to interact with the Microsoft Excel worksheet temporarily replace Word's menus and controls. Microsoft Excel, the application that is needed to edit or modify the worksheet, partially "takes over" the

Word document window, as shown in Figure 127. The user can then interact with the Microsoft Excel worksheet without switching to a different application or window. (Unlike the first release of the OLE technology, the current release of OLE does not launch users into a separate Excel window to work on the spreadsheet data.) When users move on to work on the word processing portion of the document, the focus returns to Word, and the original Word menus and controls are restored.

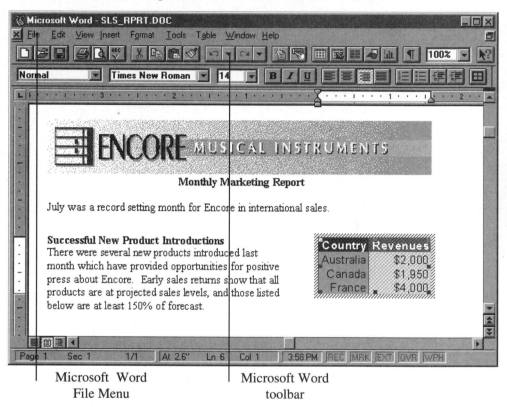

Microsoft Word   Microsoft Word
File Menu   toolbar

Figure 126. A Microsoft Excel worksheet object embedded in a Word document

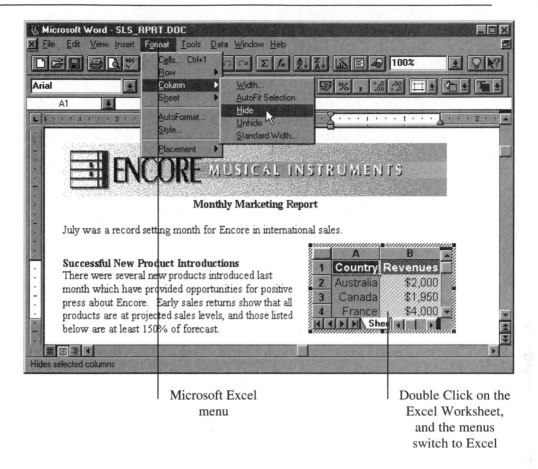

          Microsoft Excel   Double Click on the
          menu   Excel Worksheet,
          and the menus
          switch to Excel

Figure 127. Activating the Excel worksheet object, which displays the Excel menus in the Word environment

The advantage of visual editing is even greater when compound documents include large numbers of objects created by different applications, such as Microsoft Excel worksheets and charts, PowerPoint graphics, sound, video clips, and so on. Instead of switching back and forth among different windows to update the objects, users can work in a single document window, which provides one location for editing and otherwise interacting with the data. Visual editing thus offers users a more document-centric approach, putting the primary focus on the creation and manipulation of information rather than on the operation of the environment and its applications.

The *Windows 95 User Interface Design Guidelines*

As with previous versions of Windows, one of the reasons that Windows 95 applications are easy to learn is the fact that they look and act alike. Microsoft has taken great steps to improve the basic common controls that all applications can share. These controls, which have evolved based on user feedback and extensive usability testing, are among the features described in the *Windows 95 User Interface Design Guidelines.*

Applications that use the basic controls provide their users with common, improved features, such as being able to create new folders in the Save As dialog box without having to switch to the Windows Explorer or File Manager (see Figure 128).

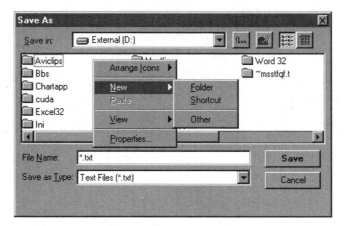

Figure 128. The Save As common dialog box

The new Printer property sheet, shown in Figure 129, illustrates some of the controls that make accessing features easier for users. At the top of the property sheet are tabs on which different categories of properties are arranged. Clicking any tab displays that category of properties. Figure 129 also shows an example of a spin control, which increments and decrements the number in the Copies box.

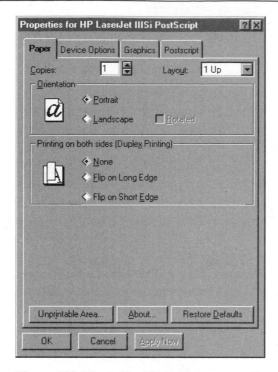

Figure 129. The tabbed Printer property sheet

The new Open common dialog box, shown in Figure 130, allows users to see long filenames and navigate around the entire PC or network to look for the files they want to open. As shown in Figure 131 on the following page, this dialog box uses tree lists to display the hierarchy of the PC's hard disk and the network to which the PC is connected.

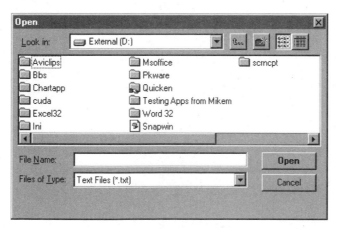

Figure 130. The Open common dialog box

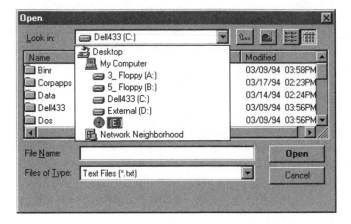

Figure 131. The tree list in the Open common dialog box

Figure 132 shows another tree list control that makes viewing and accessing hierarchical information easier. This tree list is found in the property sheet for the Device Manager in the Control Panel's System tool. As users expand and collapse the tree, they can see information relevant to their chosen topic.

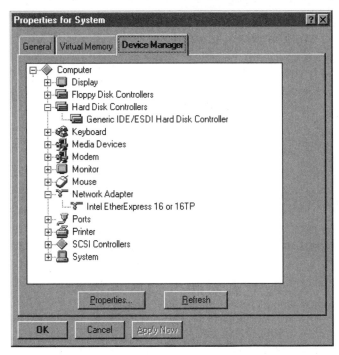

Figure 132. The tree list in the Device Manager property sheet

Applications no longer have to include their own custom slider controls. Figure 133 shows the Mouse property sheet, where the pointer's Size option is controlled by the slider control included in Windows 95.

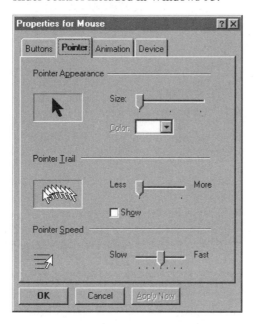

Figure 133. A slider control in the Mouse property sheet

Many new common controls are included in Windows 95, such as toolbars, the status bar, column headings, tabs, sliders, progress indicators, rich-text controls, list views, and tree views. Great Windows 95 applications will use these controls to make user access to features consistent across applications, thereby making the entire system much easier to use.

Support for Handling Plug and Play Events

Applications that provide Plug and Play event awareness help users by seamlessly adapting to hardware configuration changes. Users reap the following two key benefits:

- **Applications automatically recognize and respond to hardware changes.**
  Consider this scenario: A user has a mobile PC installed in a docking station and is using an external monitor running at a resolution of 1024x768. When the user undocks the PC, the desktop Control Panel recognizes this action and switches the resolution for the mobile PC to 640x480. When this change occurs, Plug and Play–aware applications resize their windows and toolbars accordingly. The user doesn't have to do a thing; it's all automatic.

Here's another scenario: A user is working on a document on a mobile PC. Battery power is running low. The computer sends a message to all the active Plug and Play–aware applications, telling them to save the user's data and shut down because the power is going off in a few minutes.

- **Applications warn users about open network files when hot-undocking their computers.** Consider this scenario: A user has a PCMCIA network card installed in a laptop computer. Before leaving the office, the user switches PCMCIA cards and installs a modem for dial-up network access. With Plug and Play, the user doesn't have to fuss with software configuration. Windows 95 simply knows that the network has been replaced by a modem and passes this information on to a Plug and Play–aware e-mail application. The application then knows that it now needs to use the modem to make connections.

Applications that are Plug and Play–aware provide seamless adaptation to changes in the hardware configuration so that users can focus on their work, not their configuration.

Support for Quickly Identifying Files

As discussed in Chapter 3, "The Windows 95 User Interface," the UI for Windows 95 is much improved. But the UI itself is only part of the benefit for users. Applications that take advantage of the new UI support can offer their users long filenames and direct file viewing. Long filename support means that document names are no longer limited to eight characters; they can now have up to 255 characters, as shown in Figure 134. Instead of 23ISM_JB.DOC, users can name a file *Status report July 23 regarding the ISM project for my boss Jim Bernstein*—a title that clearly identifies the document's contents. Applications that support the Quick View capabilities of Windows 95 provide users with a quick and easy way to identify files by viewing them directly from the UI without launching the applications that created them.

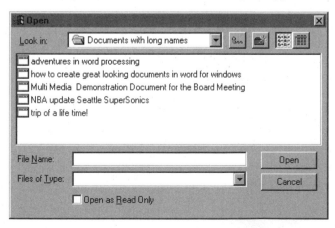

Figure 134. Sample long filenames supported by Windows 95

Consistent Setup Guidelines

In the past, users have generally had an easy way to set up new applications, but removing applications from their hard disks was not so simple. Most Windows 3.1 users eventually ended up with hard disks clogged with files that were never used because they belonged to a deleted application. Because many applications use the same library files, Windows 3.1 users quite commonly had several copies of a file stored in different places on their hard disks—an inefficient use of precious disk space. Another common problem with Windows 3.1 was that applications put files not only in their own directories, but also in the Windows directory, in the System directory, and even in the root directory, creating a nightmare for users who were trying to keep track of what was where.

The *Windows 95 Software Development Kit* offers some guidelines to developers for consistent installation locations and uninstall functionality in their applications. Common libraries can be shared by applications, thereby reducing the amount of disk space consumed by duplication. The guidelines also set standards for where developers should put files on the hard disk so as to provide an easy, powerful, and compatible structure for users. Setup programs that follow the guidelines all operate similarly, use consistent naming conventions, and offer the same setup options, thereby reducing the learning curve for users, improving manageability and support for corporations, and increasing the efficiency of remote administration of installed software.

CHAPTER 22

The Windows 95 Logo Program

Much of the industry is working very hard and very creatively to develop software, hardware, and peripheral products that are not just compatible with Windows 95 but are designed specifically for it. The Windows 95 logo program is intended to help users easily identify these great new products, which exploit the rich capabilities of the operating system. Examples of these new capabilities are Plug and Play and support for 32-bit applications.

Products developed for Windows 95 will bear the Designed for Microsoft Windows 95 logo shown in Figure 135. This logo makes it easy for customers to choose products that were designed to deliver the benefits and functionality of Windows 95. Customers can mix and match hardware and software products identified by the Designed for Microsoft Windows 95 logo and be assured that the products are fully compatible with Windows 95. They no longer have to figure out which technical details make one product more compelling than another or worry about compatibility. To make computing easier and more powerful, they can simply look for the Designed for Microsoft Windows 95 logo to choose a product built to work synergistically with Windows 95.

Figure 135. The Designed for Microsoft Windows 95 logo

The Availability of Windows 95–Based Products

Licensing of the Designed for Microsoft Windows 95 logo will begin in early 1995. Products supporting the new logo are expected to appear on the market within two to three months of the release of Windows 95, although some may appear sooner. The Windows 95 logo program is completely optional for vendors, and products without the logo will continue to be sold as they always have. Products that meet current Windows logo licensing requirements but do not meet the requirements for the Windows 95 logo can continue to use phrases such as *For Windows* or *Windows Compatible* to indicate that the product runs on the Windows platform.

Licensing Criteria for the Windows 95 Logo

To license the Designed for Microsoft Windows 95 logo for use with their products and to be a part of the logo program, vendors of hardware and software products must meet specific criteria. Customers can feel comfortable that products that use the logo offer the following capabilities:

- **Hardware products.** For hardware products, including PC systems and subsystems, the baseline criteria include supporting Plug and Play in Windows 95. Historically, installing new hardware devices has required substantial technical expertise to configure and load hardware and software. Plug and Play provides a mechanism for configuration to happen automatically. Computers, add-on boards, and peripheral devices supporting Plug and Play bring true ease of use to users of Windows 95. The logo is an easy-to-remember way to identify which products support the Plug and Play benefits of the Windows 95 operating system.

- **Software products**. Software products must be 32-bit Windows–based applications, providing better multitasking and application robustness. Applications with the Designed for Microsoft Windows 95 logo will also feature the enhanced Windows 95 UI and provide support for long filenames, automated installation, and uninstall capabilities. Many applications, especially typical productivity applications, will also support OLE component-software technology, providing better cross-application interoperability and efficiency through features such as OLE drag and drop.

For More Information

Additional information about the Windows 95 logo program, including commonly asked questions and answers and a sample of the logo, is available through the Microsoft Developer Solutions Phone-Fax Service at (206) 635-2222.

CHAPTER 23

Questions and Answers About Windows 95

Microsoft is continually enhancing the Microsoft Windows product line to deliver easy-to-use yet powerful operating systems that exploit the latest advancements in microcomputer hardware technology. Windows 95 has sparked a great deal of interest and speculation. It is the official name of the Windows "Chicago" project, which is the technology-development effort that will deliver the next major release of Windows for the mainstream desktop and portable PC. The purpose of this chapter is to answer the questions customers have asked most often about Windows 95.

Note: The list of questions and answers about Windows 95 is updated on an as-needed basis. To obtain the latest list, connect to an online information service and access the Microsoft WinNews information forum. See the end of this chapter for more information about where to find Microsoft WinNews information.

General Questions

- **What is Windows 95? Why change the name from Windows "Chicago" to Windows 95?**

  Windows 95 is the official product name of the next major version of Microsoft Windows. Windows "Chicago" was the code name for the development project to produce the successor to Windows 3.*x* and Windows for Workgroups 3.*x*, and this name was used until the official product name was decided upon and announced.

- **What are the key benefits and features of Windows 95? What features will Windows 95 not have?**

  Windows 95 presents a major step forward in functionality on desktop and portable PC platforms by providing a system that is easier, faster, and more powerful to use, while maintaining compatibility with the MS-DOS–based and Windows–based applications and hardware peripherals that customers have invested in.

Ease of use is improved through the Plug and Play architecture and a more intuitive user interface. With the introduction of Windows 95, the Microsoft Windows engine is being revamped to improve performance and provide smooth multitasking. Windows 95 is a complete, integrated 32-bit operating system that does not require MS-DOS, although it can run MS-DOS–based applications. It implements the Win32 API and supports preemptive multitasking and multiple threads of execution for 32-bit applications. Windows 95 provides reliable and open networking support and high performance, as well as messaging and dial-up network access services.

As the successor to Windows 3.*x* and Windows for Workgroups 3.*x*, Windows 95 meets a number of key requirements. First, Windows 95 is compatible with applications and device drivers for both MS-DOS and Windows. When a customer upgrades to Windows 95, performance will meet or exceed that of Windows 3.1, as long as the customer has an 80386DX or higher system with at least 4 MB of RAM. For systems with more than 4 MB of RAM, performance will exceed that of Windows 3.1. The transition to the new user interface is easy for current users of Windows, and companies that want to make the transition at their own pace can run Program Manager and File Manager during the transition period.

Windows 95 is not processor independent, nor does it support symmetric multiprocessing systems. Windows 95 is also not designed to meet C/2-level security specifications. If these features are important to a customer, Windows NT is the operating system to use.

- **How does Windows 95 compare with the Windows 3.1, Windows for Workgroups, and Windows NT operating systems?**

Windows 95 is designed to make mainstream PCs easier to use and more powerful. It is the right choice for customers who want to run business and personal-productivity applications and for use on home computers. Windows NT is designed for the most demanding business uses, such as development or advanced engineering and financial applications. Windows NT is the right choice for customers who need the highest level of protection for their data and applications. Windows NT is also the right choice for those who need scaleability to multiprocessing and RISC systems.

- **Why is Microsoft changing the numbering system for Windows?**

Until recently, version numbers helped inform customers that new versions were available and gave some sense of the significance of the improvements. However, Microsoft's customer base has broadened to include less technical users, and research indicates that even the most sophisticated customers find the current version-numbering scheme confusing. For example, Windows 3.1 provided far more new capabilities than a typical 0.1 release, and Windows for Workgroups 3.11 involved dramatically more changes than the usual .01 release. The new numbering system is designed to make it easier for customers to understand which version of the software they are using, so that they know when to consider upgrading to the next release.

- **Does this numbering system mean Microsoft will release a new version of Windows every year?**

  No. The version numbers will help give users a sense for the "model year" of their software in the same way that customers have a sense of the model year of their cars.

Upgrading to Windows 95

- **Why will individual customers want to upgrade to Windows 95?**

  The sheer quantity of the improvements included in Windows 95 represents a great value for customers. Topping the list of requested improvements was an easier way to work with the PC. As a result, a new user interface was designed for Windows 95 that helps make computing easier for both novice users and experienced users who want greater efficiency and flexibility.

  Long filename support is one of many usability improvements in Windows 95. Improving ease-of-use goes beyond fixing problems with Windows; it encompasses the hardware, applications, and network as well. Plug and Play makes hardware setup automatic, and built-in networking makes starting a new network or connecting to an existing network server, such as Novell NetWare and Windows NT Server, equally easy.

  Customers also want greater efficiency and power, so that they can get their work done faster. They want to run more than one application or task at the same time. They want to use their computers to access files, electronic mail, and public-information networks from any location—at work, at home, or on the road. They also want better multimedia, whether for playing MS-DOS–based games or for teleconferencing using TV-quality video resolution. The following are highlights of capabilities in Windows 95 that address these requests:

  - **Preemptive multitasking.** Windows 95 can perform multitasking smoothly and responsively for 32-bit applications.

  - **Scaleable performance.** The performance improvements that Windows 95 provides over Windows 3.1 increase as the amount of RAM increases because of the high-performance 32-bit architecture of Windows 95.

  - **Support for 32-bit applications.** Windows 95 supports the Win32 API, which means customers can look forward to a new generation of easier, faster, and more reliable applications.

  - **Increased reliability.** Windows 95 increases protection for running existing MS-DOS–based and Windows–based applications and provides the highest level of protection for new 32-bit applications for Windows. As a result, an errant application is much less likely to disable other applications or the system.

- **Faster printing.** Windows 95 features a new 32-bit printing subsystem that reduces the time spent waiting for print jobs to finish and improves system response when jobs are printing in the background.

- **Better multimedia support.** Just as Windows 3.1 made sound a part of the system, Windows 95 now includes support for video playback. The video system and CD-ROM file system provide high-quality output for multimedia applications.

- **More memory for MS-DOS–based applications.** The use of protected-mode drivers in Windows 95 means that customers have more than 600 KB of free conventional memory in each MS-DOS session, even when they are connected to a network and using a CD-ROM drive and a mouse.

- **The Microsoft Exchange client.** Windows 95 includes the Microsoft Exchange client, a universal client that retrieves messages into one universal inbox from many kinds of systems, including Microsoft Mail, faxes, CompuServe Mail, Internet mail, and so on.

■ Why will companies want to upgrade to Windows 95?

Companies will want to move to Windows 95 because it helps reduce their PC support burden, helps increase their control over the desktop, and helps increase the productivity of their users. Numerous studies have shown that as much as 80 percent of the cost of owning a PC over the long term are the costs associated with support, including installing, configuring, and managing the PC, and training the PC user. The Gartner Group has concluded that Windows 95 will likely lead to significantly lower total cost of ownership compared with MS-DOS and Windows 3.1 (*PC Research Note*, "Personal Computing Costs: A Windows 95 Model," Aug. 15, 1994). The Gartner Group's model estimates that the support savings will be $1,180 per user per year. Over the five-year ownership period assumed in the analysis, the total savings is nearly $6,000 per user.

Windows 95 includes numerous features designed to reduce the costs of supporting PCs and PC users, including the following:

- **A simpler, more intuitive user interface that can reduce training requirements for novice users and enable experienced users to learn new tasks with less help.** The Start button, the Taskbar, the Windows Explorer, Wizards, a new Help system, and other features make Windows 95 easy to learn and make functionality easy to discover.

- **Built-in networking support that is easier to set up and configure and is faster and more reliable to use.** Whether a company is running NetWare or Microsoft networks, whether it is using TCP/IP, IPX/SPX, or NetBEUI protocols, and whether it is using NDIS or ODI drivers, Windows 95 has integrated support for the network client, protocol, and driver. Additional networks can be added easily. Windows 95 includes 32-bit clients for both NetWare and Microsoft networks that are fast and reliable, and require no conventional memory. A Windows 95–based PC can have multiple network clients and transport protocols running simultaneously for connecting heterogeneous systems.

- **Plug and Play device installation to automate the difficult process of adding devices to a PC.** Windows 95 supports the industry-standard Plug and Play specification to enable automatic installation and configuration of add-on devices. If users install Windows 95 on their existing system and later purchase a Plug and Play add-on device, they can install that device by plugging it in and turning on the system. Plug and Play takes care of the messy details of installation and configuration. Plug and Play also enables innovative new system designs that support such capabilities as hot-docking and undocking.

- **System-management capabilities that simplify remote administration and enable new system-management applications.** Windows 95 features an infrastructure for the management of PCs that leverages a hierarchical database of system-configuration information called the Registry. The Registry holds all pertinent information about the system—hardware, software, user preferences and privileges, and so on—and provides access to its contents over the network through a variety of industry-standard interfaces, including SNMP, DMI, and Remote Procedure Call. This infrastructure simplifies many administrative tasks by including tools for remote configuration of the desktop. It will lead to a new generation of sophisticated system-management applications for managing the desktop, inventorying hardware and software, and supporting software distribution.

- **System Policies that enable an administrator to control a desktop configuration**. Windows 95 supports System Policies, which are settings an administrator configures to define the operations users can access on their PCs. System Policies can also be used to define the appearance of the desktop. For example, the administrator can set a policy to disable the MS-DOS prompt and the Run commands so that users can't arbitrarily run applications.

- **Support for roving users.** Windows 95 can present different configurations, depending on who has logged onto the PC. This option allows users to log onto different machines on the network and see their personal configurations.

- **Built-in agents for automating backup of desktop systems.** Windows 95 includes the software required to back up a desktop system using a server-based backup system. The backup agents included with Windows 95 work with the most popular server-based systems.

In addition to reducing support costs and increasing control over the desktop, Windows 95 helps users to be more productive. In usability tests, users are able to perform a series of typical tasks using Windows 95 in 25 percent less time than they can perform the same tasks using Windows 3.1. These tests did not take into account many of the tasks that users would like to perform but that are too difficult under Windows 3.1, such as installing a CD-ROM drive and sound card, or retrieving a file from their desktop system using a portable computer at home or while traveling on business. By making these capabilities much more accessible, Windows 95 enable users to be even more productive using PCs.

- **Won't it be expensive to put Windows 95 on all the PCs in a company?**

  Windows 95 has been designed to provide a safe and smooth transition to the new operating system. Windows 95 works on existing hardware and software through support for MS-DOS–based and Windows–based device drivers and applications. On mainstream systems—those with at least an 80386DX processor and 4 MB of RAM— Windows 95 performs as fast or faster than Windows 3.1. The installation program detects and maintains current system settings and enables automated installation through a variety of techniques, including logon scripts and software-distribution applications. Thorough usability testing conducted with Windows 3.1 users who have been given the learning aids included with Windows 95 confirmed that users of Windows 3.1 will quickly become productive. After a 15-minute "play period" and with the help of a computer-based tutorial, users of Windows 3.1 participating in tests have been found to be as productive using Windows 95 as they are using Windows 3.1 the first time they perform a set of typical tasks. By the time Windows 95 is commercially available, it will have been subjected to hundreds of thousands of hours of rigorous internal testing and will have undergone the most extensive beta testing in history.

  The savings achieved by using Windows 95 outweighs the costs of the migration. The Gartner Group has estimated that migration costs can be recouped in three to six months. Good planning and deployment techniques can help keep these costs to a minimum.

Ship Dates and Packaging Plans

- **When will Windows 95 ship?**

  Windows 95 is scheduled to ship in the first half of 1995. Microsoft's commitment is to ship a great product. The intense testing period helps ensure a successful release based on feedback from tens of thousands of beta testers.

- **What different packages will Windows 95 come in?**

  Packaging decisions will be made later in the development cycle, based on customer needs.

■   **I understand there is a new logo for Windows 95. What will it mean to me?**

The new logo, which features the same Windows flag and looks quite similar to the current logo, will be used optionally by vendors to identify hardware, software, and peripheral products that take advantage of new capabilities in Windows 95. For example, the logo lets customers know at a glance which CD-ROM drives are Plug and Play-enabled and which applications are 32-bit.

Vendors can obtain details of the logo requirements by accessing the Microsoft Developer Solutions Phone-Fax service at (206) 635-2222 and requesting document 130.

■   **I keep hearing rumors that Microsoft is working on versions of Windows 95 for non–Intel microprocessors. Is this true?**

No, Microsoft is not working on versions of Windows 95 for non–Intel microprocessors. Windows NT is Microsoft's portable operating system, and it is already available on high-end Intel, MIPS, Alpha AXP, PowerPC and Clipper computers.

■   **What will happen to MS-DOS?**

Microsoft will continue to enhance MS-DOS as long as customers require it. Future versions will be derived from the protected-mode technology developed during the Windows 95 project.

User Interface

■   **How will the new user interface in Windows 95 make the PC easier to use?**

The goal for the user interface for future versions of Windows is to make computers easy for all people to use. The user-interface design in Windows 95 achieves this goal through the most extensive usability-testing effort ever and through feedback from various sources, including testing at customer sites, reviews with experts on training in Windows, audits by user-interface consultants, feedback from focus groups, and analysis of product-support calls.

Microsoft expects that both novice and experienced users will find that the user interface in Windows 95 makes it easier to learn and use. The Taskbar makes all the functions most users need accessible with a single click of a button. The Taskbar shows all open windows and allows users to switch to a different window just by clicking the button representing that window. Instead of mastering different kinds of tools—for example, Program Manager, File Manager, Print Manager and the Control Panel—to work with different resources on their computers, users of Windows 95 can browse for and access all resources in a consistent fashion with a single tool. All resources in the system have property sheets, which present tabbed-notebook-style interface settings that can be directly changed. And a new integrated Help system makes getting help easy and fast at all times.

■ **Won't a new user interface mean a lot of retraining for current users of Windows?**

The Windows 95 user interface is designed to make experienced users of Windows 3.*x* productive immediately, and usability testing has found this to be the case. After a few iterations of working with the Windows 95 environment, users of Windows 3.1 are able to complete common tasks faster with Windows 95. With subtle refinements in the user interface and the addition of migration training aids during the continued testing process, productivity can be expected to improve even more.

Windows 95 enables corporate customers and individuals who want to move gradually to the new user interface to continue running Program Manager and File Manager while they become familiar with the new user-interface features.

Architecture

■ **Your performance goals sound very ambitious, considering all the functionality you're adding to Windows 95. How will you achieve those goals?**

The stated performance goal of Windows 95 is that when a customer upgrades to Windows 95, performance will meet or exceed performance of Windows 3.1, as long as the customer has an 80386DX or higher system with at least 4 MB of RAM. (For systems with more memory, performance will exceed that of Windows 3.1.) Windows 95 meets this performance goal by implementing new technologies to better optimize the use of memory on low-end system configurations. The networking, disk, CD-ROM, and paging caches are fully integrated to scale better as more memory is added to the system. Protected-mode device drivers are dynamically loadable to ensure that only the drivers that are immediately needed are consuming memory. Great attention will be paid to effective tuning, including hand-tuning source code.

- **I've heard Windows 95 described as a 32-bit operating system, yet I've also heard that portions of Windows 95 are implemented with 16-bit code. Are both these statements correct?**

Windows 95 is a 32-bit, preemptive multitasking operating system that implements some 16-bit code to provide compatibility with existing applications. Windows 95 deploys 32-bit code wherever it significantly improves performance without sacrificing compatibility. It retains existing 16-bit code where it is required to maintain compatibility or where 32-bit code would increase memory requirements without significantly improving performance. All of the I/O subsystems and device drivers in Windows 95, such as networking and file systems, are fully 32-bit, as are all the memory management and scheduling components. Many functions provided by the Graphics Device Interface (GDI) have been moved to 32-bit code, including the spooler and printing subsystem, the TrueType font rasterizer, and key drawing operations. Windows 95 includes a 32-bit implementation of OLE. Much of the window-management code (user) remains 16-bit to help ensure application compatibility.

- **Does Windows 95 improve limits on system resources?**

Yes. Windows 95 improves system-resource limits dramatically while maintaining compatibility with existing Windows–based applications. This improvement means that users can not only run more applications than under Windows 3.1 or Windows for Workgroups 3.11, but can also create more complex documents.

Plug and Play

- **What is Plug and Play? What benefits does Plug and Play provide?**

Plug and Play is a technology jointly developed by PC product vendors to dramatically improve the integration of PC hardware and software. Windows 95 is a key enabling technology for Plug and Play. Plug and Play is built into all levels of Windows 95 and covers both common desktop and laptop devices, such as monitors, printers, video cards, sound cards, CD-ROM drives, SCSI adapters, modems, and PCMCIA devices.

With Windows 95, users can connect Plug and Play devices to the system and let the system automatically allocate hardware resources with no user intervention. For example, users can turn a desktop PC into a multimedia playback system by simply plugging in a CD-ROM and sound card, turning on the PC, and "playing" a video clip.

Windows 95 also enables new Plug and Play system designs that can be dynamically reconfigured. For example, if a Windows 95 Plug and Play laptop is removed from its docking station while still running so that it can be taken to a meeting; the system automatically reconfigures itself to work with a lower-resolution display and adjusts for the absence of the network card and large disk drive.

- **Will Plug and Play devices work with my current system, or will I need a new system? What benefits will I receive when I purchase a Plug and Play device with my current system after I have installed Windows 95?**

Windows 95 and Plug and Play devices provide complete backward compatibility to work with systems that were not designed to the Plug and Play specification. When users purchase a Plug and Play device for a non-Plug and Play PC running Windows 95, they still benefit from the automatic installation features of Plug and Play add-on devices.

Application Support

- **What support does Windows 95 have for applications?**

Windows 95 supports MS-DOS–based applications, 16-bit Windows–based applications designed to run under Windows 3.*x,* and a new generation of 32-bit applications. It provides this support through the Win32 API, which is also available in Windows NT. The new generation of 32-bit applications provide many benefits, such as greater robustness, smoother multitasking, long filename support, a new look and feel, and threads.

- **When will applications that exploit Windows 95 be available?**

Applications written for Windows 3.1 and Windows NT that follow guidelines provided by Microsoft can run on Windows 95. Hundreds of 32-bit Windows–based applications are available for Windows NT, and more are released every day. In addition, leading software vendors are developing 32-bit applications for Windows 95, and many will ship within 90 days of the Windows 95 ship date.

Networking

- **Will I need new networking software to connect Windows 95 to my network server?**

No. Windows 95 will continue to run existing real-mode networking components while enhancing the 32-bit protected-mode networking components first delivered with Windows for Workgroups.

- **What improvements will the networking support in Windows 95 offer over the support in Windows for Workgroups 3.11?**

In addition to being backward compatible with today's network clients, Windows 95 enhances the open and flexible, high-performance, 32-bit networking architecture provided by Windows for Workgroups 3.11, which enables customers to mix and match networking components. Windows 95 includes fast 32-bit, native clients for both NetWare and Windows NT Server networks; supports NDIS 2.*x*, 3.*x* and ODI drivers; and provides 32-bit TCP/IP, IPX/SPX, and NetBEUI protocols. In addition, the network architecture in Windows 95 makes it possible for users to connect simultaneously to multiple networks using multiple protocols.

- **Will there be a Windows 95 server product?**

  Windows 95 will not be provided in a separate server product. Windows NT Server is the Microsoft product to use for production servers. Windows 95 does improve upon the peer-server capabilities provided in Windows for Workgroups by offering additional features for remote installation, control, and administration. These features make Windows 95 an even better product for an easy-to-use, file and print sharing LAN that is ideally suited for a small business, small department, or remote office.

- **Can Windows 95 connect to the Internet?**

  Yes. Windows 95 includes the networking support needed to connect to the Internet. It includes a fast, robust, 32-bit TCP/IP stack (TCP/IP is the language used by the Internet) as well as PPP or "dial-in" support. Windows 95 supports the large number of tools used to connect to the Internet—for example, Mosaic, WinWAIS, and WinGopher—through the Windows Sockets programming interface. Windows 95 also includes standard Internet support, such as telnet and ftp.

Systems Management

- **What specific desktop-management features will Windows 95 enable?**

  The Windows 95 operating system can be set up from a network server and can be configured at the desktop to run locally or across the network. In each case, the administrator can establish a specific configuration for the installation, controlling which features are installed and which features can be accessed or altered by the end-user.

  Windows 95 supports System Policies, which are settings an administrator configures to define what applications or services users or groups of users can access using their PCs. For example, the administrator can use policies to disable the MS-DOS prompt and the Run command to prevent users from arbitrarily running applications, and to disable file and print sharing.

  To enable users to rove on the network and use any system, Windows 95 provides User Profiles. These profiles are centrally stored, accessed when a user logs onto a Windows 95 system, and used to install the appropriate configuration and set the appropriate policies for that user. Windows 95 also enhances the security provided by Windows for Workgroups to include user-level security.

Windows 95 also includes key desktop agents for popular server-based backup programs as well as SNMP and DMI. Finally, hardware installation and configuration have been made much easier and less costly with the implementation of the Plug and Play architecture in devices and systems. The Registry provides data about hardware resources that can be accessed by third-party vendors to provide inventory-management solutions.

Messaging and Mail

■ **What is Microsoft Exchange?**

Microsoft Exchange is a universal information client built into the Windows 95 user interface. It can read and send electronic mail from different e-mail systems, including LAN-based systems such as Microsoft Mail, Internet mail, or remote online system services such as CompuServe or The Microsoft Network. It can also send and receive faxes and other remote messages. Microsoft Exchange in Windows 95 also includes Microsoft At Work Fax software for sending and receiving electronic fax messages. Microsoft Exchange also provides an effective way to organize, sort, categorize, and filter messages.

The Microsoft Network

■ **What is The Microsoft Network?**

The Microsoft Network (MSN) is a new online service that Microsoft is developing to help bring the rapidly expanding world of electronic information and communications to mainstream PC users. MSN brings all Windows 95 customers affordable and easy-to-use access to electronic mail, bulletin boards, chat rooms, file libraries, and Internet newsgroups. Windows 95 customers worldwide will be able to access MSN with a local phone call. MSN will offer a wide range of online information and services, and in particular, Microsoft customers will find MSN the single best place to get information and support for Microsoft products. The MSN client's tight integration with Windows 95 allows customers already familiar with Windows 95 to leverage their learning and feel comfortable online immediately.

■ **How does The Microsoft Network differ from other online services?**

Microsoft has long had a vision of "Information At Your Fingertips" and believes that The Microsoft Network represents a major opportunity to deliver on that vision. Enabling PC users to easily communicate and access information is the next great opportunity in the PC industry. The online service business shows great promise as far as providing consumers with that easy communication and information access is concerned, but it is still in its infancy, and many factors must come together to make it a mainstream phenomenon. Online services must offer a more compelling multimedia-rich set of publications, shopping services, games, and so on, that will both attract and retain a large audience. Achieving this goal will require product investments by the providers of information and services, and new tools and infrastructure investments by the online service companies. Microsoft hopes to help expand this market by making better technology and tools available to the providers of information and services, while motivating them with a more attractive business model.

Mobile Computing

■ **What improvements will Windows 95 offer for people who use a mobile or remote computer?**

Windows 95 provides support for mobile computers and makes it easy for users to access resources when they are away from the office. The implementation of Plug and Play in Windows 95 supports inserting and removing devices such as PCMCIA cards while the operating system is running. It also supports automatic reconfiguration of dockable computers when they are inserted or removed from the docking station, without rebooting the system. An enhanced version of Advanced Power Management (APM) further extends battery life.

Remote networking is a special focus of Windows 95. The operating system includes a dial-up network client that allows a mobile computer to dial into popular remote networking products, such as Shiva Netmodem, NetWare Connect, and Windows NT Remote Access Services, using the same network protocols and advanced security features provided for desktop PCs. In addition, Windows 95 provides file-synchronization services.

■ **How are the remote-client capabilities in Windows 95 different from those in Windows for Workgroups 3.11?**

Clients running Windows for Workgroups can remotely dial into a Windows NT Server or a Windows for Workgroups–based server only. Windows 95 supports a much more diverse remote-access environment; it can connect not only to a Windows NT Server and other PCs running Windows 95, but also to a NetWare server running NetWare Connect, a network device such as the Shiva Netmodem (using the PPP Dial-Up Networking support in Windows 95), and the Internet.

For More Information

- **How can I obtain the latest information directly from Microsoft about Windows 95?**

  Microsoft has established a number of easily accessible electronic-distribution points for new white papers, press releases, and other pertinent documentation. Use the

CompuServe	GO WINNEWS
Internet	ftp.microsoft.com/peropsys/win_news
Worldwide Web	http://www.microfot.com
GEnie	WINNEWS Download area in Windows RTC
Prodigy	Jumpword WINNEWS
AOL	Keyword WINNEWS

  To subscribe to Microsoft's WINNEWS Electronic Newsletter, send an e-mail message to enews@microsoft.nwnet.com with the words SUBSCRIBE WINNEWS in the message.

Index